A Gay History of Britain

A Gay History of Britain

Love and Sex Between Men
Since the Middle Ages

Edited by
Matt Cook

with
H. G. Cocks
Robert Mills
and
Randolph Trumbach

Greenwood World Publishing
Oxford / Westport Connecticut
2007

First published by Greenwood World Publishing 2007

1 2 3 4 5 6 7 8 9 10

Introduction, Chapter 5 and Chapter 6 © Matt Cook
Chapter 1 © Robert Mills
Chapter 2 and Chapter 3 © Randolph Trumbach
Chapter 4 © H. G. Cocks

Greenwood World Publishing
Wilkinson House
Jordan Hill
Oxford OX2 8EJ
An imprint of Greenwood Publishing Group, Inc
www.greenwood.com

British Library Cataloguing-in-Publication Data: a catalogue record for this book is available from the British Library

Library of Congress Cataloguing-in-Publication Data

Cook, Matt.
    A gay history of Britain: love and sex between men since the Middle Ages/
Matt Cook with contributing authors Robert Mills, Randolph Trumbach, and
H. G. Cocks.

    p. cm.
    Includes bibliographical references and index.
    ISBN 1-84645-002-0 (alk. paper)
    1. Gay men – Great Britain – History. 2. Gay men – Great Britain – Social conditions. 3. Homosexuality – Great Britain – History. I. Mills, Robert.
II. Trumbach, Randolph. III. Cocks, Harry, 1968–. IV. Title.

    HQ76.2.G7C66 2007
    306.76'620941 — dc22

                                            2006039653

ISBN 978-1-84645-002-0

Designed by Fraser Muggeridge studio
Picture researched by Zooid
Typeset by TexTech
Printed and bound by South China Printing Company

For John, Madeline and my mum, Gwladys

Contents

Acknowledgements

Matt Cook. Thanks to Ajamu, Michael Brown, Justin Bengry, Sue Donnelly, Matt Houlbrook, Sam Hoyle, Victoria Field, Simon Mason, Scott Nunn, Will Nutland, Lisa Power, Nick Rathbone, Tris Reid Smith, Ian Townsen and Chris Waters. Also to Allegra Madgwick and Pam, Jaya and Chetan Rathbone.

Robert Mills. Thanks to Neil Young, my ideal reader.

Randolph Trumbach. Thanks to Anton Masterovoy for helping me to assemble chapters two and three.

Introduction

Standing in the dock of a packed court in 1895, Oscar Wilde attempted to justify love between men by invoking a queer heritage stretching back 2,000 years. He connected Plato, David and Jonathan, Shakespeare and Michelangelo to the 'love that dare not speak its name' in 'this century'. Wilde used the past to suggest that homosexuality had a long and noble pedigree and was not a modern malaise borne out of urban degeneracy as some of his contemporaries were suggesting. Since the end of the nineteenth century – though mostly since the 1970s – historians and others have tried to flesh out this past and to reclaim lives and communities which had been 'hidden from history'. This work has been crucial in constituting a sense of 'gay' identity and pride in the face of abuse and discrimination. It has also helped to sustain a reform movement in Britain, which has arguably led us to an equal age of consent and the right to register our partnerships and to adopt children.

It is not to diminish the importance of these histories or the huge personal and political significance of recent legal change, however, to question presumptions that have commonly gone with this reclamation of the past. The main problem in Wilde's pragmatic deployment of figures from history is the suggestion that each of these men understood desire and identity, their loves and relationships, in the same ways; that – in modern parlance – they were all 'gay'. Yet if Shakespeare had male and female lovers, he certainly did not see his identity in terms of homo- or bisexuality: these were frames of reference which came later. Men have always had sex with other men but whether or not they have associated this with being a particular type of person as we tend to in the Western world now depended very much on the time and place in question. The 'gay' in the title of this book can only really be said to apply to the last thirty years of the millennium under discussion, and looking for gay men in medieval monasteries or the court of James I is a fruitless task. What the following chapters do instead is to explore the ways in which intimate sexual and/or emotional relationships between men were understood at different times by those involved and by those around them. They show, for example, the high value placed on platonic bonds between men in the medieval period, the way sex between men and adolescent boys was a commonplace in the renaissance and the idea emerging in the 1700s that there was a minority of men who differed sexually from the rest (even though this minority was not the only group of men having homosexual sex). Different labels were given to these men in the eighteenth, nineteenth and twentieth centuries, and so we get mollies, sodomites, inverts, maryannes, homosexuals, queens, trade, gays and queers. These labels were not synonymous, though, and each represents a different understanding of identity and desire.

The book explores this terminology and explains how and why 'gay' has come to be the most common label and the means of understanding homosexual identity and subculture. Because 'gay' is so recent, though, it is only used in the final section of the book. It carries with it a strong sense of its opposite ('straight') and hence suggests a clear division of sexual identities which is not appropriate for most earlier periods. Instead, the authors have tended to use language that was in circulation at the time they are examining. In addition, Randolph Trumbach uses homosexual to conjure the beginnings of an oppositional system of sexuality, whilst Robert Mills and I have found 'queer' useful as a broader term because it does not carry quite the same idea of a definitive and singular identity that 'gay' does. Mills explains this further in the introduction to his chapter on the medieval period.

Looking at the history of homosexuality in terms of different understandings, identities and subcultures at different times also problematises the idea of a progressive movement from oppression to liberation for 'gay' men. Whilst the sex men were having with other men may have been criminal or considered sinful, the men involved did not necessarily see themselves being part of a repressed minority. They would not have conceptualised a closet to be in or out of as we do now. Many were blind to sexually 'deviant' behaviour, others treated it pragmatically. The police and government, as we see in Chapters 3–6 especially, were not consistent or systematic in their attempts to repress homosexual activity. Arrests and prosecutions for homosexual offences in fact reached record levels after the supposed watershed of the Sexual Offences Act of 1967, which allowed two men to have sex in private in England and Wales as long as they were over 21 (men in Scotland, Northern Ireland, Guernsey, Jersey or the Isle of Man had to wait until 1980, 1982, 1983, 1990 and 1993 respectively). Some men in oral history interviews meanwhile hark back nostalgically to the interwar years and to what some found to be a more vibrant and exciting 'queer' scene. This is not to idealise the past or to diminish the significance of recent social and cultural change, but it is to call into question knee-jerk assumptions about 'progress' or the idea that lives and loves are necessarily easier and happier now than in the past.

In exploring these issues and identities, we have drawn on a wealth of sources – including literature, theatre, diaries, legal records, newspapers, scientific writing and oral testimony. Different sources come into particular focus for different periods. The courts and the newspaper press provide some rich evidence for the eighteenth, nineteenth and twentieth centuries, for example; for the earlier periods, art, theatre, diaries and chronicles are a primary means of reconstructing attitudes and experiences. The move in the 1980s to record the experiences of gay men and lesbians means that oral history comes into play alongside a growing canon of gay literature, film, art and journalism. With varying source material, different kinds of history necessarily emerge. It is possible to say things about the domestic life of queer men in the twentieth century, which we simply cannot do for men having sex or relationships in the twelfth. Each of the four contributors also has a different approach, and as a result the book charts not only Britain's queer past but also a series of different ways of engaging with it. All the chapters consider prevailing concepts of identity, community and subculture, and hence the cultural and geographical organisation of queer life; they each also look at the relationship between 'queer' and 'normal' lives and explore the broader perception and treatment of men who had sex and relationships with other men. In addition, though, each contributor has focused in on particular themes and ideas. Robert Mills in the first chapter looks especially at the distinctions and overlaps between male–male love and male–male sex; Randolph Trumbach focuses on the ways in which sexual relations were structured; H. G. Cocks concentrates on the intersection of politics, art and religion with homosexual life and scandal; I try to pinpoint the factors – such as location, class and ethnicity – which differentiated queer lives, communities and experiences.

What comes across strongly in the book is the sense that this is not a minority history, and neither should it be seen to be of minority interest. The changing ways in which sexual and emotional intimacy between men were viewed, experienced and policed affected everyone and tells us much about how, for example, concepts of masculinity (and gender categories more broadly) have shifted over time. Homosexuality cannot be neatly separated out from the broader history of Britain; it is implicated in understandings of class, gender, national and urban identity, politics, art, the law and journalism, as we will see. It is also – perhaps more obviously – caught up in other histories of social and sexual deviance; the history of lesbianism, for example, is dealt with in a separate book in this series, but it is intertwined with the history explored here. One short book cannot do full justice to Britain's gay history. What we have tried to do, though, is to highlight some of the key ideas, themes, events and stories which can help us to understand what sex and love between men has meant in Britain over the past thousand years.

Chapter 1

Male–Male Love and Sex in the Middle Ages, 1000–1500

Robert Mills

When Richard Lionheart of England, as a young prince, made peace with the youthful king Philip Augustus of France in 1187, during a diplomatic stand-off between England and France, the contemporary chronicler who reported the incident described the newly forged relationship in terms that apparently left little to the imagination:

> Richard, duke of Aquitaine, son of the king of England, remained with Philip, the king of France, who so honoured him for so long that they ate every day at the same table and from the same dish, and at night their beds did not separate them. And the king of France loved him as his own soul; and they loved each other so much that the king of England was absolutely astonished at the vehement love between them and marvelled at what it could mean.[1]

Not only was the love vehement and astonishing, but in a continuation of the narrative the chronicler recalls how several years later Richard, now king, resumed his relationship with Philip, when they met on a crusading expedition in the holy land, and 'it seemed that the affection of mutual love between them was so strong that it could not be broken, nor could they ever betray their love'.[2]

Nothing could be plainer, it seems, than this expression of ardent male–male passion: the meeting of 1187 set in motion a violent love affair between Richard and Philip, a bond that was to last across the years. Moreover, while the young Richard's father, Henry II, professed wonderment at his son's newfound passion (he was apparently surprised by the suddenness with which the love came about, wondering what 'plots' it might herald), the chronicler himself displays none of the disapproval that one might reasonably expect to encounter in a description of same-sex love written in a period more commonly associated with brutal sexual repression. How 'tolerant' this medieval writer was, that he recorded the public expression of love between two male royals with no hint of moral censure. Chronicle entries such as this appear to be evidence enough that Richard Lionheart, the future king of England, was one of the nation's most renowned homosexuals in history. Surely common sense dictates that love stories of this kind, between two men of equal age and status, do not really change much over time!

Yet the world we are about to enter in this chapter suggests that common sense is not always the most useful interpretive key for unlocking the medieval past, and that it can sometimes obscure a good deal more than it actually illuminates. Richard Lionheart has been regularly recruited by historians of homosexuality – and occasionally by historians of the king's reign – to demonstrate the existence of male–male erotic relations at all levels of the medieval social hierarchy.[3] But these are claims that other scholars have spent equal amounts of energy refuting, or at least rendering unstable, in response. Some have interpreted the absence of moral condemnation of the princes' relationship on the part of the chronicler as evidence that what we are witnessing here is not an expression of 'gay love' at all, but instead a different kind of passion, wholly alien to the twenty-first-century sensibilities – an ostentatious display of passionate male friendship that was exalted, idealized and publicly sanctioned, but that had little in common with homosexuality in the modern sense.[4] Others have argued that the expressions of love that took place between Richard and Philip, that is to say eating from the same dish and sharing the same bed, were in fact ritualized gestures – conventions with a long and venerable history – expressing political reconciliation rather than spontaneous personal emotion or erotic love.[5] Others still have countered claims for Richard's homosexuality with evidence that medieval writers were in little doubt about the king's overriding heterosexuality, relaying, for example, the legend of how Richard was once so captivated by a nun from the abbey of Fontevrault in Anjou, France – where he was eventually buried – that he threatened to reduce the institution to ashes unless the nun was handed over to him forthwith. This is a story of attempted rape or abduction on Richard's part, rather than 'heterosexuality' per se, which explains the extreme measures taken to resist the king's advances: the nun, hearing that it was her eyes that Richard found especially attractive, cut them out and had them delivered to the king as a gift.[6]

The debate Richard Lionheart's sexual identity has provoked serves to convey in microcosm what is at stake in writing the opening chapter in a gay history of Britain. What exactly do we mean when we apply a term such as 'gay' to the distant medieval past? If gay identity is an entity that can be subjected to historical enquiry, what are the contours of that history, how far back does it extend and at what point does its appropriation by modern scholars spill over into anachronistic modes of identification? Modern gay identities embrace relations of fellowship and love, as well as particular configurations of sex, gender, age, social status and style. This chapter suggests that if we experience as time- and culture-bound those forms of existence now subsumed under the category 'gay', we may well experience same-sex relations in the present a little less schematically – and a little more queerly – as a result. 'Queer', like gay, is a category that has no precise medieval equivalent, but I occasionally use it here to capture the ability of historical sources to trouble or resist frameworks that assume a neat divide between homosexual and heterosexual persons, or between emotional and erotic bonds. As we shall see in the later chapters, the hetero/homo-binary assumed a more public character in Britain in the modern period, especially after the late nineteenth century (though even today it does not have universal applicability). Arguably, some medieval thinkers understood male–male sex as a behaviour that denoted a special type of person, for instance the figure of the 'sodomite'. But sodomy is a notoriously slippery concept, even in the modern period; as will become clear in what follows, sodomites and 'gay people' are connected to one another only partially and incompletely. Likewise, expressions of male–male love in the Middle Ages potentially conveyed meanings different from those assumed in later centuries; it would therefore be a mistake to view expressions of male–male intimacy in medieval sources entirely through the lens of homosexuality.

'Homosociality' is a term coined by historians and literary critics to describe intense emotional relationships between people of the same sex that have social, economic or political consequences, but that are not explicitly sexual in nature. These relations between males are often compatible with – and indeed structured by – expressions of sexual desire by men for women. However, it is also possible to perceive moments when the line separating homosocial relations from homoerotic relations becomes blurred. One of the strategies employed by medieval moralists to separate male–male sex from male–male love was to exploit the category of sodomy in contexts where it was theologically or politically useful. But, there are occasions where the policing of male–male relations in medieval culture produces its own queer effects – where gestures of homosocial intimacy themselves get characterized as dangerously sodomitical. The working assumption here is that the tale of Richard Lionheart's love for

Philip of France has something to contribute to a gay history of Britain, not because the princes' relationship mirrors modern gay identities absolutely, or even in a looser, more shadowy fashion, but because the question of love between males is not necessarily or inevitably divorced from the question of sex between males. Each potentially tells us something about the other.

Before fleshing out these points, it is worth making some preliminary remarks about geography and timescale. The Middle Ages is a period of almost a thousand years, stretching from some time after the fall of the Roman Empire until the religious, political and cultural upheavals of the 1500s. During this long interval, the island of Britain bore witness to the rise and fall of several different cultures. The Celts lived in Britain under Roman rule until the fifth century, when the Romans withdrew their troops. Faced with being overpowered by certain hostile tribes, the Celts sought the aid of Germanic troops from overseas, who eventually also themselves invaded and overpowered the Celts (later called the Welsh), presaging the beginning of the Germanic or Anglo-Saxon period, during which time a language called by modern scholars Old English developed. This period lasted until the eleventh century, when England was invaded by the Norman French under the leadership of William, Duke of Normandy ('the Conqueror'). After the twelfth century, influenced by this Anglo-Norman culture, Middle English developed as a distinct linguistic medium. Nonetheless, this was a period of political division, and immense cultural and linguistic variation. Middle English literature existed alongside texts written in French, Welsh and Latin, and outside the realms of history, political aspiration and myth, Britain was little more than a geographical expression.

The material surveyed here spans the sixth century to the fifteenth and makes use of texts in Latin as well as in Old and Middle English; as with documents about Anglo-Norman monarchs such as Richard Lionheart, texts from the eleventh century onwards are often implicated in the history of male–male relations in France as well as in England (although they do occasionally also look outwards to Wales, Scotland and Ireland). Furthermore, this chapter's evidence base differs from later chapters in that, as we shall see, male–male relations were not subjected to any secular legal proscription in Britain before 1534. This means that the rich prosecution records available to the historians of later periods are, for the most part, not available for this; statistical surveys of the kind possible for subsequent eras cannot be produced with any confidence for medieval England. We will have to rely instead on a combination of documentary sources and chronicles, texts produced in religious contexts and literature written in a courtly milieu, as well as on a number of striking visual images. The stories these sources tell are somewhat varied: it is not possible to discover for the Middle Ages a fixed pattern or 'sexual system' of the sort Randolph Trumbach finds for the Renaissance in Chapter 2. Although there is evidence that age-differentiated relations were significant in the Middle Ages, and that same-sex and cross-sex sexual behaviours were compatible in certain contexts, my own analysis reveals a series of patterns in which male–male attraction comes into view, rather than a single, overarching system. I take the view that there is not a consistent, unitary history of male–male relations at any one point in time. Instead, the history of sexuality is best interpreted as a series of competing, if partially overlapping, models – all of which have contributed, in some measure, to current ideas about gay identity through a process of accretion and historical overlay.[7] One significant framework in which male–male relations are rendered visible, albeit incoherently so, is sodomy. We will focus on its elusive qualities, its appropriation as a tool of political and moral reproach and its association – or not – with phenomena such as anal penetration and effeminacy. The concluding section assembles the extant records of male–male erotic experience and expression in 'everyday' contexts, in order to reveal a world of same-sex relations beyond the sodomy accusations dreamed up by propagandists and polemicists. We will glimpse here the institutional spaces within which age-differentiated relations were especially significant, as well as instances of cross-dressing and gendered passivity or 'inversion'. But taking the view that histories of same-sex relations are not simply histories of explicit sexual activity, it is with the blurred spaces between brotherhood, friendship, love and marriage in medieval society that our journey properly begins.

Brotherhood, friendship, love and marriage

Intimate relations between males in medieval society took a variety of forms, and it is not possible to reduce the driving force behind those relations to a single, overriding motive. What it is possible to trace are the outlines of a far-reaching rhetoric of same-sex intimacy, which spanned all manner of practices from rites of voluntary kinship, adoptive brotherhood and peacemaking to expressions of homosocial bonding, physical closeness and loving union between males. This rhetoric has the following general traits: it is concerned with establishing enduring peace, friendship and reciprocity; it is frequently allied to practices with ritual and public significance; and on the surface it has nothing whatsoever to do with sodomy. That said, it is also clear that at certain critical moments in the long span of time between the Anglo-Saxon period and the early sixteenth century, the rhetoric of intimacy ran the risk of misinterpretation. It is these moments of confusion that afford some of the most telling insights into medieval attitudes to male–male love.

Perhaps the most celebrated example of a medieval same-sex interaction that tips over into queerness is the relationship between the English monarch Edward II (1284–1327) and his so-called favourite Piers Gaveston. The precise nature of this relationship was a matter of debate, even within the king's lifetime, but most modern ideas about it have been shaped by the accounts of Edward's reign produced in the late Elizabethan period, notably Christopher Marlowe's *Edward II*, written in or around 1592.[8] A common theme runs through these post-medieval reconstructions: political history is recast as a meditation on sexual ethics. Edward's erotic inclinations can be glimpsed in these lines from the opening scene in Marlowe's play, where Gaveston, having received a letter from the king, inviting him to 'share the kingdom with thy deerest friend', lists the enticements with which he plans to influence the 'pliant' Edward:

> Sometime a lovelie boye in *Dians* shape,
> With hair that gilds the water as it glides,
> Crownets of pearle about his naked armes,
> And in his sportfull hands an Olive tree,
> To hide those parts which men delight to see,
> Shall bathe him in a spring [...]
> Such things as these best please his majestie.[9]

The adaptation of *Edward II* by the film director Derek Jarman appropriated Marlowe's melding of homoeroticism and politics as a means of highlighting the experiences of contemporary gay men in Britain who suffered under the oppressive policies of the Tory government in the late 1980s and early 1990s. Conversely, Mel Gibson's *Braveheart*, a film whose homophobic subtext did not go unnoticed at the time of its original release,[10] depicts the flamboyantly attired and heavily made-up Edward, heir to his father Edward Longshank's throne, cavorting with an effete male companion, who is subsequently tossed out of a window to his death by Longshanks himself.[11]

The image we have inherited of Edward II clearly assumes that the relationships he had with his male companions were sexual, and that he and Gaveston were homosexual lovers.[12] But is this the impression conveyed by fourteenth-century sources? In truth, it is not possible to pin down what, if anything, went on between Edward and Gaveston when they were alone. There are no eyewitness accounts of the king's sexual encounters, nor are there specific references in any contemporary chronicle to Gaveston and Edward's status as lovers in a strictly erotic sense. As with so many of the examples assembled in this chapter, there is not any conclusive proof that Edward II was 'gay' or that he had a sense of enduring 'sexual orientation' towards other males. This is not to say that Gaveston and Edward never had sexual relations over the course of their acquaintance – we simply do not have proof either way. What can be demonstrated with some confidence is that the pair's relationship was sometimes viewed in terms of the language of ritualized love and friendship that we have already encountered in the life of Edward's ancestor Richard Lionheart.

Early fourteenth-century chronicles commonly attribute the troubles that afflicted Edward in the first few years of his reign to the nature of his connection with Gaveston, which was characterized, they say, by a passion 'beyond measure and reason', a love 'inordinate', 'immoderate' and 'excessive'.[13] The very first encounter between the pair is said to have taken place at the close of the thirteenth century, at a time when the old king Edward I was at war with Scotland, and one anonymous chronicler has this to say of the meeting:

> When the king's son gazed upon him, he straightaway felt so much love for him that he entered into a covenant of brotherhood with him and chose and firmly resolved to bind himself to him, before all mortals, in an unbreakable bond of love.[14]

Comparable terminology also crops up in chronicle accounts describing Edward and Gaveston's continuing passionate attachment, such as the following comment – from a generally reliable account of the Edward's reign – appended to a description of Gaveston's murder by the young king's enemies: 'For they put to death a great earl whom the king had adopted as brother, whom the king loved as a son, whom the king regarded as friend and ally'.[15]

Elsewhere, this same chronicle describes the love that transpired between Edward and Gaveston as being comparable in intensity to that of the biblical Jonathan for David, or the classical Achilles for Patroclus.[16] But here the language is of adoptive brotherhood, a ritualized bond cemented in public, 'before all mortals'. It is perfectly possible that Edward and Gaveston were sexually entangled – we shall never know for sure – yet the picture that can be pieced together from contemporary documents suggests that 'brotherhood' was an equally important frame of reference. Conceptualization in these terms is not simply attributable to the reticence of medieval chroniclers. We also know that Edward explicitly named Gaveston as his brother in public documents, such as an official writ of 1308, which refers to him as 'our dear brother and faithful'.[17] What this establishes is that Edward and Gaveston probably entered into a compact corresponding to the Middle English expression *weddyd bretheryn* or 'wed brothers', a mode of voluntary kinship formed through a ritualized promise rather than relations of blood.[18]

References to bonds of artificial kinship between males can be traced back to the early Middle Ages and assume a variety guises.[19] An account of the life of Columba, the sixth-century Irish saint, includes a description of how a certain priest called Findchán brought with him from Ireland to Britain Áid the Black, to be a 'pilgrim' with him for a number of years at Findchán's monastery on the isle of Tiree, off the west coast of Scotland. Áid, a man of royal lineage who had murdered the king of all Ireland, was subsequently ordained by Findchán as a priest. In due course, we learn of Columba's displeasure at the ordination, an outcome that can be attributed in part, the text implies, to Findchán's 'carnal love' for Áid; the saint reacts by laying a formidable curse on the pair.[20] In context, the phrase carnal love does not necessarily denote sexual passion. More likely, it refers to the priest's love for Áid as a member of his family, a relation of earthly kinship that highlights Findchán's misplaced priorities in the ordination of his murderous friend.[21]

Moving forward to later centuries, it is possible to find references to comparable bonds in monastic chronicles, such as twelfth-century accounts of ritualized kissing, and oaths of brotherhood and friendship, between the Anglo-Saxon king Edmund Ironside and the Danish king Cnut in 1016.[22] What is more in Middle English literature, accounts of 'sworn' or 'wed' brothers appear with some regularity, notably in writings by Chaucer. Chaucer's *Canterbury Tales* contains several instances of the phenomenon, including 'The Knight's Tale', which tells of the fatal enmity that develops between the two Theban protagonists, Palamon and Arcite, over their love for Princess Emily, who they glimpse for the first time from the windows of their prison cell. Palamon, who is the first to catch sight of Emily, responds to Arcite's own declaration of love by appealing to the terms of their friendship:

> 'It nere [were not]', quod [said] he, 'to thee no great honour
> For to be false, ne for to be traitour
> To me, that am thy cousin and thy brother
> Ysworn ful deep, and each of us til [to the] other,
> That never, for to dyen [die] in the pain,
> Till that the death depart shall us tweyne [two],
> Neither of us in love to hinder other,
> Ne in none other case, my leeve [dear] brother,
> But that thou sholdest [should] truly forthren [help] me
> In every case, as I shall forthren [help] thee –
> This was thine oath, and mine also, certeyn [indeed]'.[23]

The language of this passage alerts readers to the strength of the bond. 'Till that the death depart shall us tweyne' is a phrase evocative of the vows exchanged between husbands and wives in the later Middle Ages, which included the expression 'tyll dethe vs departhe'.[24] In the light of such parallels, it is difficult not to hear the concept of a 'brother Ysworn' chiming partially with the sounds of marriage.

A satirical account of Irish social mores in the writings of the Anglo-Norman propagandist Gerald of Wales also bears witness to symbolic resonances between sworn brotherhood and marriage in other areas of medieval culture. In his *Topography of Ireland*, written *c.*1186–1188, Gerald records how Irishmen

> come together in some holy place with the man with whom they
> are eager to be united. First they join in covenants of spiritual brother-
> hood. Then they carry each other three times around the church.
> Then going into the church, before the altar and in the presence of
> relics of the saints, many oaths are made. Finally with a celebration
> of the mass and the prayers of priests, they are joined indissolubly
> as if by a betrothal.[25]

The ritual concludes, we are told, when the participants drink each other's blood. Unfortunately, however, the bloodshed that results is so violent that one or other becomes drained of blood, so that what starts out as a 'betrothal' ends up as a 'bloody divorce' Gerald's anecdote is designed to play up the barbarity of the Irish, who he characterizes as seriously missing the symbolic significance of the ritual they perform. His point is that this 'novel' Irish custom culminates not in the sharing of Christ's blood in the ceremony of Holy Communion in church (probably the most common conclusion to rites of sworn brotherhood in Europe after the twelfth century), but in a pagan ritual of 'blood brotherhood'. Though the truth value of Gerald's story is questionable and may have more to do with justifying Henry II's conquest of Ireland in 1171, what it does show is that there was a degree of correspondence, in the minds of Gerald's audience, between the ritual brotherhood sanctioned by 'normal' Christian societies and that other form of voluntary kinship, marriage.[26]

Other texts in which betrothed males, 'wed-brothers' or oath-bound friendships are depicted are more self-evidently literary. For example, the popular Middle English romance *Amys and Amylion* tells the story of two identical young nobles, biologically unrelated, who swear an oath of allegiance to one another that they will stick together, from that day forth, 'in well, woe, word and deed'.[27] Clearly, in such texts, sworn brotherhood is not incompatible with cross-sex partnerships. Both protagonists in *Amys and Amylion* marry, and one of them has children. At the narrative climax, however, Amylion is cured of leprosy by the blood of Amys's children (who are slain by Amys himself, but miraculously revive); the pair subsequently live together happily ever after, die on the same day and get buried in the same grave.

The concept of homosocial desire provides one framework for interpreting such narratives of male–male love and friendship. Women are often significant in tales of sworn brotherhood, notably as objects of desire in an erotic love triangle (as in Chaucer's 'The Knight's Tale'). The inclusion of female love objects helps underscore the similarities and differences between male erotic desires for women and homosocial bonds between males. *Amys and Amylion* includes a scene where Amys is seduced by Belisant, the daughter of the duke in whose court he and Amylion both serve; prior to the seduction, an evil male steward had offered to be a 'better friend' to Amys than Amylion, and, having been rejected, now threatens to expose Amys's relations with Belisant to the court. The parallel between the eroticism that motivates Amys and Belisant's liaison, and the ties of friendship that the steward attempts to cement with Amys, draws attention to the potential slippage between homosocial and homoerotic relations in courtly contexts. This becomes especially apparent in a scene where the steward jealously spies on Amys and Belisant through a hole in the wall as the pair kiss and 'play' in the next room. The episode represents one of a number of moments in the text where male–male relations of the sort exemplified by Amys and Amylion – oath-bound kinship ties with no explicit sexual dimension – have the capacity to become erotically charged relations, when misrecognized as such by one of the participants (in this instance, the steward).[28]

Texts like *Amys and Amylion* demonstrate the hold on the imagination that motifs of male–male love had in fourteenth-century England. The parallels with actual relations of sworn brotherhood in this period, such as that between Edward II and Gaveston, may not have been lost on some contemporary readers.[29] But, the court was not the only context in which the language of male–male love and friendship surfaced in medieval culture: it also exerted a steady influence on religious sensibilities. The bible itself contains a number of representations of intense male–male passion, such as the love of David for Jonathan, the death of whom inspired David to declare Jonathan his 'brother', 'exceedingly beautiful, and amiable to me above the love of women', and it is in writings by the Anglo-Saxon churchman Bede that one finds one of the earliest mentions of the notion of *spiritalis amicitia* or 'spiritual friendship'.[30]

Monastic environments proved especially conducive to the practice of this kind of idealized but sensually charged intimacy.[31] Aelred of Rievaulx (1110–1167), whose book *On Spiritual Friendship* became a cornerstone in the medieval Christian ethics of friendship, made a distinction between earthly, carnal modes of relation and what he called 'sublime' love, a love that transcends social and fleshly bonds. Aelred was a member of the Scottish nobility, who, in his youth, occupied an important position in the court of King David II of Scotland. At this time, it has been suggested, on the basis of his own reminiscences and those of his biographer Walter Daniel, Aelred was subjected to a number of accusations, notably that he was involved in a sexual liaison with another member of the court, possibly an older man. That the accusations may have contained a grain of truth is confirmed by Daniel's admission that at this period in his life Aelred indeed 'occasionally deflowered his chastity'. It was also in these years that Aelred developed attachments to certain other male figures, notably the king's son Henry, who he later described as 'a most beautiful young man, lovable to all'.[32] Later in life, when he arrived at the Cistercian abbey of Rievaulx in Yorkshire, Aelred developed a formula for friendship that he saw as especially appropriate for monastic environments. He was inspired in part here by the classical idea of friendship developed by Cicero. At Rievaulx, Aelred entered into relationships in turn with two monks, Hugh and Simon, and when the latter died, in the early 1140s, the holy man composed a protracted lament in which he characterized Simon as a 'remarkably handsome' young lad, who was a son, brother and father to him. 'It is as if my body has been eviscerated', he grieved, 'and my hapless soul rent to pieces'.[33]

What distinguished the relations Aelred enjoyed with monks like Simon from the relations he had entertained at court was the fact that these monastic attachments, though described using erotically charged language, were ultimately distanced from the physical in their day-to-day practice. Modern secular friendship is likewise frequently divested of close physical attraction, both in the words used to describe it and in the experiences that underpin it. In Aelred's ideal of spiritual friendship, though, it is acceptable for Aelred to express the depth of feeling between men with passionate and even sexual language, just so long as this language does not slip into actual physical expression.

Of course, monasticism was literally structured as a form of nonbiological, oath-bound kinship – a union sealed with the love of Christ – in which monks became each other's spiritual 'brothers'. Viewed in this light, it is possible to perceive elements of crossover in the language of same-sex intimacy developed by twelfth-century spiritual leaders and the vocabulary of sworn brotherhood and passionate friendship in courtly literature and chronicle accounts.[34] The 'vehement love' between Philip of France and Richard Lionheart, who Philip 'loved as his own soul', is comparable in tone to Aelred's descriptions of spiritual union with his fellow monks, as is the love that transpires between Amys and Amylion. While Aelred's *On Spiritual Friendship* ranks among the most developed accounts of sublime love in medieval devotion, earlier practitioners included Anselm, prior of Bec, an influential monastery in France, and later archbishop of Canterbury (d. 1109), who once wrote a missive to a recently departed friend in which he asked that 'when we see each other again we should once more revive, face to face, lip to lip, embrace to embrace, our unforgotten love'.[35] Earlier still, Alcuin of York (732–804) produced poetry on the Continent with comparable affective vigour.[36] In one letter to a bishop, he writes of how he longs for that 'lovely time' when he will be able to 'clutch the neck of your sweetness' with the 'fingers' of his desires; 'if only it were granted to me', he continues, 'to be transported to you, how would I sink into your embraces ... how would I cover, with tightly pressed lips, not only your eyes, ears and mouth but also your every finger and toe'.37

Perhaps the most illuminating account – revealing for what it says about the perceived risks that spiritual friendship potentially entailed – emerges in the context of an anecdote about the influential Cistercian abbot Bernard of Clairvaux (d. 1153) getting into bed with another male. The story appropriates a gesture familiar from secular peacemaking rituals – the practice of sleeping, like Richard and Philip, in a shared bed – by describing how Bernard once persuaded his friend Hugh of Vitry to join the Cistercian order by snuggling up to him 'in a bed so narrow it could scarcely hold one of them'.38 But the story easily played into the hands of those wishing to criticize Cistercian monasticism for its emotional excesses. While Geoffrey of Clairvaux, the source of this anecdote, omitted the story in his official biography of the abbot,39 the English cleric Walter Map transformed it into a dirty joke about Bernard's failure to perform a miracle, by recasting the saint's bed-partner as a seriously ill boy who Bernard had been asked to cure. Walter reports a story he heard second-hand, via the bishop of London, of how Bernard took the boy into a private chamber and lay upon him, but the boy did not move. In a punch line that clearly alludes to the capacity of monks to sexually arouse boys in the bedchamber, Walter quips, 'he was then the most unlucky of monks, for I heard before now of a monk throwing himself upon a boy, but always, when the monk rose up, the boy rose up too'.40

It is clear from these stories that relations between males could be described using gestures that were passionate, even eroticized, but that were ultimately differentiated from illicit physicality. By reinventing Bernard's sleeping arrangements phobically, as a form of intimacy that could only give rise to monkish erections, Walter Map conjures up the obverse of Aelred's spiritual friendship – the spectre of Sodom. Medieval people were not totally innocent of the erotic potency of sublime love, or of the potential risks involved. It is therefore not necessarily anachronistic to view stories of spiritual friendship as being linked, by partial analogy, to certain aspects of gay history. Rather, twelfth-century monasticism aimed to harness the power of Eros in the service of religious devotion, by appropriating a language of bodily feeling as a means of drawing monks closer to one another and ultimately, by extension, closer to God. This is not to say that Aelred of Rievaulx, Anselm of Canterbury or Bernard of Clairvaux were 'gay' in the sense of an enduring sexual 'orientation' or even that they had sporadic sexual encounters with other males (though it is not beyond the realms of possibility that in his youth Aelred of Rievaulx had male sexual partners in the Scottish court). What is clear is that the line separating sex from love in medieval encounters between males was sometimes blurred: although sodomy and homosociality were not the same thing, evidence suggests that their paths occasionally crossed.

Delusions of sodomy

Sodomy is a concept whose significance in the Middle Ages must be learned afresh with each text in which it appears, each context in which it is deployed. While the theologian Thomas Aquinas defined 'sodomitic vice' as a subspecies of the sin 'against nature', a vice performed with a 'person of the same sex, male with male and female with female',[41] sodomy was not consistently associated with same-sex relations in medieval sources; nor did it inevitably conjure up images of anal sex (which is often how the term has been read in modern contexts). Initially, sodomy was a theological construct, serving only intermittently to refer to a clear variety of sexual activity or to bring into focus the behaviour of a particular kind of person. Medieval 'sodomites' were normally guilty of the sin of sodomy, for sure, but the activities that constituted that sin were notoriously vague.[42] The biblical narrative of Sodom, for example, arguably confounds attempts to pin down absolutely the reasons for the city's destruction. Genesis 19 tells of how two angels come to Sodom one evening to investigate the city's sins; Lot, seeing the angels at the city gates, offers them lodging in his house. But before the household goes to bed, the inhabitants of the city besiege the residence and call on Lot to deliver his guests 'that we may know them'. Lot offers his two daughters up as an alternative (a motif of female sexual exchange often downplayed by writers principally concerned with the significance of the episode for homosexuality), since he announces that his overriding concern is for the well being of his visitors: 'I will bring them out to you, and abuse you them as it shall please you, so that you do no evil to these men'. Threatened with violence, however, Lot is escorted out of the city by the angels with his family; subsequently, we are told, the Lord 'rained upon Sodom and Gomorrah brimstone and fire … and he destroyed these cities, and all the country about, all the inhabitants of the cities, and all things that spring from the earth'. In the dramatic climax to the tale, Lot's wife, ignoring the angels' warning to 'look not back', is turned into a statue of salt.

Although the destruction of Sodom is traditionally interpreted as a punishment for homosexual depravity, some modern commentators have argued that the episode is chiefly concerned with hospitality to strangers: the inhabitants of Sodom were simply exercising the right to 'know' who Lot's guests were, motivated by an awareness of Lot's own alien status in the city.[43] All the same, in the early Middle Ages, the narrative was usually perceived through a more familiar, sexualized lens. One of the earliest appropriations of the story in an English context occurs in a letter from St Boniface to the king of Mercia, Æthelbald, in the mid-eighth century, which accuses the people of England of 'despising lawful marriage, and preferring incest, promiscuity, adultery and impious union with religious and cloistered women' – sins perceived as echoing the lustful fashions of the people of Sodom. The Anglo-Saxon abbot Ælfric, writing around the year 1000, is more specific, contrasting the Sodom story with the narrative of Noah's Flood:

> In Noah's days God punished men's lechery with the gentler element of water because they sinned with women, and the Sodomites sinned shamefully against nature, and they were therefore consumed with sulphurous fire … [Of the people of Noah's Day] God said: 'I will give them their due punishment for their folly here in this world'. This is not written about the Sodomites, who shamefully sinned against nature, for they are condemned for all eternity.[44]

Each event is interpreted by the abbot as a chastisement for a different kind of sexual transgression. The Flood punished acts of fornication with women, but this was relatively mild compared with the penalty exacted on the people of Sodom, who sinned against nature and were therefore damned for all time.

Certain visual images from the Anglo-Saxon period clearly underscore the homoeroticism of the story. For instance, a drawing in an eleventh-century manuscript containing an abridged version of the Hexateuch (the first six books of the Old Testament) depicts Lot seated within a building, while the men of Sodom huddle outside, staring intently into each other's eyes.[45] By comparison, the phrase 'against nature' in Ælfric's discussion is somewhat vague and does not make unambiguous reference to same-sex relations; Boniface's letter to Æthelbald interprets Sodom-like vice as sexual activity of any kind that is practiced outside 'lawful marriage'. This predisposition to vagueness is also apparent in the other method commonly deployed by medieval writers to refer to the sins of Sodom: allusions to the vice as something that 'should not be named'.[46] In the later Middle Ages, the motif of unmentionability was especially favoured by writers of confession manuals – instruction books for parish priests offering guidance on how best to extract confessions from parishioners – since it prevented priests from corrupting innocent minds by disclosing illicit, previously unheard of practices. John Myrc's *Instructions for Parish Priests*, written before 1450, asks that priests 'shalt [to] thy parish no thing teach' of the sin 'against kind [nature]', while the fifteenth-century *Book of Vices and Virtues* warns that it is an 'abomination' to speak of the sin, so much so that the devil himself is 'squeamish' when anyone does it.[47] Chaucer's Parson, in the lengthy moralizing tract that concludes the *Canterbury Tales*, appears to have an especially broad category of sins in mind, characterizing 'fornication, that is bitwixe man and woman' as a sin 'against nature'; he concludes his discussion of lechery with a discussion of that 'abominable sin, of which that no man unnethe ought [scarcely ought to] speak ne write'.[48]

The term 'sodomy' is not part of the vocabulary of these texts, though the writers' assumption is that readers know exactly what they mean. Chaucer's Parson admits that the vice in question is 'openly rehearsed in holy writ', although he also explains, more ambiguously, that it is performed, 'in diverse entente [intention] and in diverse manner', by women as well as by men. While the Parson's reference to the scriptures is apparently designed to clarify his comments, in the event he leaves us confused as to whether the vice embraces same- or cross-sex relations; likewise we never find out what the 'diverse' motives and methods of its practitioners really are, or what exactly goes 'against nature'. The *Vision of the Monk of Eynsham* – an account of a vision of purgatory purportedly witnessed by a monk in 1196 and translated from Latin into English for a fifteenth-century printed edition – is less circumspect. In a chapter on 'the unclean and foul vice and sin of sodomites', the visionary makes reference, allusively, to 'that foul sin, the which ought not be named'. But in a section on the punishments exacted, canny readers are afforded insights into the sorts of activities involved: the sodomites are set upon by 'great beasts, unnaturally shapen' and, 'in a foul damnable abusion', compelled to 'meddle' with them.[49]

Sodomy in these discussions encompasses a broad spectrum of acts and intentions, but it can also accommodate something rather more precise. Several of the Old and Middle English texts quoted, after all, do appear to associate the vice with same-sex relations. Moreover one fourteenth-century poem defines sodomy specifically as male–male anal sex. *Cleanness* is a text built around an opposition between cross-sex unions, valued as an instance of divine craftsmanship, and male–male intercourse, presented as a rejection of the perfect pleasure bestowed by God on humans in conventional lovemaking. The section of the poem focusing on the 'sin of Sodom' partly scorns relations between males for their affront to their 'natural' gender: 'Uch male mas his mach a man as hymselven' we are told, 'And fylter folyly in fere on femmales wyse' ['Each male takes as his mate a man like himself, and they join together wantonly in female fashion'].[50] But the poet also puns repeatedly on the vice's anal associations, as in the following passage describing how the Sodomites make their demands of Lot:

'If thou lovyes thy lyf, Loth, in thyse wones,
Yete uus out those yong men that yorewhyle here entred,
That we may lere hym of lof, as oure lyst biddes,
As is the asyse of Sodomas to segges that passen'.
Whatt! thay sputen and speken of so spitous fylthe;
What! thay yeyed and yolped of yestande sorwe,
That yet the wynd and the weder and the worlde stynkes
Of the brych that upbraydes those brothelych wordes.[51]
['If you love your life in this place, Lot, send out those young
men that recently entered here that we may teach them of love,
as our desire bids, as is the custom of Sodom for men who pass'.
What! They spat out and spoke such spiteful filth. What! They cried
out and boasted such festering dirt that the wind and the sky and
the world stinks of the breach that brings forth those poisonous
words.]

The word 'asyse' puns on asses; 'segges' refers to privies; the poet's comparison of the Sodomites' poisonous words to the smell of a 'brych' (an opening, rupture or violation) plays on the word for underpants ('breeches') as well as for the buttocks themselves. Although the word 'sodomy' itself is avoided by the *Cleanness* poet, in keeping with the familiar medieval device of circumspection, he paradoxically discloses what he appears to hide with these references to the sin's anal associations. The Sodomite is literally depicted talking out of his ass.[52]

Cleanness is one of the exceptions to the rule. More often than not it makes sense to keep an open mind on what we *think* writers mean when they refer to sins 'against nature' or sins that 'should not be named'. Indeed, it is precisely these indeterminacies that made sodomy such a versatile and rhetorically useful vice in the Middle Ages, ready to answer any number of political, moral and social requirements. The term's flexibility of reference and its associations with unmentionability provided medieval commentators with a means of critiquing power structures obliquely, by way of enigma and allusion, without putting themselves directly in the political firing line.

There are clear links, for example, between the deployment of sodomy as a term of political reproach and the reigns of weak kings. Late medieval chroniclers were occasionally quite audacious in their mud-slinging activities, even running to allegations of sodomy within the royal circle when circumstances allowed. The reign of Richard II, which ended with the king's deposition in 1399, was dogged by attacks on the king's counsellors, in particular his friend and confidante Richard de Vere, but what particularly stands out is the sexual content of the slurs. The accounts of the king's reign produced by Thomas Walsingham in the late fourteenth century ridiculed the lascivious practices of the king's favourites by showing how they posed a threat to courtly masculinity.[53] An entry in his short chronicle for the year 1387, for example, grumbles that courtiers were 'more powerful in the bedchamber than on the field, more vigorous with words than weapons, quick in speaking but slow in performing the acts of war', which implies that the court's exchange of macho activities such as warfare for lovemaking and verbal dexterity was potentially feminizing.[54] Conceptions of sodomy in the later Middle Ages were often shaped by the notion of a divinely inspired hierarchy between men and women, and writers who condemned sodomitic vice frequently did so in terms designed to disparage 'unnatural' perversions of gender. Theologians presented sodomy as feminizing, but also figuratively as feminine, a symptom of the belief that desire itself was inordinately female.[55] Alan of Lille (d. 1203), for instance, complained how sodomy turned 'hes into shes', while Peter Damian, in his *Book of Gomorrah* (1049), conjured up the image of an 'utterly diseased Queen of Sodom' who caused knights to be stripped of the 'armour of virtue' and 'pierced by the spears of every vice'.[56]

Depictions of sodomy as a violent assault perpetrated by a feminine persona on male bodies derived their force from medieval notions of femininity as already dangerously perverted. Against this backdrop, Adam of Usk, writing after Henry IV's usurpation of the throne, could easily turn from courtly perversions of gender to actual allegations of sodomy in his assessment of Richard's deposition. The closest Walsingham gets to characterizing the king's intimacies with his favourites as sodomitical occurs in a passage recounting de Vere's elevation as Duke of Ireland in 1386, which describes how the pair engaged in 'obscene intimacies'.[57] Usk, however, lists the king's *sodomidica*, his 'sodomies', as a cause of his downfall – an allegation which says next to nothing about the king's actual sexual habits.[58] The writer deploys sodomy in hindsight, as a justification for the Lancastrian accession and an instance of Richard's incompatibility with sovereign ideals.

The most famous visual image of Richard II appears in the Wilton Diptych, an artwork probably commissioned c.1395 by the king himself. The left panel of the diptych shows Richard with three saints – Edmund the martyr (king of East Anglia), Edward the Confessor and John the Baptist – being presented to the Virgin and Child in the right panel. What is striking about this arrangement is the fact that the saints in question were all celebrated in this period as models of male chastity. Why would a married king self-consciously wish to align himself with these representatives of saintly purity? Richard's first marriage to Anne of Bohemia (d. 1394) was childless, which generated considerable speculation about the identity of his heir. In medieval culture, as today, sexual potency and virility were closely linked, and the king's childlessness may have presented a further threat to his identity as a proper man. Medieval virginity potentially connoted heroism, moral worth and even virile power. So Richard's self-presentation as a virginal figure, in a company of eminent virgin saints, might be viewed as a retrospective attempt to pass off his childless marriage as a chaste union, deliberately chosen, in order to counter contemporary allegations attributing it to personal failure.[59] Moreover, the alleged sexual misdemeanours and contraventions of gender in Richard's court could have further fuelled this desire to present the king as a born-again virgin, undefiled by the sins of the flesh yet heroically battling, like his saintly models, to establish a sort of spiritual virility.

Richard's reign established a link between the practice of kingship and the performance of manhood in the minds of both his detractors and his supporters. But there were important precedents for associating courtly exuberance with moral laxity and gender transgression in medieval chronicles. Allegations of courtly degeneracy were especially prevalent in the decades after the Norman Conquest, when conservative clerics, buoyed up by the period's monastic reforms, protested in their writings against the codes of courtliness then being imported from regions of France.[60] The Norman monk Orderic Vitalis was at the forefront of this movement to denounce courtly style. He protested, for example, that a newfangled shoe, with pointy, turned-up toes, was being foisted on the court of Foulk le Rechin, count of Anjou (d. 1109), by groups of trend-setting 'effeminates'. Moreover 'foul catamites', he spluttered, 'doomed to eternal fire, unrestrainedly pursued their revels and shamelessly gave themselves up to the filth of sodomy. They rejected the traditions of great and illustrious men, ridiculed the counsels of priests and persisted in their barbarous way of life and style of dress'.[61] Orderic's comments on the demise of William Rufus, William the Conqueror's successor as king of England, continued in this vein. He attributed Rufus's death in 1100 to the 'effeminates' in the king's company, who 'carried on their debaucheries without restraint', as well as 'loathsome Ganymedes' who 'abused themselves with foul sodomite-things'. (Ganymede was a figure of classical Roman myth who was abducted by the God Jove and who became synonymous with homoerotic relations in this period.)[62]

William of Malmesbury, another chronicler of William Rufus's reign, likewise assumed a link between courtliness and gender transgression, taking a swipe at the fashion for long hair, fancy clothes and curly-toed shoes then sweeping through court. 'To compete with women for softness of body', he moans, 'to break stride with a cultivated negligence of gait, and to walk with the hips thrust forward: this was the epitome of style for youth'.[63] But effeminacy was not always associated explicitly with sodomy in these accounts. Although Orderic Vitalis condemned the 'barbarous' customs of courts in Anjou and England as sodomitical, it is not clear from his words what the 'filth of sodomy' actually implies, beyond its association with 'new' chivalric customs imported by foreigners. Uppermost in moralists' minds was courtly obsession with luxury and materiality, at a time when monastic ideals dictated increased austerity. Male clerics were expected to wear tonsures, not elegant coiffures, and it was with reference to courtly hairstyles rather than sodomy that William of Malmesbury attacked Henry I, Rufus's heir. William accused Henry of bringing over from Normandy a craze for wearing the hair long, a fashion that inspired English courtiers to make women of themselves in the way they dressed. (By contrast, William congratulated David II of Scotland, in whose court Aelred of Rievaulx had spent his youth, for resisting the spread of such extravagance in his own country.)[64]

Modern claims for William Rufus's 'homosexuality' begin to look a little unwieldy in this light.[65] They are based on an interpretation of the sources that associates allegations of effeminacy and courtly excess with male–male sexual relations, a connection that was not inevitably assumed by monastic chroniclers at this time. (As H. G. Cocks shows in Chapter 4, even in the 1800s effeminacy was not consistently associated with homosexual desire.) The nineteenth-century historian Edward Freeman, for example, characterized Rufus as a notorious invert, guilty of 'vices before unknown, the vices of the East, the special sin, as Englishmen then deemed, of the Norman', in order to represent homosexuality and effeminacy as undesirable Norman imports, imposed from above on the Anglo-Saxon population. Freeman's pernicious blend of nationalism and homophobia renders attempts to perpetuate the myth of Rufus's 'homosexual' legacy problematic.[66] At the same time, as with Richard II and Edward II, we should not be tempted simply to discount the possibility of the monarch's sexual nonconformity altogether. Allegations of effeminacy in the Anglo-Norman court tell us much about clerical attitudes to courtliness in the wake of monastic reform, but in truth there is no 'evidence' either way that would help us to secure or deny the notion that Rufus had sexual relations with other males. So an agnostic position on the question of Rufus's sexual preferences may ultimately be more helpful than one that assumes for all historical figures, unless 'proved' otherwise, a default position of monolithic straightness.

We have seen how Edward II's relationship with his favourite Piers Gaveston was characterized by contemporary chroniclers as an intense friendship, ritually sealed within a covenant of brotherhood. But with others looking back on his reign, we find the suspicion that such bonds were simply a cover for sodomy.[67] One chronicle mentions the king's preference for 'illicit and sinful unions' as an alternative to the embraces of his wife, while another describes how Edward indulged in sodomitic vice 'excessively'.[68] Moreover, the French chronicler Jean Froissart portrays the execution in 1326 of Hugh Despenser – another of the king's close advisers, who later in his reign provoked a renewed wave of baronial antipathy – in terms that clearly underscore the sexual as well as political nature of his crimes. Dragged in an elaborate procession through the streets of Hereford, Despenser was tied naked on a ladder in the town square and had his genitals removed, all because, Froissart announces, he was a 'heretic and sodomite'.[69]

Sodomy also seems to surface in accounts of Edward's own death. Deposed by his wife, Isabella of France, and her lover Mortimer in 1326, the king was imprisoned in Berkeley Castle in Gloucestershire and subsequently murdered. Certain chroniclers describe the manner of the king's death in terms that allude explicitly to anal penetration. To make sure no visible signs of foul play appeared on the king's body, for instance, Geoffrey le Baker describes how Edward's captors 'passed a red-hot soldering iron through a trumpet-like instrument ... into his anus, through the intestines and into his wind-pipe'; Ranulf Higden refers to his having been 'slain with a hot broche [spit] put through the secret place posterielle [posterior]'.[70] But the impalement motif is not necessarily meant to communicate the victim's sexual preferences – originally it was intended to emphasize the tyrannous nature of Isabella and Mortimer's usurpation. Baker's account is the first to make use of the red-hot spit anecdote, but he also aligns Edward explicitly with Christ, betrayed by his own people, as well as comparing him with the archetypal biblical sufferer Job. The chronicler may therefore have used the impalement image to highlight the king's status as a martyr, not a sodomite, by conveying the extreme agonies endured by Edward at the hands of evil tormentors. Between the twelfth century and the fifteenth, after all, a number of stories exist in which tyrants deploy impalement as a mode of punishment, notably Vlad the Impaler, prince of Wallachia. So the motif of impalement may simply be a literary convention, designed to defame the tormentors rather than the victims.[71]

Nevertheless, there are contemporary examples of anus-to-mouth impalement being used to punish sinners guilty of sodomy, in depictions of hell in Italian Last Judgment frescos.[72] The branding of Nicholas's buttocks with a red-hot coulter (the blade of a plough share) in Chaucer's 'Miller's Tale' likewise has sexual connotations.[73] Even if certain chroniclers appropriated the impalement motif to highlight the king's sanctity, other medieval writers may still have perceived a connection with sodomy. Higden, who was writing around the same time as Baker, makes reference to the hot spit episode, but comments that 'opprobrious death cause not a martyr', thus distancing himself from claims for Edward's posthumous sanctity.[74] The point is not that Edward's relationships with his peers were unambiguously sexual. 'Sodomy' was a massively meaningful category in medieval culture, but partly to the extent that it was not clearly defined – it was not consistently or inevitably associated with a distinct configuration of sexual partners, or even with a particular kind of sexual act. Those chroniclers who alluded to sodomy in the courts of kings did so because there was a sense in which male–male love and friendship, unlike sodomy, *did* signify plainly on the medieval radar screen. Ritually cemented bonds between males, as we have seen, were celebrated publicly in both literary and documentary sources. So when writers threw suspicion onto bonds between kings and courtiers with recourse to a language of sodomy, they generally did so with a view to undermining the capacity of those relations to be socially and politically meaningful.[75]

Unhooked from the purely sexual, sodomy could also be mobilized in different ways, to condemn ethnic difference, for example, or to shore up a sense of national identity. In his *Description of Wales*, written in 1194, Gerald of Wales describes the native Welsh people's praiseworthy traits, before going on to outline their more blameworthy characteristics. Among the various allegations is the following: that 'because of their oppressive sins and especially that detestable and wicked sodomitic sin, the Welsh lost Troy and then Britain in times past through divine punishment'.[76] His characterization of Welsh 'sodomitic sin' as a vice inherited from the Trojans and Britons – a vice he suggests they have not actually practiced for some time, despite having an inherent tendency to do so – transforms sodomy into a mark of ethnicity, a disposition dependent on lineage and – ironically – procreation. It is worth noting that the so-called Gerald of 'Wales' was himself only part-Welsh, since his mother was Norman. This may explain his willingness to take up the role of spokesman for the Norman-Welsh Marchers, the lords who ruled the frontier lands between England and Wales.[77] Gerald's sodomy allegation seems to be an attempt on his part to distinguish the Marchers with whom he was ideologically linked from the native Welsh, characterized as barbarously other.[78] Sodomy also appears in a related way in a petition by the Good Parliament in 1376 requesting that Edward III banish Lombard bankers from England, on account of the fact that some of them were Jews, Saracens and spies and that they had introduced to the kingdom 'the too horrible vice that is not to be named'.[79] Sodomy is much more than a category of transgressive sexual acts in these contexts: it has also become a mark of foreign or alien status.

If sodomy could be an ethnically charged category, it was just as readily associated with religious nonconformity. Connections were made between heresy and sodomy in medieval culture from at least the eleventh century, grounded in the assumption that religious deviance and sexual deviance were comparably sacrilegious. The groups that proved most troublesome to Church authorities were Cathars, or Albigensians, a heretical movement based in northern Italy and southern France which, it was claimed, licensed hedonistic sexual activity. The sect's alleged origins in Bulgaria gave rise to the use, in Old French, of the word *bougre* to describe Albigensian heretics, from which the modern English word 'bugger' is derived.[80] Clearly, by the thirteenth century, the term had already acquired associations with sodomy, as seen in the *Bible moralisée*, or 'moralized bible', an enormous illustrated manuscript first produced in Paris around 1225. The *Bible moralisée* worked by juxtaposing images illustrating Old Testament texts with corresponding images and texts commenting on and providing a 'moralized' interpretation of the preceding biblical narrative. One such bible contains a scene moralizing an episode in Judges 20, where a group of Benjamites who survive a devastating battle with the tribe of Israel flee into the wilderness. The scene links back to an earlier episode in Judges 19 in which the Benjamites demand that they might 'know' the Levite man lodging in their city (interpreted as a mirroring of the treatment of strangers by Sodom's inhabitants), and end up raping the Levite's wife. The bible's commentary text labels the Benjamites 'Sodomites', which plays on their association with sexual depravity and compares them explicitly with 'Bulgars and Albigensians' who 'adore and believe in the devil'; the commentary image depicts a cluster of men and women embracing beneath a cat (often associated with heresy) and a male–male couple kissing. An earlier page in the same bible contains a scene commenting on the episode in Genesis 12 where Abraham's wife is given over to pharaoh. The commentary image depicts a king kissing and stroking the chin of a bearded man, and a tonsured cleric and capped male embracing. But the accompanying text announces that the scene signifies 'the princes of the world and the heretics who endeavour to infest the Church with their persecutions'.[81]

The arrest of the Knights Templar by Philip IV of France in 1307 shows just quite how much could be at stake in the conflation of heresy and sodomy for political ends. Founded as a military order in 1118, to defend the newly created Latin kingdom of Jerusalem in the aftermath of the First Crusade, the Templars were one of the most respected religious orders in medieval Christendom, establishing communities throughout Europe as well as in the Holy Land. It is little wonder that Edward II of England's initial reaction to the arrest of all members of the French branch of the Order by his father-in-law on the grounds of 'detestable heresies' was astonishment, 'more than it is possible to believe'.[82] The official articles of accusation laid against the French branch of the Order in 1308, produced as a prelude to the brothers' interrogation and torture in Paris, outlined the precise nature of these 'heresies'. The Templars were charged with denying Christ, spitting on the Cross and idolatry, but also with illicit kissing 'on the mouth, on the navel or on the bare stomach and on the buttocks or the base of the spine', as well as permitting new brothers to have 'carnal relations together' and arguing that it was 'licit' to do so.[83] Only a handful of members of the French Order actually confessed to this final allegation (although they admitted to many of the other charges). The claims were part of a stock armoury of accusations designed to discredit political and religious enemies, and on the whole the Templars were probably *not* guilty as charged.[84] But the events leading to the Order's suppression are instructive for what they say about medieval attitudes to sodomy. It appears that the fall of the crusader states in 1291 was being interpreted as divine judgment for the failures of the Order, a judgment that had its counterpart in the biblical destruction of Sodom; Philip felt that unless he moved swiftly to stamp out the order and its associated sexual habits from his kingdom, God's wrath would be manifested in France.[85]

In England itself, Edward II eventually agreed to the arrest of the Templars, after he received a bull authorizing him to do so in the name of the pope; instructions were also issued to take members of the Order into custody in Scotland and Ireland. Although some efforts were made to enforce the papal inquisitors' demands for torture, in England there were few precedents for judicial torture, and the trials for the most part failed. The inquisitors had to rely in large measure on witnesses outside the Order, whereas in France many of the Templars arrested had confessed at least in part.[86] These witness statements do occasionally include references to sexual slurs. One man describes how twenty-five years ago he heard a member of the Hospitallers (another military order) calling the Templars 'anus kissers', while another – a London notary called Robert de Dorturer – said that the Master of the Templars in England 'wished to seize him for sodomy' but that he fled. The statements appear in a summary of the English trial proceedings, the only section to survive from a body of evidence compiled by prelates to bring before the ecumenical Church council of Vienne in 1311.[87] As such, the descriptions do not offer instances of actual male–male relations in the English branch of the Order. What they hint at instead is a perception that ritual and sexual same-sex interactions potentially share common grounds and that the line dividing sodomy – illegitimate, unmentionable and confused – from homosociality – legitimate, publicly sanctioned and comprehensible – can become hazy and imprecise. As with the moralized bible scenes, which depict sodomy visually with scenes of same-sex kissing and embracing, the accusations against the Templars are framed in part as a response to gestures of intimacy between males, some of which (for instance, kisses) are also part of the language of ritual brotherhood and passionate friendship. In these contexts, it seems easier to *know* what medieval writers and image makers mean when they make reference to sodomitical liaisons.[88]

In late fourteenth-century England, allegations of sodomy could also run in a different direction, from those accused of heresy to their accusers. Lollards were followers of John Wyclif, an Oxford academic who questioned the role of the institutional church in English society. In 1395, a document called the *Twelve Conclusions of the Lollards* was apparently posted on the doors of Westminster Hall while Parliament was in session; the *Twelve Conclusions* ended with Latin verses describing how the 'English people bewail the crime of Sodom'.[89] The reference to the English people – the *Anglorum gentes* – reveals this as another instance of sodomy's exploitation as a marker of national or ethnic difference: the poem expresses a desire for a nation free from sodomy. (One is reminded here of the Reverend Ian Paisley's calls to 'Save Ulster from sodomy!' in a 1970s and 1980s campaign against legalizing homosexuality in northern Ireland.)[90] But the verses also align sodomy with idolatry, the second line announcing how 'idols are the cause of these ills'. The conceit is that just as idolaters take pleasure in images that they rather ought to utilize as a springboard to enjoying God, practitioners of sodomy take pleasure in bodies that should be utilized for procreative ends.[91]

In 1401, a statute was drawn up in response to Lollard dissent, which condemned recidivist heretics to death by burning. Between the posting of the *Twelve Conclusions* and the passage of this statute, a second, anti-Lollard verse was copied into a manuscript citing the original Lollard lines decrying sodomy, this time naming the 'race of Lollards' as the 'vile race of Sodom ... whom you, prelates, should be prepared to condemn'.[92] Again the category is racialized, sodomy being appropriated to promote orthodox as well as heretical agendas. The term gets traded between both parties as a defamatory insult, in a spiral of accusations that places us at one remove from a world of actual same-sex sexual relations and desires.[93]

The echoes of Lollard anti-sodomy polemic were felt 150 years after the *Twelve Conclusions* were first drawn up, in the writings of the sixteenth-century reformer John Bale. Bale, who celebrates Lollard heresy as a heroic precursor to Protestantism, describes how the heretics not only posted the *Conclusions* at Westminster, but also copied out the verses and posted them on the windows, gates and doors of well-known 'hypocrites and fleshly livers', in an outbreak of guerrilla-style sodomyphobia.[94] Bale became somewhat obsessed with condemning the sodomitical practices of Catholic monks and prelates. He habitually presented the Church of Rome as a haven for diabolical sexual activity and was especially critical of the medieval prohibition against clerical marriage, which, he said, led to 'abominable sodometry'.[95] In one such polemic, Bale recounts a story first recorded by Bede in his *Ecclesiastical History* of 731, about Pope Gregory the Great, who once, Bede tells us, saw among the merchandise in a market in Rome some boys exposed for sale, with 'fair complexions, fine-cut features and beautiful hair'. The boys hailed from the land of Britain, members of the race of 'Angles' – a name that the future pope deemed appropriate on account of their 'angelic faces'; once Gregory succeeded to the papacy, moreover, memories of the encounter inspired him to send missionaries to Britain to convert the English people.[96] Bale's own interpretation of Bede's anecdote constructs for it a sodomitical subtext, by alluding to Gregory's sexual motivations for displaying an interest in the boys. Priests in those days, he announces, 'had no wives' and consequently sought other 'remedies' – the implication being that Gregory himself, denied a wife by demands for clerical celibacy, was looking to purchase a boy for sex.[97]

As these examples show, sodomy was especially useful in times of moral and political crisis, helping to polarize the divisions between orthodoxy and dissent, to promote religious reform, or to fuel resentment against kings and their close advisers. The appropriation of sodomy as a weapon of politics is a theme that continues well into the modern period, as we will see in subsequent chapters. But in the Middle Ages, it is striking how often the figures who were accused of sodomy, or played a role in suppressing it, were also embedded in the world of male–male love and friendship mapped out at the outset. Medieval social relations were premised on ritually marked interactions between males, but these interactions only signified as sodomitical when it was politically useful for them to do so. Hence, it is not surprising that kings whose best friends were elevated to positions of wealth and political clout – as witnessed in the partnerships between Edward II, Gaveston and Despenser, or Richard II and de Vere – were haunted by sodomy, especially in retrospect, to justify dynastic change or to feed the demands of barons for greater involvement in the running of the kingdom.

We can contrast this with a situation in which Richard Lionheart is explicitly linked with sodomy in historical writing. The same chronicler who makes such a song and dance about Richard's intimate relations with Philip also relates a story, in a different context, about a hermit who warns the king to abstain from 'illicit acts' – what these are, we are not told – and to 'remember the destruction of Sodom' or risk divine punishment.[98] It is not beyond the realms of possibility that the chronicler was deploying the motif of unmentionability to draw attention to Richard's sexual relations with other men. Why assume that if we do not have proof positive of Richard's homoerotic inclinations that he must therefore, by a process of elimination, be stably 'heterosexual'? What is of interest here is the fact that, in this particular context, sodomy and friendship are viewed as distinct, even dissimilar entities: sodomy is not part of the chronicler's vocabulary in his evocation of Richard and Philip's 'vehement love'.

In other times and places, sodomy polemic was a means for men who were intimate with other males to accentuate the distance between their own affections, presented as legitimate and pure, and the curse of Sodom, conceived as utterly repugnant. We have already seen how Edward II was caught up, albeit reluctantly at first, in the repression of the Templars in England on grounds of sexual as well as spiritual impoverishment. (Perhaps, like his great grandson Richard II, he wished to shore up his own spiritual purity, by expunging a readily locatable sodomitical threat; or he may simply have wanted to appease Philip IV of France, who was apparently opposed to his son-in-law's partnership with Gaveston.)[99]. But it is telling that Alcuin of York, Anselm of Canterbury and Aelred of Rievaulx, the medieval churchmen most often cited in support of the existence of a medieval 'gay sensibility', were themselves ardent anti-sodomy polemicists. Ælfric's discussion of the moral contrast between Sodom and the Flood was an adaptation of Alcuin's own commentary on Genesis, written in the late eighth century, which contrasts male lechery with women (which is natural) with male lechery with men (which is not).[100] According to his biographer Eadmer, Anselm raised 'the matter of sodomy' with William Rufus and, in the opening years of Henry I's reign, saw through ecclesiastical legislation on the subject. The Council of London of 1102 passed a statute condemning those who 'commit the shameful sin of sodomy', especially those 'who of their own free will take pleasure in doing so'; clerics found guilty of the vice were to be deposed, laypeople deprived of 'legal status and dignity'. Although it has been argued that Anselm was involved in suppressing the council's decrees, motivated in part by a recent papal decree urging humane treatment of repentant clerics who had not indulged in the vice many times,[101] such claims are designed to fit the image of Anselm as an advocate of 'gay' love. In fact, it was at his instigation that the Council of London met in the first place, and indeed Anselm may have felt that the decrees did not go far enough.[102] Finally Aelred preached a number of sermons in which he railed against sodomy in the clergy. These sinners 'confound the order and use of the sexes', he announced, and 'abuse themselves by every form of filth'; he went on to specify the terrifying torments that these 'sodomites' could expect in hell.[103]

The anti-sodomy diatribes associated with Alcuin, Anselm and Aelred could be interpreted as instances of internalized homophobia.[104] But this assumes that we know homosexual identity fully when we see it, and that sodomy and same-sex love are inevitably two sides of the same coin. There is certainly support for the idea that sexual and emotional relations could become confused. As we have seen, medieval writers did embrace male–male sexual interactions in their definitions of sodomy (though they often embraced much more besides). There were also clearly moments when a certain amount of equivalence between emotional and sexual intimacy was assumed. This is seen most visibly in the *Bible moralisée* scenes referred to earlier, which show sodomites engaged in hugging and kissing. Such activities mirror gestures also characteristic of sworn brotherhood and passionate friendship, so that allusions to sodomy in such depictions clearly 'sodomize' interactions that in other contexts were predominantly asexual. Yet it remains to be seen how ordinary medieval people negotiated the perilous divide between sodomy and same-sex fellowship in their daily lives; whether they experienced their relationships solidifying into self-conscious identities, orientations or erotic inclinations; and what the impact of sodomy polemic was on medieval social arrangements. It is with this world of everyday practice that I shall conclude.

Everyday experiences and expressions

Representations produced by, for, or about people at the top of the social hierarchy – kings and princes, for instance, or archbishops and abbots – necessarily loom large in histories of medieval love and sex. Texts in which males are represented entering into compacts of brotherhood, love and friendship with one another privilege relationships that mattered politically as well as personally. So they inevitably focus for the most part on high-ranking figures. Moreover in these contexts, it is not normally possible to get beyond the shadowy cloud of sodomy allegations that haunt these depictions, to 'evidence' of certifiable same-sex sexual contact. This is not to say that the protagonists, regardless of their sexual conduct, did not relate to one another in ways possessing a certain affinity with modern gay expression. But rather than putting our faith in positively identifying 'homosexual' persons when sources permit (we cannot subject the historical record to the equivalent of DNA testing, and even if we could it probably would not get us very far), it may be more productive to think in terms of 'gay-like' experiences and expressions – practices that overlap partially and incompletely with more recent understandings of same-sex behaviour, identity and desire.[105] This has the advantage of resisting the compulsion to produce histories of heterosexuality by default (acknowledging, for example, that notions of a heterosexual 'norm' are as time- and culture-bound as homosexuality itself). But it also permits glimpses into aspects of existence that register less frequently or plainly on the map of same-sex intimacy – manifestations of male–male togetherness that, while not exactly average from the point of view of the social classes represented, nonetheless escape the notice of historians relying on chronicles and documentary sources.

One such manifestation comes into view on the inscribed marble tomb slab of two knights in the coterie of Richard II, Sir William Neville and Sir John Clanvowe, who died in October 1391, a few days apart, in a suburb of Constantinople (modern-day Istanbul). The pair were buried together, in the nearby Dominican church, in a common grave. The tomb slab represents their coats-of-arms 'impaled', that is to say divided in half, with the armorial bearings of Neville, on each shield, juxtaposed with the bearings of Clanvowe. Above the shields, which also lean towards each other, are two helmets, topped off by elaborate crests; the helmets, arranged in profile, look as though they are about to kiss.[106]

The device of impalement in heraldry was more commonly used to depict a union of husband and wife. But here it conveys the relationship between two knights. There are other examples of males impaling or exchanging their arms with the arms of male associates in medieval England.[107] After 1395, Richard II himself displayed his allegiance to Edward the Confessor – and presumably to his 'virginal' status – by joining his own arms with the Confessor's mythical heraldic device.[108] There is also an English treatise on heraldry that records an anecdote about two knights, who were 'sworn brethren', one of whom, because of 'the great love that his sworn brother had to him', swapped his own arms with the arms of his companion, in commemoration of the 'great love betwixt them'.[109] This suggests that the representation of the combined arms of two males, rare though it was, can be situated squarely in the context of the language of male–male love and friendship explored earlier in this chapter; the motif of kissing, a gesture with ritual as well as emotional significance, adds further support to the idea that Neville and Clanvowe were sworn brothers. But it is a written record for 1391 – a passage from the *Westminster Chronicle* – that really brings the significance of the tomb slab home. Neville, we are told, was so upset by the death of Clanvowe, 'for whom his love was no less than for himself', that he never took food again and died, two days later, of inconsolable grief.[110]

Taken together, the chronicle entry and tomb slab underscore the public significance of Neville and Clanvowe's relationship, revealing the capacity for amatory unions between two males to signify visibly and legitimately in pre-modern cultures. This is about as far from sodomy as one can get. Both knights appeared in the line-up of 'Lollard knights' listed by certain fourteenth-century chroniclers; Clanvowe himself authored a pious religious treatise called *The Two Ways* that betrays a certain amount of reformist sympathy. (As has already been noted, Lollards backed a wave of anti-sodomy polemic in late fourteenth-century England.) We also know that the pair moved in the same circles as Chaucer, being close enough to witness a deed releasing the poet from a rape charge brought against him in 1380.[111] Significantly, Clanvowe quoted from an early version of Chaucer's 'The Knight's Tale', called by Chaucer the tale of 'the love of Palamon and Arcite of Thebes', in his own *Boke of Cupide, God of Love*.[112] This suggests that Neville and Clanvowe viewed their relationship in terms reminiscent of the kinds of male–male intimacy that Chaucer portrays so vividly in his poetry. Yet the fact that the couple elected to be buried in this fashion – sharing, like Amys and Amylion, a grave – also highlights the extraordinary intensity of their bond. Monumentalizing their love in public, displaying it for the gaze of future generations, the grave mates were probably motivated by concerns transcending those of individual mutual affection (the establishment of a union between two families, for example, or the formation of an artificial kinship with social weight). But this is not to say that their love was not genuinely felt.

Clanvowe's preference for homosocial union with a single male partner – an orientation with enduring, one might say death-defying force – stands in stark contrast to his intense distaste for cross-sex sexual relations in his moral outlook. His treatise *The Two Ways* contains a harsh indictment of 'foul lecherousness', a sin which he expressly connects with the transgressions of Adam and Eve at the Fall, and which he associates later on with promiscuity.[113] This makes it seem unlikely that the union between Neville and Clanvowe was consummated sexually – which is not to say that the bond was not, in a broader sense, erotically motivated or charged. In this particular instance, the sodomitical and the not-sodomitical seem poles apart.

When we do catch a glimpse of 'ordinary' males engaged in sexual activity with one another in medieval sources, it is usually in the context of secular or ecclesiastical proscription. This means that the main focus is in all likelihood the illegal sex act that took place. Other modes of intimacy related to the liaison are of interest to the recorders only insofar as they reveal something about the participants' intentions, or the manner in which the sex act was performed. This has led some historians to make claims for a time before sexual identities, a medieval past when acts alone defined one's place in the hierarchy of sinfulness. The French philosopher Michel Foucault famously distinguished between sodomy as a category of 'forbidden acts', defined by ecclesiastical or civic regulation, and the homosexual as a 'personage' and 'way of life', which he suggests enters into the public imagination most forcefully through the medium of nineteenth-century psychiatry.[114] It should be emphasized that Foucault is not making an empirical claim for the historical existence or not of sexually deviant individuals in particular periods. As such, this is not an argument for the modern 'origins' of homosexuality. Rather it is a claim about two different modes of disqualifying sexual practices in written texts. If we read documents of legal proscription, the picture that generally emerges is of illicit sex acts rather than coherent identities defined by a way of life, as was suggested by late-nineteenth century sexologists for example. Our understanding of medieval same-sex relations thus fundamentally depends upon the kinds of evidence we examine.

Certainly, the impression conveyed by medieval penitentials – reference guides for priests and monastic confessors on the types and gradations of penance appropriate to different sins – is that sex acts were predominantly at issue. Anglo-Saxon penitentials, which may be viewed partly as documents of living practice, regularly target same-sex sexual activity as part of a general effort to restrict sex to marriage and, within marriage, to procreation.[115] Occasionally, these texts contain canons requiring penance for sexual relations between two females.[116] But the vast majority of canons making reference to same-sex acts do so in the context of male–male liaisons. Even with a single penitential, there were usually a number of options available to the confessor for assigning penances for male–male sex. The tenth-century *Old English Penitential* mentions the individual who fornicates 'unlawfully' with animals, 'one who soils himself with young ones' and the 'male who has intercourse with another male'. The text goes on to distinguish the penances appropriate for the twenty-year-old practitioner (who should fast for fifteen years), the married forty-year-old participant (who is refused Mass and required to fast for the rest of his life) and 'young' and 'witless men' (who are beaten).[117] The *Canons of Theodore*, a translation of the Latin *Penitential* of Theodore, mentions, among other things, male–male fornication, inter-femoral intercourse 'between the limbs' and the practice of sending 'seed into the mouth' (deemed 'the greatest evil'); the practitioners of these sins include boys, adult men, those who have sexual relations with members of monastic orders, biological brothers and a category called in Anglo-Saxon *bædling*, which may refer to a special variety of male who took on a passive role in sex and was known to do so on a regular basis.[118]

With their matter-of-fact condemnations of same-sex sexual activity, these documents put pay to any notion of 'tolerance' towards male–male sex on the part of the early medieval Church.[119] But they also afford insights into the organization of same-sex behaviour along axes such as age, gendered style and sexual role. The word *bædling*, which appears in only one other closely related translation of the *Penitential* of Theodore, may derive from another Old English word meaning 'hermaphrodite' or 'effeminate fellow, womanish man'; the suffix '-ling' in Old English is diminutive, suggesting subordination or even youth. This may betray an awareness of a sexual minority, even a separate sexual identity, in

Anglo-Saxon writings – a category of person known to have sex with ordinary males, as well as with others like himself.[120] But the distinction between *bædling* and other categories of males who have sex with males also suggests that there were many people who were not included – or did not view themselves – under this specific and little-used heading. The *Old English Penitential* makes reference to a man who is married engaging in same-sex relations, as well as the *wæpnedman*, or manly male, having sex with 'another' like himself (the *wæpned* prefix has associations with being armed). This suggests that the notion of a distinct or self-conscious homosexual minority, set apart from the heterosexual majority, was not the most prominent organizing principle in Anglo-Saxon penitential writings. Some handbooks of penance do make reference to outbreaks of 'habitual' sodomy, performed by 'sodomites', which may exhibit a fear that frequent same-sex activity will solidify into an identity of sorts.[121] But there were also clearly males who had sex with other males outside these parameters, groups for whom the notion of modern gay identity, in the sense of sexual orientation, probably would not make immediate sense.

One of the contexts in which same-sex activity took place without necessarily hardening into a distinct identity or way of life – at least, according to the terms by which it was officially acknowledged and identified – was the single-sex monastery. We have already seen how certain penitentials attempted to regulate sexual relations with males in orders. Some texts also address same-sex relations within orders, such as a Latin penitential attributed to Bede (but not written by him) prescribing penance for nuns who fornicate with other nuns by means of a *machina* or 'device' – presumably a reference to the use of a dildo-like object.[122] But there are also indications that it continued to be necessary in later periods to regulate same-sex sexual activities in monasteries. A good example surfaces in the account by the monk Jocelin of Brakelond of the goings on in the Abbey of Edmundsbury (Bury St Edmunds) in the last decades of the twelfth century. At one point in his *Chronicle*, Jocelin recounts how, following the election of a new abbot, Samson, one of Samson's rivals for the election, William Wiardel, was dismissed from his role as sacrist. When moves were made to oppose the dismissal by Wiardel's friends, Samson publicly declared that his action was justified by the fact that, as sacrist, Wiardel had engaged in dodgy financial dealings without the abbey's leave. But the chief cause, Jocelin says, 'he did not mention, not wishing to make a scandal of him'. The cause in question comes into focus in the context of Wiardel's punishment after the dismissal – the destruction of his houses 'as being unworthy to stand upon the earth, an account of the frequent wine-bibbing, and other things of which it is best not to say'. The references to unmentionableness and the eradication of buildings produce a veiled allusion both to sodomy and to the destruction of Sodom. But the fact that Abbot Samson refuses to go public with the allegation indicates that this may not simply be a case of sodomy being appropriated rhetorically. Samson is clearly concerned for the reputation of his abbey, but medieval theologians also defined 'scandal' as an event that gives rise to sins in others. What is more, given the abbot's destructive inclinations, it seems reasonable to assume that he at least believed the allegations to be true: these are things 'which willy-nilly he had witnessed', we are told.[123]

A concern to avoid scandal was also uppermost in the mind of John, Duke of Bedford, who in 1422 wrote a letter to the Prior of a monastery in Durham conveying his distress that one of the inhabitants, by the name of John Marley, 'was not long ago proved and found guilty of the horrible sin of sodomy'. Bedford noted that he himself was a lay brother at the monastery and insisted that the Prior seek out the monk in question and punish him 'sharply'.[124] Other monastic records point towards a distinction between sodomy, conceived as unspeakably vile and deserving of expulsion, and male–male relations that provoked complaint but not outright condemnation. An inspection of religious houses by the Bishop of Lincoln in his diocese turned up the case, in 1440, of one John Dey, a canon of New College, Leicester, who was 'defamed' of sodomy and, after an investigation, excluded from the College. The bishop's sentence charges Dey with 'that damnable and hateful sodomitic vice, by the name whereof alone the air is defiled, committed in damnable wise by you, as it was said, with divers persons'; earlier we learn that Dey's partners included two choristers and another canon.[125] But there is also a reference in the same record to the investigation of a claim that at Markby Priory in 1438 'secular youths do lie in the dorter among the canons, and some with the canons in the same beds, and especially John Alforde, who more often than others has such in bed with him'; the allegation is repeated several times in the course of the deposition, for instance with the detail that Alforde often lay with John Kyrkeby's brother's son. However, in these contexts, the word 'sodomy' is not explicitly deployed. Alforde's bed-sharing activities failed to induce the same kind of outcry as Dey's sodomitical activities, which may indicate that the former was not viewed as an identical kind of sin.

Indeed, Alforde is simply told that henceforth he should not allow anyone to sleep with him except in times of 'pressing and unavoidable necessity'.[126] The Lincoln visitation records thus offer a glimpse of the opportunities that certain institutions such as monasteries offered for male–male relations, without those relations inevitably falling under the heading of sodomy.[127]

The reference in the Lincoln visitations to Alforde's sleeping with youths also draws attention to the fact that in medieval cultures, same-sex relations between males were often age-differentiated relations, structured according to a distinction between youth and adulthood. Although it is not possible to demonstrate the existence of a coherent 'system' of dual desire for both boys and women in the lives of individual monks, of the sort Randolph Trumbach attributes to the majority of men in the sixteenth century, this is a theme that likewise emerges forcefully in Renaissance representations of sodomy. We have already encountered instances of male–male liaisons that fall into the categories of pederasty or age-differentiated desire. Aelred of Rievaulx's spiritual friendships were cemented with monks younger than himself, and Walter Map's homophobic joke about Bernard of Clairvaux's bed-sharing activities makes reference specifically to 'boys' being stimulated by monks. Moralized bible manuscripts that include scenes of male–male couples embracing and kissing sometimes make the older participant in the exchange taller than his more diminutive companion, or depict him as a bearded figure.[128] Although the illustrations of the Sodom story in the eleventh-century Hexateuch manuscript depict both the Sodomites and the angels as beardless, we should not necessarily read too much into the youthful appearance of the latter: winged angels with beards are rare in medieval art. Nonetheless, the poem *Cleanness* describes Lot's guests explicitly as beardless 'yong men'. The Old English term *bædling* may have been associated with youth as well as effeminate passivity. Finally, Anglo-Saxon penitentials regularly differentiated sexual activities between boys from relations between boys and men; sometimes a further distinction was made, regarding the penances to be administered to younger and older boys.[129]

The prominence of age-differentiated relations helps explain the special measures that were taken to regulate contact between adults and children in monastic environments. Child oblation, the practice of parents dedicating their offspring to religious houses at an early age, was especially common in early medieval monasticism, provoking the drawing up of rules designed specifically with the monastery's younger inhabitants in mind. Abbots were charged with watching over boys and adolescents, making sure they never went unsupervised; there were even regulations about boys going to the toilet in the night, such as the requirement that boys 'perform the necessities of nature with a light, and their masters with them' – presumably a strategy to prevent masturbation, among other things.[130] But, there were also rules acknowledging the possibility of sexual desire between adult masters and their younger charges. For instance, a tenth-century rulebook, specifically drawn up for English monastic houses, commands that 'not even on the excuse of some spiritual matter shall any monk presume to take with him a young boy alone for any private purpose', before going on to stipulate that children remain under the care of a master. At the same time, the text continues, the master himself should not be permitted to be in the company of a boy 'without a third person as witness'.[131] Anxieties about man–boy relations were even reflected in the spatial arrangements of early medieval religious houses. Among the reforms undertaken by monastic reformers in ninth-century France was the drafting of the St Gall Plan, an attempt to embody in architectural form the ideals of the Benedictine Rule. This plan pays considerable attention to the segregation of children from adults, as well as to the regulation of children's areas of activity with each other. Viewed in conjunction with penitential literature of the period, the underlying sexual logic of these arrangements is apparent.[132]

Monasteries were spaces set apart from the rest of medieval society, and we should be wary about abstracting from regulations designed to prevent sexual activity between monks and boys conclusions about the nature of male–male interactions in other areas of social existence. It is not possible to produce statistical surveys for medieval England of the sort available for late medieval Florence, where legal documentation suggests that most adult males engaged in sexual relations with younger, adolescent males as well as with women.[133] We can therefore only guess at the significance of man–boy or man–youth relations in society at large. In the next chapter, Trumbach argues for the existence of a system of 'dual desire' for boys and women in Renaissance Britain to which the majority of men were prone. However, while there is certainly evidence that *some* men surveyed in the present chapter fit this pattern, I take the view that it is one of a number of competing models of desire rather than being symptomatic of a single, unified system. I prefer to keep in view the particular institutional contexts in which same-sex relations assume significance, rather than projecting the Florentine situation onto other localities in Europe and drawing identical conclusions.

Bearing these qualifications in mind, my argument about the significance of age differentials specifically concerns the medieval English monastery. Here, a number of different sources combine to produce a picture of passion and erotic possibility between younger and older males. Indeed, efforts to divide children from adults may ironically have increased the capacity for young males to elicit sexual attraction. Although organized around divisions between different generations, gender distinctions still tend to be strongly present in all-male institutions. After all, it is often the case that adult men appear more visibly and audibly 'masculine' than boys. But these gender splits also commonly map onto other kinds of difference – distinctions of intellect, power and responsibility. The single-sex monastery may thus have generated situations in which the appeal of age-differentiated pederasty was especially powerful.[134]

Of course, in the confines of a monastery's walls, the main concern was with maintaining a monk's chastity. Paradoxically, this may explain why medieval religious institutions proved especially conducive to the composition of homoerotic poetry. We have already seen how figures such as Alcuin, Anselm and Aelred promoted erotically charged friend-ships with other males, while fiercely opposing sodomy in other contexts. The writings of the twelfth-century cleric Hilary the Englishman are comparable in intensity: in a Latin poem entitled 'To an English Boy', in which the poet makes explicit reference to Pope Gregory's praise for the 'angelic' English in Bede, Hilary declares:

When nature created you, it wavered for a moment,
Deciding whether to bring you forth as a girl or a male.
But while she fixed her mind's eye on this choice,
Look, you came forth, a boy born for all to see.

…

You stand out, an object of general devotion for young men
and girls;
They sigh and long for you, recognizing you as unique.
Those who call you English truly make a mistake; no, they even sin.
Let them change the vowel and say angel.[135]

Again such developments cannot be accounted for simply with recourse to a notion of early medieval tolerance. That monastic institutions were able to generate expressions of such vitality is best explained by the fact that from the eleventh century, in particular, general efforts were made by churchmen to harness the language of Eros as a medium for mystical transport and spiritual transcendence. The idea was to appropriate a vocabulary of homoerotic affect as a meditative starting point – a stepping stone, so to speak – that was in the last analysis differentiated from actual physical expression.[136]

This was a situation in which divisions between spiritual relations and sexual relations were delicately balanced. Although efforts were evidently made to channel same-sex attraction into disembodied forms, there are indications that in the early Middle Ages certain monastic communities openly acknowledged same-sex desire between monks, or monks and boys, in texts, visual images and even drama.[137] The late eleventh century, however, saw a shift towards the reconfiguration of such longing as dangerously sodomitical. Peter Damian's *Book of Gomorrah*, which has been called 'the first comprehensive guidebook to Christian homophobia',[138] denounced what he perceived as the institutionalization of sodomy in monasteries. Damian reserved special venom for 'spiritual fathers who contaminated their sons' calling for the expulsion from orders of monks and clerics who had sex with other males.[139] This was also a period when the distinctions formerly erected between physical sexual activity and nonphysical expressions of same-sex intimacy began to lose some of their practical force. In the eleventh century, the age at which children were admitted to monasteries was raised, and more monks entered these institutions as adults. As a result, the length of training a monk received was dramatically curtailed, generating a demand for measures aimed at repression and eradication, rather than techniques designed to redirect sexual desire towards spiritual union with God.[140] This might account for the apparent decline in the language of passionate friendship in Christian monasticism after the twelfth century. Within the new climate of moral panic whipped up by figures such as Damian, verbal expressions of homoerotic passion risked being read as a prelude to sodomitic deeds.

When we turn to secular society, and to the sexual regulation of ordinary people, it is striking how rarely sodomy appears in judicial spheres. We should not be tempted to attribute this simply to low levels of same-sex sexual activity. Anglo-Saxon penitentials, with their concern to regulate the sins of lay people as well as clerics, assumed that male–male sexual contact took place in a variety of social contexts, involving married partners, for example, or relations between same-sex siblings. Single-sex education, military service and the extended household were all situations in which male–male contact probably took place in medieval cultures without being prohibited under the pretext of sodomy.[141] Sodomy's absence from secular justice is explained by the simple fact that there were no secular laws against sodomy, or other categories of same-sex relation, until February 1534, in the reign of Henry VIII, when parliament passed a bill against 'buggery'. Anglo-Saxon law codes occasionally punish sexual offences such as rape and incest, and often include provisions for penalizing adultery. But same-sex offences are never mentioned in these laws.[142] A thirteenth-century English legal compilation called *Fleta* recommends burial alive for 'those who have dealings with Jews or Jewesses, those who commit bestiality, and sodomists'; the almost contemporary treatise *Britton* prescribes burning, this time lumping sodomites together with sorcerers, apostates and heretics.[143] But these are textbooks, not legal codes, and there is no evidence that such penalties were actually enforced. (A different picture emerges elsewhere in Europe in certain urban settings, especially after 1400.)[144] In a culture where male–male sexual relations had no explicit legal consequence, it is not surprising that sodomy appears almost nowhere in records of temporal justice. It is only in documentation associated with church courts, where sexual matters were explicitly part of the remit, that we are afforded a glimpse of the situations in which male–male relations were deemed culturally troubling.

Fifteenth-century London church court records turn up a single reference to sodomy among many thousands of cases. Yet in this instance, the court appears to have been less concerned with sodomy itself than with its use as a means of defamation: in 1471, William Smyth 'publicly preached' that he had committed a 'sodomitic crime with master Thomas Tunley', but the case was dropped from court. Defamatory insult was also at issue in the other case relevant to the study of same-sex relations in this set of records: an allegation by one Agnes Andrew that Margaret Myler's husband was a 'woman', who, she said, was accustomed to 'grab' priests between the legs.[145] Once again, the case was dismissed from court, and it is therefore not clear whether Myler's husband *actually* cross-dressed as a woman, or whether the allegations of interfering with priests had any substance. The suit is mainly of interest for the light it sheds on the connections between effeminacy and male–male sexual relations in this period. It bears comparison with perhaps the most famous literary depiction of a man whose lacking masculinity bespeaks a general queer lack of fit in medieval society: Chaucer's Pardoner in the *Canterbury Tales*, who is described by the narrator in the General Prologue as 'a gelding or a mare', that is to say a eunuch or a female horse.[146]

London in the later Middle Ages probably did not have anything resembling modern gay 'subcultures'. A chronicle written at Winchester in the 1190s, during the reign of Richard Lionheart, lists within an inventory of London's 'grave obscenities' its 'smooth-skinned lads', 'hustlers', 'effeminates' and 'male-lovers',[147] which has sometimes been read literally, as referring to a tradition of subterranean same-sex networking in medieval cities.[148] The description is actually a fiction-alized account, placed in the mouth of a French Jew; the Jew advises a Christian boy, who he has taken on as an apprentice, to migrate to England but to pass through London quickly on his way to Winchester. The text is full of classical and scriptural allusions: categories such as 'effeminates' (*molles*) and 'male-lovers' (*mascularii*) are derived from I Corinthians 6:9, where they count among the 'unjust' who will fail to inherit God's kingdom. Moreover, the chronicle continues with a satirical account of the disappearance of the 'poor lad' while he is staying with the Winchester Jewry – a passage designed to stimulate thoughts in the reader of ritual Jewish child murder. The chronicler, who was a Benedictine monk, wished to expose through such means the 'fictive' nature of Christian representations of Judaism: by conjuring up narratives of ritual murder, the chronicler wanted to draw attention to the ways in which hysterical fantasies replace or disguise historical realities. This alerts us to the problems of treating such material as 'true history', a reflection of actual social experience.[149]

What the passage about London's citizenship does hint at is another institutional context within which male–male sexual relations conceivably prospered, from time to time, in medieval cities: that of prostitution. One of the most extraordinary documents to come to light in recent years, where selling sex for money is very much at issue, is an entry in the Plea and Memoranda Rolls for London in 1394. The case provides a fitting conclusion to issues raised in this chapter about the terms in which we conceive male–male relations in pre-modern cultures. The document concerns the testimony of one John Rykener, 'calling him/herself Eleanor', who, 'having been detected in women's clothing', was discovered by city officials 'committing that detestable, unmentionable, and ignominious vice' with a man called John Britby. Britby, 'thinking he was a woman', asked if he could 'as he would a woman ... commit a libidinous act with her'; John/Eleanor, we are told, asked for money for his/her 'labour'. In the course of the encounter, the pair were captured and taken to prison, but the narrative does not end there. The scribe also provides further titbits, such as the fact that s/he was taught how to dress up in women's clothing by one Elizabeth Brouderer and that in Brouderer's house a priest from Essex had sex with him/her 'as with a woman'. Furthermore, dressed as Eleanor, s/he worked as an embroideress for a few weeks in Oxford, where several scholars 'practiced the abominable vice with him often'; several friars and 'six foreign men' also committed the vice with him/her, in exchange for money, as did countless other clerics; strikingly, John/Eleanor also 'as a man' had sex with a number of married and unmarried women, as well as with numerous nuns.[150]

Both sodomy and prostitution offer important lenses for reading this extraordinary document. Exchange of money is clearly at issue in John/Eleanor Rykener's sexual relations with other males (if not with his/her female partners); the familiar motif of unmentionability, deployed repeatedly in these contexts, announces a clear sodomitical subtext. But the document also reveals the potential compatibility of same-sex sexual relations with cross-sex sexual relations in the experience of a single individual. Just as sodomy and friendship make strange but curiously intimate bedfellows in the medieval sources we have encountered in this chapter (and just as many of the relations discussed refuse to be packaged neatly into boxes like 'homosexuality' or 'gay love'), it makes no sense to try to accommodate John/Eleanor fully within 'common-sense' parameters. Is s/he a male sodomite, a female impersonator, a resourceful prostitute or a libido-driven sex addict? Where exactly, in John/Eleanor's gendered and sexual performances, does the 'male' end and the 'female' begin? Asking questions of this sort may well raise the issue of whether this is a document about male–male relations at all. But what it says about medieval experiences of sexual identity is thoroughly instructive. Male–male sex in the document is modelled so as to emphasize configurations of male and female (witness Britby's repeated insistence that he thought Eleanor a woman). On the surface, it seems that 'heterosexuality' exerts a powerful organizing influence on the text, while 'homosexuality' awaits discovery as a deeper kind of truth. But, the document may also benefit from being opened up to other, less prescriptive frameworks. John/Eleanor partially accommodates the categories we attempt to impose on him/her, but also resists them too, in the same way that labelling Richard Lionheart gay or straight may ultimately be beside the point. What we end up with in this effort to resist proscriptive labels may not be 'gay' in the sense of a history that mirrors modern sexual identities absolutely. But it may provide points of departure for a queerer, more unruly understanding of sex and love in the medieval past.

Chapter 2

Renaissance Sodomy, 1500–1700

Randolph Trumbach

Between the Middle Ages and the Renaissance, there was no real break in the way in which sexual relations between males were organized. There were some changes. Monasteries were abolished, and priests were allowed to marry, but priests, like other men, continued to have sexual relations with both adolescent boys and women as they had done before 1500. The establishment after 1576 of permanent theatres in London produced a venue (as the Puritans complained) for the public discussion of sodomy since about one-third of the 300 plays for which texts exist for the period from 1601 to 1642 have some reference to sexual relations between men and boys. More information on the history of sodomy therefore survives for the Renaissance than for the Middle Ages, but the kinds of information remain the same. There is gossip and biographical information about kings and gentlemen. There are sodomy trials and visitation records. And there are plays and poems.

The previous chapter has made the point that in medieval cultures, relations between males were often structured by differences in age. This chapter argues in addition that men attracted to adolescent boys also desired women and that this dual desire was probably experienced by all men. The statistical information from fifteenth-century Florence establishes in fact that in a mere 5 percent of cases did sexual relations occur between two adult males – all the other sodomy was between men and boys. In medieval England, the sin of the men of Sodom in the book of Genesis was invariably represented as occurring between beardless youths and bearded men, both in the visual and in the written sources. The illustrations from the Anglo-Saxon period in the Old English version of the Heptateuch paint two beardless youths as Lot's visitors and put beards on both Abraham and Lot. The author of *Cleanness* in the fourteenth century describes Lot's visitors in Sodom as having 'berdles chynnes' (L. 789). The sodomy of Sodom was structured by differences in age, and all the men at Sodom desired these youths. These Sodomites also desired women, and for this reason Lot attempted to save the youths by offering his daughters in their place. The Florentine material similarly establishes that the men who pursued boys also desired women and that these two forms of desire were experienced by all Florentine men.[1]

Sexual systems in which all the men in a society engaged in relations with both women and boys have existed in many different times and places. This evidence makes the English Renaissance world more credible to readers in the twenty-first century. It allows us to see how the varying forms of relations between males in age-structured systems fit together since across time and space, there is an interesting consistency in the roles that such systems produce. This is true whether one considers the ancient pagan Romans, the Renaissance Florentines or, in the twentieth century, the worlds of either the Muslim Mediterranean or the Hindu India. In all of these worlds (as in Renaissance England), there were four different roles that individuals could play in sexual relations between males. There was the adult penetrating man. There was the passive penetrated boy. And there were two kinds of passive penetrated adult males. One kind of passive adult usually married a woman but secretly had relations with other active adult males. If his passivity was discovered, he was treated with great contempt. He was an individual who had failed to make the transition once his beard had grown from passive boy to active man. It was essential to male honour to make this transition, and men went to some pains (as Shakespeare's sonnets show) to make the certain that the boys they loved did so. In Renaissance Florence, these passive adults were 3 percent of the men charged with sodomy, and this would seem to be a likely enough percentage for this kind of man in all these age-structured systems. The second kind of adult passive man became a transvestite prostitute. He left the world of the family and often became a member of a band of such men who served as an alternative family. These two kinds of passive adults do show up occasionally in the English Renaissance world, but one would not expect to find many men of either kind.

In ancient Rome, free men had sexual relations with boys who were slaves or foreigners. They were supposed to avoid free boys. But, some free boys must have had relations with men, and a percentage of these grew up to be passive adult men who usually married women but were held in great contempt for their passivity with men. These passive men were the cinaedi. The galli were the transvestite men who joined a band. They served the Mother Goddess and were also prostitutes. The historian John Boswell agreed that the Roman sources presumed that all men desired both boys and women. In the twentieth century, a survey of Arab university students (some of whom were Christians) showed that 75 percent had had sexual relations with women (usually prostitutes) and 44 percent with males, usually beginning at twelve or thirteen. Across the Muslim world, the four roles of age-structured sexual relations between males appear, whether in Turkey, Oman or Morocco. Studies of late twentieth-century India have concentrated on the role of the hijra, the transvestite prostitute who joins a band, is often castrated and serves a goddess. The men who go to the hijra have usually not been studied. A hijra in one of the earliest studies (1983) makes the point that 'we are in demand by men who get fed up with women and who find it difficult to get boys'. In a single sentence, three of the four roles make their appearance, and there is now at least one study of the fourth role of passive adult men who continue to live with their families. In a series of brilliant reports and articles (1996–2001), the sex researcher Shivananda Khan has made two overwhelming points. Sixty percent of Indian men have sex with males, and most of it is with adolescent boys. The evidence has long been there for those who wished to see it: the psychologist Shakuntala Devi casually mentioned (and mis-interpreted) thirty years ago that 'in India, boy-brothels are very common in the bigger cities, the Bhindi Bazar and Foras Road areas of Bombay have entire rows of houses strictly catering to the needs of homosexual clients'. The 'homosexual' clients were ordinary Indian men.[2]

As late as 1400, this was still the prevailing system in Western Christian societies, as the historian Michael Rocke has now demonstrated with statistical certainty for fifteenth-century Florence. In the second and third generations of that century, at least 15,000 Florentine males were accused of sodomy, and over 2,400 were convicted by the principal magistracy responsible for overseeing sodomy. From this, Rocke has estimated that at least two-thirds of all Florentine males were implicated by the time they reached the age of forty, and these figures do not cover all the magistracies. This strongly suggests that almost all males had sexual relations with other males at some point in their lives and did so repeatedly. Sodomy was nonetheless illegal in Florence. Preachers such as Bernardino of Sienna regularly denounced it. But Bernardino also accepted that it was wide-spread. The Florentines apparently lived out their sexual lives under two different moralities, one that was Christian and disapproved of sodomy and another that was masculinist and patriarchal and promoted it.

The distinction between a homosexual minority and a heterosexual majority cannot have existed in Florence. If this distinction can be shown not to have existed in a single European society, it is extremely unlikely to have existed in any of them, and for this reason, the Florentine evidence can be used to understand English society. Similarly in the twenty-first century, all European societies share the same division into a homosexual minority and a heterosexual majority. It is apparent when one compares Renaissance Florence with either the ancient pagan or the later Muslim Mediterranean that the sodomy of Florence was nothing new. It was simply more open and therefore better documented. The question needs to be raised whether it had grown more open in the course of the fifteenth century. There had certainly been relatively few cases in the fourteenth century when the penalties had been far more severe. But as the penalties were moderated into a series of graduated fines (which were often not paid), the number of denunciations increased. Many Florentines therefore thought that sodomy was wrong, but they did not think it was so wrong as to merit a severe punishment. This was the compromise between the two moralities by which many Florentines lived. But in their adolescence and young manhood, most Florentine males lived entirely according to the masculinist morality and not the Christian one.

The sodomy which most Florentine males practiced was strictly organized by differences in age. From the time boys entered puberty at fifteen until their beards began to grow at nineteen or twenty, they were anally penetrated by older men. These men were usually unmarried and in their later twenties. Between nineteen and twenty-three, there seems to have been a transitional phase when a young man could be both active and passive, but he was always active with someone younger and passive with someone older. Adolescent boys occasionally took turns at being active and passive with each other. But young adult men never allowed themselves to be passive with their adolescents. Older men sometimes fellated their adolescent partners instead of penetrating them. Most men seem to have stopped pursuing boys once they married in their thirties. A few adult men (12 percent) never married, and some of these had boys throughout their lives. Some men in their twenties had sex both with female prostitutes and with boys. A very few adult men (3 percent) allowed themselves to be penetrated; they had presumably failed to make the transition from passive boy to active man. No adult transvestite men appear in fifteenth-century records, but there is evidence for such men in the sixteenth and seventeenth centuries.

With these comparisons in mind, it is possible to say that sexual relations between males in England in the sixteenth and seventeenth centuries were usually structured by differences in age. Adult males whose beards had grown had sexual relations with adolescent boys who usually they penetrated anally. The sources make it clear that puberty began around the age of fourteen or fifteen, or much later than it does in the twentieth century. Boys' voices broke in the later teenage years, usually around nineteen. Full beards did not grow until twenty-three to twenty-five.[3] The men and the boys who had sexual relations with each other were also sexually attracted to women and often had sexual relations with both males and females in the same period of life. It was presumed that all adult males felt desire for adolescent boys even though not all men acted upon this desire. Renaissance sodomy therefore differed profoundly from the kind of homosexual behaviour that first came into existence in western (and English) society in the early eighteenth century. In the Renaissance, all men desired both women and boys, and a substantial majority of men (if not all) acted at some point in life on their desire for boys. It is not possible to prove statistically for England the existence of this sodomitically acting majority. The literary sources suggest its existence, and the investigations into the sexual lives of English monks at the moment of the dissolution of the monasteries give it some slight but important statistical support. It is possible to show statistically the existence of this sodomitically acting majority in Renaissance Florence. Nonetheless, both in England and in Italy, sodomy was officially declared immoral by the Christian church and punished, often with death, by the state. Yet men practiced it and openly recommended it. The English Puritans quite rightly claimed that sodomy was often promoted on the London stage. There were therefore two competing sexual moralities. One morality maintained that all sexual acts should be at least potentially procreative and should therefore occur only in marriage to a woman. The other masculinist morality gave adult men prestige for all sexual acts in which they were the dominant and phalically penetrating partner, whether with women or boys.

The sexual context of sodomy: monasteries, the royal court, the great household, the village

The history of sodomy in England during the Reformation and the Renaissance begins with the passage in 1534 of 25 Henry VIII, *c.6*. This Act of Parliament took jurisdiction over sodomy away from the ecclesiastical courts and gave it to the secular state. It was a first step in justifying the dissolution of the monasteries and the seizure of their endowments. The first act was not intended to be permanent, and it had to be renewed three times in 1536, 1539 and 1540. In 1548, under the reign of Henry's young son, a new version of the Act was passed (2&3 Edward VI, c.29). When Henry's daughter Mary succeeded her brother and restored England's papal allegiance, all these Protestant Acts were repealed. But when Henry's daughter Elizabeth became queen, a new version of the Act (5 Elizabeth, c.17) was passed in 1563. It made sodomy between males and between males and animals a crime punishable by death. The courts, and especially Sir Edmund Coke in his commentary on the laws (1644), did not understand the law to penalize sexual acts between women. Most of the few cases brought to court under the Elizabethan statute over the next century and a half seem to have been cases of rape against prepubescent boys.[4]

The passage of the Henrician statutes was accompanied in 1535 and 1536 by an extensive enquiry into the sexual lives of England's monks and nuns. (The enquiry's accuracy is accepted by the latest account of the Henrician reformation.) The results of this enquiry were used to justify the dissolution of the monasteries, and they became part of the story by which Protestant England justified its breach with the Rome over the succeeding centuries. John Bale, a former Carmelite prior who became a reformer, promoted the story of the monks and nuns who broke their vows of chastity in popular and learned works in English and Latin.[5] The reports on the monastic houses in northern England and in East Anglia have survived. The nature of the sexual relations between males that are described in them fits precisely the structure that the model of age-structured relations would predict. This can be seen in the story of two houses. Garendon in Leicestershire was a house of Cistercian or white monks (so called from the colour of their habits). In 1535, there were fourteen monks, twelve of whom were priests. Five of the monks were reported to have had sexual relations with boys, one of them with ten boys some of whom must have come from outside the monastery. The other house was Chertsey, a Benedictine abbey of black monks in Surrey. In 1535, it had twenty monks. Of these, thirteen were charged with various forms of sexual irregularity. Seven had had relations with both married and single women. Three others had had relations both with women and with boys; one with five married women and two boys; a second with a married woman and three boys; a third with women both single and married and with two boys. This third monk had also masturbated as had a fourth monk who also had relations with four women but not with boys. Finally, two monks were said to have been passive in sodomy. Only seven of the twenty monks were sexually continent. Of the thirteen who were sexually incontinent, seven had been so only with women and six with males. These six sodomitical monks divided into two groups: four who had relations with boys and women and two who were sexually passive with men.

These thirteen monks constitute a very small sample. They could be used to argue, however, that among sexually active men in sixteenth-century England, half would have had relations only with women and half with both males and females. The sodomitical five either had relations with boys or were sexually passive adults. These passive adults at Chertsey do not, however, show up at Garendon where all five sodomites had had relations with boys. These two abbeys together housed thirty-four monks, of whom ten had had sexual relations with other males. All these monks were sworn to sexual continence. Among Englishmen who had not made such vows, it is likely enough that some would have been faithful to their wives or have lived continently in their single state. But by the standard of the monks, at least half of lay Englishmen probably had had sex outside of marriage, and at least half of these had had sex with both boys and women.[6]

The historian David Knowles tried to raise doubts about these findings in regard to both Garendon and Chertsey by pointing out that in previous and subsequent investigations conducted by more sympathetic inquisitors than those of 1535 and 1536, these two houses and others accused of sexual misconduct had been assessed as well behaved. But these favourable reports could also be used to argue that local opinion was very likely not to make too much of a little monastic incontinence whether with women or with boys. The inquisitors of 1535 used the official Christian standard against the monks. Their neighbours were more likely to asses them by the other standard of masculine acceptance of sex outside of marriage as being no great matter. The monks were likely, in any case, to be more restrained than their lay neighbours. This was certainly what Robert Burton argued in 1621 in *The Anatomy of Melancholy*. Taking his evidence from Bale's reports, he noticed the 'self-defiling monks' and the friars who left girls 'not able to sleep in their beds'. In these monasteries, one 'found among them so great a number of wenchers, catamites, debauchees, buggers, lovers of boys, pederasts, Sodomites (as it saith in Bale), Ganymedes, &c, that in every one of them you may be certain of a new Gomorrah'. But from this, Burton argued that outside of monasteries, the incidence of sodomy must be much greater, for 'if 'tis thus among monks, votaries, and such-like saintly rascals, what may we not suspect in towns, in palaces? what among nobles, what in brothels, how much nastiness, how much filth!' To this evidence of extensive if not nearly universal sodomy in England outside of its monasteries, we now turn.[7]

The history of the relations between King James and the males, young and old, who caught his eye and who became his favourites neatly summarizes the career through which men passed, from passive boy to the active male lover of boys whom he later encouraged to enter manhood, marry a wife and sire a family as he himself had done. In 1579, in Scotland, the thirteen-year-old James met and fell in love with Lord Aubigny, later Duke of Lennox, who was thirty-seven and married with children. Later in the 1580s, it was said that James was 'too much carried by young men that lies in his chamber and is his minions'. One of them, Alexander Lindsey, was the 'best beloved minion' and 'his nightly bed-fellow'. James was also taken with the Earl of Huntly who was four years older. It is probable that in this decade, when James was between fourteen and twenty-four, he would have been passive still with a man like Huntly but active with a younger boy like Lindsey. James married Anne, princess of Denmark, in 1584 when he was twenty-three and she was fifteen. During the next sixteen years, Ann became pregnant every two years which suggests regular intercourse with the king. James seems not to have had male favourites during most of these years.[8]

In 1603, James became the king of England, and famously entered into a series of relationships with at least four young men in turn.[9] James' friendships with Robert Carr, created Earl of Somerset, and George Villiers, created Duke of Buckingham, caused the greatest sensation because of James' openly affectionate behaviour. Somerset was about twenty, 'straight-limbed, well-favourede, strong-shouldered, and smooth-faced'. The smooth face was especially important to James. The French ambassador claimed that James' interest waned when Somerset's beard began to grow. James liked his young men to be effeminate and well dressed. Francis Osborne said that James treated Somerset and Buckingham like ladies and that the two young men laboured in 'the effeminateness of their dressings' to play such a role, though in 'w[horish] lookes and wanton gestures, they excseded any part of woman kind'. With Somerset, James leaned 'on his arm, pinches his cheek, and smoothes his ruffled garment'. He made it possible for Somerset to marry Lady Essex by declaring her husband impotent and imprisoning Thomas

Overbury. Somerset could not deal with James' increasing attention
to Buckingham and James complained. Somerset came to a disastrous
end when he and his wife were tried and imprisoned for the murder of
Overbury.[10]

James and Buckingham became friends when the king was forty-eight
and Buckingham twenty-three. Buckingham was chosen and promoted
by the political opponents of Somerset. James gave Buckingham as the
Venetian ambassador wrote, 'all his heart' – he 'will not eat, sup, or
remain an hour without him and considers him his whole joy'. Six years
after the affair began, Buckingham married with the King's approval, and
James made himself a part of the new family. Buckingham also made
himself indispensable to James' son, the future Charles I. While Charles
and Buckingham travelled in Spain, James wrote frequently with news
of Buckingham's wife and daughter. He hoped that he and Buckingham
would 'make at this Christmas a new marriage ever to be kept hereafter'.
He desired to live only for Buckingham's sake and declared that without
him, he, James, would 'live a sorrowful widow's life'. Then changing
roles, he blessed him as 'my dear sweet child and wife, and grant that ye
may ever be a comfort to your dear dad and husband'. It is likely enough
that sexual relations between them had now ended, and that James had
transformed the relationship into a chaste marriage. Buckingham
described James as his 'dear Dad and Gossip', and longed to lay at James'
feet and to be in his arms as a man longed for 'the arms of his Mistress'.
He was 'your humble slave and dog'. His 'thoughts are only bent on
having my dear Dad and master's legs soon in my arms'. In the first of
these letters, Buckingham reminded the King of an earlier incident asking
'whether you loved me now … better than at the time which I shall never
forget at Farnham, where the bed's head could not be found between
master and his dog'.[11]

James nonetheless in his *Basilikon Doron* advised his son prince
Henry that sodomy was one of the 'horrible crimes that yee are bound
in conscience never to forgive'. The public conscience of the king was
demonstrably different from the actual behaviour of the man. Not every
young man whom the king approached was willing. The Earl of Holland
lost his chance of advancement 'by turning aside and spitting after the
king had slabbered his mouth'. James could tell when young men had
been encouraged to court him by their relations. Young William Monson
in 1618 was thrown in the king's way by his Howard relatives, but James
told him to avoid his presence and advised him to leave the court. Lord

Middlesex, the Lord Treasurer, tried 'to set up a new ydoll', his wife's brother, Sir Arthur Brett. But he was forbidden to see the king and sent to the Fleet prison. The relatives of both these good-looking young men never doubted that it lay in their power to sexually entice the king since that power arose from the ordinary operation of male desire.[12]

Gentlemen, both married and unmarried, had sexual relations with the adolescent male servants of their households. The most spectacular revelations about a noble household began to be made when nineteen-year-old Lord Audley complained in 1630 to the Privy Council about the behaviour of his father, the second Earl of Castlehaven. This led within a year to the trial of the Earl and two of his young male servants on charges of sodomy and rape. Four young men were involved, three had begun as pages either to Castlehaven or to his wife; the fourth was a footman. Lord Audley charged that Castlehaven gave Henry Skipwith control of his finances and transferred to him property worth £12,000. Castlehaven encouraged Skipwith to have sex with Audley's young wife (she was about thirteen or fourteen and had to be oiled to be penetrated) and promised that he would give their child an estate. Skipwith admitted the affair. He also said that Castlehaven had watched him have sex with the Countess, but that he and the Countess had fooled Castlehaven into believing that penetration had occurred. He and Castlehaven had shared a bed but had not had sex, though others in the household thought they had. John Anktill had also been a page, and there were rumours of sex between him and Castlehaven. Some claimed that he also had had sex with the Countess at Castlehaven's request, but they both denied it. Anktill courted and married one of Castlehaven's daughters. Giles Broadway, one of the Countess's pages, admitted that on occasion Castlehaven had 'used his body as a woman'. Broadway also had sex with the Countess as Castlehaven held her down. He denied penetration, she insisted that it had occurred. Florence Fitzpatrick was Castlehaven's footman. He admitted to sex with him but denied there was penetration. Broadway was tried for rape, Fitzpatrick for sodomy, Castlehaven for both crimes. All three were executed. Anktill had a successful career in Ireland collecting rents for Castlehaven's family. His son inherited an estate. Skipwith for an undisclosed sum of money restored the houses and land the Earl had given him.

In his relations with his male servants, Castlehaven was probably typical of many men. He differed when he encouraged them to have sex with his wife and his daughter-in-law. He had also erred in giving Skipwith property that his eldest son believed was rightfully his to inherit. The lords who served as the jury at Castlehaven's trial took the rape charges far more seriously than the sodomy. Twenty-six of twenty-seven voted against him on the rape; but while fifteen voted for conviction on sodomy, twelve were for his acquittal. The evidence of penetration was equally problematic on both charges. To violate a countess with powerful friends was more outrageous to these men than sodomizing a footman.[13]

Men in ordinary villages regularly made passes at younger males. A man could do this over many years before the complaint of a boy brought to official light what the man's neighbours had clearly long known. In the end, the neighbours did not approve of sodomy, but they did not disapprove of it to the extent that they felt obliged to try to stop it. These stories show as well as anything else the coexistence of two different moral opinions on sodomy – the official and Christian position, and the ordinary masculinist libertine point of view. In 1622, George Dowdeney, a married innkeeper in his forties from Somerset, was accused of sodomy. A yeoman's son had gone into a field and 'untrussed his points and put down his hose' in order to relieve himself. Dowdeney followed and did the same. He caught the boy at the waist and tried to penetrate him. Dowdeney must have been attracted to the boy's entire family. The boy's father remembered that when fourteen years before he had travelled with Dowdeney, they had shared a bed. Awakening at midnight, Dowdeney had grabbed the man's penis and compared it unfavourably with his own. Dowdeney then had kissed and hugged him around the neck and gotten on top of him. Dowdeney did not penetrate him but ejaculated on his thighs and shirt, saying that 'he had done him as much pleasure as if he were a woman'. When the local blacksmith shared a bed with Dowdeney, he awakened to find Dowdeney on top of him as he lay on his belly. Dowdeney tried to penetrate him, but the blacksmith was uncertain whether he had succeeded. On other occasions, Dowdeney suggested that they close the stable door and bugger one of the mares, or go and watch Dowdeney bugger a sow in the sty. The blacksmith resisted and told him 'though you take a course to hang yourself you shall not take any course to hang me'. On twenty or thirty other occasions, Dowdeney had thrust his hand into the smith's hose, taken hold of his penis and urged that they 'go to some private place to the end Dowdeney might bugger him'. One presumes that Dowdeney sometimes succeeded with the young men in his village, but this all went on for years before it came officially to light.[14]

An incident in 1716, in a rural Gloucestershire village of eighty inhabitants, provides another example. George Andrews, a tenant farmer, met a young farm labourer, Walter Lingsey, as he lay at midnight on a bridge. Andrews took Lingsey's hand, fondled it, complimented the softness of the skin and put his hand into Lingsey's breeches. Andrews then said they would be more comfortable in his house. Once there, they got into bed, and Andrews sodomized the young man. The story came out when Lingsey explained to another labourer where he had spent the night. Andrews was an overbearing and an unpopular man. He had also been 'infamous for these practices formerly'. But no one had ever denounced him, and in this case, no one at first brought him to the magistrate. Instead, a group of local men planned a 'mock groaning'. Lingsey was dressed in a 'mantua petticoat, white apron and headclothes' to look like a woman. Another man played the midwife who delivered Lingsey of a child in the form of a wad of straw dressed in baby's clothes. Another man was appointed the parson. He christened the child saying as much of the Prayerbook ritual as he could remember. The two godfathers gave the child the name of George, since his father was George Andrews. They then feasted and sent for some women to 'wait with the lying-in woman as they termed Lingsey'. Andrews was eventually charged with sodomy, brought to trial and found not guilty. It is apparent that the villagers in Gloucestershire saw sodomy as an inversion of sexual relations between men and women. But Andrews was well known to have done those things, and for years no one had complained. The Christian morality involved in the groaning was not so strong as to make impossible the life of a local man with enough confidence to seduce the pretty passive youths of his neighbourhood.[15]

Sodomy on the London stage, 1576–1642

Sex between men and boys in London, of gallants with their pages, masters with their boys, boy actors with adult actors and their admirers in their audiences and of transvestite boy prostitutes in the streets with their customers, of all this there is a good deal to be found in the plays and the satires. The most sympathetic discussion of sexual relations between males in the seventeenth century appeared in the plays of the London stage, and a good deal of the opposition to the theatres by the Puritans was inspired by this tolerance. On the London stage, women's roles were played by transvestite boys, and it was claimed that this excited men's desire for boys. The plays also had sodomitical exchanges between men and boys who were playing the role of a boy. In a number of plays, a young girl (played by a transvestite boy) dressed as a boy or a page. With these girls dressed as boys, men in the play often flirted, thinking them actual boys. The potential sodomy of these scenes was redeemed when the boy was revealed to be a girl; the man (and the playwright) could then say that they had been reacting to a girl's good looks and not a boy's. But, of course, the good looks of the young actor were in fact those of a boy: the sodomy could never be entirely displaced. These plays with girls dressed as boys have been counted. Between 1590 and 1642, there were seventy-four such plays.[16] In fourteen years (26 percent), there were none, but in the remaining thirty-nine years, there were from one to four each year. If to this list one adds the other plays with sodomitical references, it is likely that about 120 plays (some of which were frequently performed) would have been acted over the course of the entire century that can be used for our purpose.

The Puritans insisted that the book of Deuteronomy (22:5) forbade women to put on men's clothes and men to put on women's clothes, 'for all that do so are abomination to the Lord thy God'. Stephen Gosson protested in *Plays Confuted* (1583) that boys acting on the stage went even further and 'put on not the apparrell onely, but the gate, the gestures, the voyce, the passions of a woman'. John Rainoldes in *Th' Overthrow of Stage-Playes* (1599) explained the nature of the abomination forbidden by Deuteronomy. He cited Paul to the Romans (1:27) and to the Corinthians (1 Corinthians 6:11) the stories of Sodom (Genesis 19:5) and Gibeah (Judges 19:22) in which Canaanites and Jews demanded that male guests be handed over for sexual use, and the condemnations of the sacred male prostitutes in the first and second books of Kings (1 Kings 14:24; 2 Kings 23:7). He did not cite Leviticus (18:22), and it is not apparent why. Rainoldes left no doubt from these examples that he thought that the transvestism of boy actors was forbidden because it led to sodomy between men and boys. Men by their 'naturall corruption and vitiousness' were 'prone to monstrous sin against nature'. 'Beautiful boyes transformed into women' were 'an occasion of drawing and provoking corruptlie minded men to most heinous wickedness', for 'beautiful boys by kissing doe sting and powre secretly in a kind of poyson, the poyson of incontinencie'. William Prynne in *Histio-Mastix* (1633) knew of 'some moderne examples of such who have been desperately enamored of players boyes thus clad in womans apparel, so farre as to follow them by words, by letters, even actually to abuse them', especially a certain scholar of Balliol College.[17]

Prynne pointed out that every playhouse was surrounded by a group of bawdy houses to which men took their 'strumpets and adulteresses': 'witnese the Cock-pit, and Drury-Lane: Black-friers Playhouse, and Duke-humfries: the Red-bull, and Turnball-street:the Globe, and Bank-side Brothel-houses'. Prynne did not mention any brothels specifically for boys, but Clement Walker in 1649 knew of 'new-erected sodoms and spintries at the Mulberry Garden', a spintry (a word from Tacitus) being a brothel for boys; the Mulberry Garden was later the site of Buckingham Palace. In 1649, the playhouses had been closed for seven years, but in 1654, the Mulberry Gardens was the one place left 'for the ladys & Gallants' when John Evelyn went there to seek 'refreshment' since 'Cromwell & his partisans' had shut up Spring Garden. It is likely enough that in Prynne's day, the female strumpets and the boys had also mixed together in bawdy houses adjacent to playhouses. The behaviour men learned in the play-houses they carried even to church: 'many come into the Church to behold more curiously the beauty of women, and the fairness of young men'. It was therefore the 'accursed fruit of Stage-plays, not only to make the Play-house but even the very Church of God a kind of Brothell'.[18]

In the plays and the playwrights, there were several kinds of sodomy presented, but almost all of it was structured by differences in age between an adult man and an adolescent boy. The adult male characters in the plays are for the most part gentlemen. Many of the boys are represented as poor boys, but some pages have the same social standing as their masters. When the man and boy are of the same social class, it is expected that the master will see to the page's education. As the boy grows up, the master will promote his marriage. Boy and master are sometimes represented as deeply in love, with one boy longing to marry his master. A page will be expected to sleep in the same bed as his master, to dress and undress him, to accompany him in public, to entertain him by playing on the lute, by singing and by reading him to sleep. Pages who are poor boys are most likely to be represented as crafty, and their sexual relations with their masters are less likely to be idealized. Boy actors are represented as the sexual companions of the adult actors who are their masters. It is often said that they are prostitutes for the men who have come to see them act. Some of them seem to have worn women's clothes in the street. There is evidence of transvestite boy prostitutes in the street who were not necessarily young actors. The page's body size and his clothes were so sexually appealing to men that some female prostitutes dressed as pages in the street. It was suggested that trasvestism in boys could affect their gender identity as men. Women seem to have found these adolescent pages as appealing as men did and sought to seduce and keep them. The pages were therefore sexually responsive to women. The men who pursued pages are also usually represented as being attracted to women as well. Very occasionally, there are representations of adult men who are sexually passive with another adult man, but this attraction is usually explained as the result of drunkenness or bewitchment. In all these presentations, sodomy is shown in a relatively matter of fact way as a fairly typical male behaviour. It can never be directly praised for that would be contrary to the law and true religion. This is the unofficial masculinist position on sodomy, the alternative that men believed, felt and often practiced, when they were not being officially Christian.

Christopher Marlowe was one of the playwrights explicitly charged with sodomy. According to Richard Baines, Marlowe had declared 'that all they that love not Tobacco & Boies were fools'. Sodomy in Marlowe was one sign of his general rejection of conventional religion. It allowed him to make critical interpretations of the scripture and to find in the life of Christ justification for his own sodomy. Marlowe, according to Bates, claimed 'that John the Evangelist was bedfellow to Christ and leaned always in his bosome, that he used him as the sinners of Sodoma'. Thomas Kyd had also heard him say that St John was 'our savior Christes Alexis ... that is that Christ did love him with an extraordinary love'. But Christ's sodomy for Marlowe did not exclude the love of women since he claimed (so Bates said) 'that the woman of Samaria & her sister were whores & that Christ knew them dishonestly'. For Marlowe, Christ liked both boys and women, as presumably he himself did. This theme of Jesus and St John turns up throughout Renaissance Europe. But, it must have been possible to assert this in public when the sexual part of the friendship was not stressed since King James said to the Privy Council in 1617 that he was not to be blamed for his love of the Earl of Buckingham, 'for Jesus Christ had done just what he was doing ... Christ had His John and so he, James, had his George'.[19]

Sodomy in Marlowe's plays occurs between master and page and the king and his minion. When *Edward II* (1593) opens Gaveston, on the accession of his friend the new king, has been recalled from the exile in France into which the previous king has sent him. Gaveston plans how he will entertain 'the pliant king' and draw him 'which way I please'. Gaveston's pages are to be dressed as nymphs and his men like satyrs. 'A lovelie boy' will appear as a naked Diana, hiding with an olive tree

'those parts that men delight to see'. Edward tells Gaveston that he has
mourned his absence as Hercules did Hilas and heaps honours on him.
The lords at court loathe this 'base minion'. Edward's wife is also angry
that now the king pays her no regard 'but dotes upon the love of Gaveston'
and says she will become as frantic as Juno since her husband makes
more of Gaveston than Jove did of Ganymede. But if Gaveston is to be
a great man, he must have a wife, and so Edward gives him his niece in
marriage. The lords go into rebellion. Edward blames the Queen as the
'cause of all these jarres' and tells her that Mortimer, the leader of the
rebels, has become her lover. By the end of the third act, Gaveston has
been captured in battle, thrown into a ditch and his head struck off.[20]

The Queen and Mortimer are lovers and dominate the last two acts
of the play. Edward is captured and forced to abdicate in favour of his
young son. Mortimer and the Queen decide to kill Edward. Lightborn,
who has learned in Naples to kill without leaving a trace, does the deed.
He orders a spit to be made red hot and acts out on stage, but does not
describe in words the insertion of the spit into the king's anus. But
Mortimer is betrayed by one of his associates. The young king turns
on him and on his mother. He orders Mortimer executed and his head
placed on his father's hearse and sends his mother to the Tower. The play
is plainly as much about adultery as it is about sodomy. It is sometimes
argued that Gaveston is an adult man and not a boy and that therefore
something like a modern homosexual consciousness is on display.[21] The
Queen, however, compares Edward and Gaveston to Jove and Ganymede,
which suggests that an age-structured relationship is all that Marlowe
imagines. The ancient pairs of lovers with whom the older Mortimer
compares Edward and Gaveston all had differences of age between them.
Other seventeenth-century accounts of Edward and Gaveston (of which
there were many) presumed that the two were separated by differences
in age.[22] On the other hand, Gaveston in the play has reached the age of
marriage, and Edward gives him his niece for a wife. Marlowe probably
means to indicate that sexual relations between the friends have ended
but not affection. It is time for the younger friend to marry and the other
promotes that marriage as similarly happened in plays by Chapman,
Beaumont and Fletcher, and Shakespeare and in the life of King James.
It is an ordinary stage in age-structured relations. These relations between
men and boys are not meant to exclude marriage to women. Modern
commentators often cite Marlowe's statements about boys and tobacco
and on Jesus and St John. They usually ignore his remark that Jesus

sexually knew the woman of Samaria and her sister. Marlowe is not a modern homosexual but a Renaissance libertine who liked both boys and women and hoped to marry and have an heir.

Throughout Ben Jonson's works, there are references to sex between men and boys and to men who have sex with both women and boys.[23] These plays can be used to document the world of male prostitution. In Jonson, the transvestite boys of the playhouses were the most usual boy prostitutes or ingles. Ovid in *Poetaster* (1601) ties ingle to the sexual desirability of boy actors: 'What? Shall I have my sonne a stager now? And enghle for players? a gull? a rooke? A shot-clogge? To make suppers and be laughed at?' Later in the play, Tucca offers at first to sell or rent his two boy actors, but after Histrio asks to 'let one of them do a little of a ladie', and then enquires what Tucca will charge for a week of the boys' services, Tucca withdraws his offer, saying 'No, you mangonizing slave, I will not part from 'hem: you'll sell 'hem for engles you'. In *The Devil is an Ass* (1616), Merecraft proposes to hire a boy actor to play the Spanish lady and suggests Dicke Robinson. Robinson was a real enough actor. In the play, Robinson is called 'a very pretty fellow' who went often to the chamber of a gentleman who was a friend of Merecraft's. With this gentleman, the boy went once to a supper party dressed as a lawyer's wife. Does this show that boy actors visited gentlemen and went about the street dressed as women? Merecraft describes it as all high spirits. It suggests that a boy's stage transvestism might move into the real world and be part of his attraction for his adult male admirers.[24]

Boy prostitutes (some of whom were actors) are referred to by others like John Marston who in one of his satires writes 'But ho, what Ganimede is that doth grace the gallants heeles. One, who for two daies space is closely hyred'. Older actors seem to have slept themselves with the boy actors. J. Cocke in his character of 'a common player' (1615) says that after marriage actors treated their wives like boys (or had anal intercourse with them) but before marriage made do with boys and female whores: 'If he marries, hee mistakes the Woman for the Boy in Womans attire, by not respecting a difference in the mischiefe: But so long as he lives unmarried, hee mistakes the Boy, or a Whore for the Woman'. But there were boy prostitutes who were not actors. In 'Ingling Pyander' (1599), Thomas Middleton bitterly told of a man who had fallen in love with a boy he then encountered 'ingling' or whoring in the street dressed in 'a nymphs attire' or in woman's clothes. Previously the man had 'lov'd Pyander well', so he 'loathes' to 'shame' him, but in retrospect he feels that he was a 'fool … in his affection'. With women it would not have been so bad: 'for had he been a she injurious boy, I had not been so subject to annoy'. He warns other men, 'trust not a painted puppet, as I've done'. (Sir Simonds D'Ewes in 1622 told a friend 'that boyes weere growen to the height of wickedness to paint'.) The streets, Middleton said, 'are full of iggling parasites' dressed as women. If you must hire a boy, 'be curious in your choice, the best will tire'. The best boy prostitutes are bad, 'therefore hire none at all'. No actual examples of boy prostitutes in the streets have so far been recovered for London. They appear frequently in the Spanish and Portuguese records. The boys in Lisbon dressed as women and used women's mannerisms. Middleton's poem therefore probably described the actual world.[25]

The plays of John Fletcher and his circle of friends (Francis Beaumont, Philip Massinger and Nathan Field) present a wide range of sexual possibilities between men and boys. But there are also adult men who make passes at adult men usually under the influence of magic or drunkenness.[26] Fletcher at his most daring in 1611 in *The Night Walker* or *The Little Thief* showed the penetration of one adult man by another. In a darkened room, Tobie, the household's coachman, and therefore a man and not a boy, the Nurse, a merchant's wife, Mistress Newlove, and Jack Wildbraine, a wild rake, wonder back and forth frightening themselves and each other, thinking that they hear the Devil in the room. Wildbraine puts out his candle and offers to hold the merchant's wife to protect her from the Devil. He hopes to use the occasion to make love to her, but she slips away. In the dark, Tobie, the coachman, returns. Wildbraine thinks it is the merchant's wife comeback and Tobie thinks Wildbraine is the Devil. Wildbraine catches hold of Tobie: 'Are you there?' he asks, and then begins to try to penetrate him, saying 'In, in, presently'. Tobie moans: 'I feel his talents through me, tis an old haggard devil, what will he doe with me?' Wildbraine delays a moment: 'Let me kiss thee first, quicke, quicke' and then presumably putting his hand on Tobie's ass exclaims 'what a hairie whore tis, sure she has a muffler' (or a hairpiece for the vagina). Tobie worries that he might become pregnant by the Devil: 'If I should have a young Satan by him, for I dare not deny him, in what case were I? Who durst deliver me?' Wildbraine discounts his doubt and forces his way in: ''Tis but my fancie, she is the same, – in quickly, gently my sweete girl'. Tobie surrenders and exclaims 'Sweete Devill be good to me'.[27]

Tobie and Wildbraine say to themselves and to others that they have had sex with a devil. But they know that they have had sex with each other. Tobie tries hard to persuade Wildbraine to stay with him, if not forever, at least for one night more. When Wildbraine bids him, 'Adieu honest Toby', Tobie answers 'and shall we part with dry lips, shall we that have been fellowe devils together flinch for an old woman's fart'. But Wildbraine insists that 'we must part Toby'. So Tobie offers to keep Wildbraine. Wildbraine declines the offer gently and says that if they meet 'a day or two hence, may be wee'le cracke a quart yet'. Toby starts to cry, so Wildbraine tells him, 'nay cry not Toby, twill make thy head giddy'. Tobie insists, 'sweat Master Wildbraine', but Wildbraine brushes him off again with 'no more Toby, go, the times may alter'. The night after their sexual encounter, when a boy in the street offers to sell Tobie 'a ballad of the maide was got with child', he replies, 'That might have been my case last night, Ile ha't what ere it cost me'.[28]

Boys are depicted feeling and expressing passionate desire for their masters, though the odds were always against them. Nathan Field in *The Honest Man's Fortune* (written in collaboration with Fletcher and Massinger) presented a young page in love with his master who resents the women in his master's life. Veramour (or true love) is intended to be so good looking that both men and women think that he must be a girl dressed as a boy. When Charlotte flirts with Veramour's master, she says 'I do most dangerously suspect this boy to be a wench; art thou not one? Come hither, let me feel thee'. Veramour responds that he will feel her to see 'whether you be a boy or no'. The two had once been intimate, but now they were in competition for his master Montaigne. Veramour urges Montaigne when Charlotte enters to 'steale away, you were wont to be a curious avoider of women's company'. Montaigne responds, 'Why boy, thou darst trust me any where darst thou not?!' To Charlotte the boy says 'Pray doe you leave my Master, and me; we were very merry before you came, he does not covet womens companie'. Veramour tries unsuccessfully to get his master to leave with him, promising to 'sing to you again' and swearing that his master's 'mind is stronger than to credit womens vowes, and too pure to be capable of their loves'. But Charlotte wins. She notes that 'the boy is jealous', condescends to him as 'a good child' and gives him a piece of gold to 'go buy thee a feather'. Veramour sees that his master wants him to leave and does so, saying 'now I perceive you love her better than you doe me; but God blesse you whatever you do, or intend; I know you are a very honest man'.[29]

Veramour had delighted in the hard times into which his master Montaigne had fallen since that situation had thrown them together. To a woman who he thinks might make his master a wife, he says he knows 'no Juno worthy such a Jove', implying that he hopes to be his master's Ganymede. He offers to carry Montaigne: 'good sir, leane on my shoulder … oh that I were a horse for half an houre that I might carry you home on my backe: I hope you will love me still?' He tells him that 'when you are weary, I will lay me down that in my bosome you may rest your head, where whilst you sleep, Ile watch that no wild beast shall hunt or trouble you; and thus we'l breed a story to make every hearer weep, when they discourse our fortunes and our loves'. The boy, in other words, hopes to be impregnated by his master's love, and the fame of their devotion will be the child they breed. Veramour offers his master the gold he has earned with his singing and to get more. He praises Montaigne for not teaching him the things other men taught their boys: 'how to handle cards, to cheat and cozen men with oathes and lies'. In reply to all this devotion, Montaigne says 'oh what a scoffe might men of women make if they did know this boy?'; he tells him, 'oh lad, thy love will kill me'; and says to him that 'Nature made thee a beauteous caskanet to lock up all the goodness of the earth'. But after all this, Charlotte enters and the boy realizes that the idyll is over and that his master wants him to leave.[30]

In this world, Veramour can never marry his master. The nearest the boy comes to marriage with a man is in his mocking of Laverdure, 'a knavish courtier'. Laverdure is excited by Veramour's good looks and decides that the boy must really be a female whore in boy's clothes. He tells him 'thou art a pretty boy', offers to employ him as a page and 'maintain thee in the bravest Cloaths' and explains that Veramour 'shouldest lie with me'. Veramour replies that he would then lodge in a brothel and that ' 'twas never a good World since our French Lords learned of the Neapolitans to make their Pages their Bed-fellowes'. Later in the play when Laverdure persists, the boy makes a mock confession: 'belive it sir indeed I am a woman'. Laverdure is ecstatic, says he wishes an honourable marriage and tells the boy that 'now we may lawfully come together without feare of hanging'. The play ends with the overthrow of this intended marriage and Montaigne's actual marriage to a woman. It raises the question whether men and boys in England sometimes lived as man and wife. In Renaissance Florence, men sometimes lived with boys and treated them as wives. Is this not what Veramour wants from Montaigne in the play?[31]

A boy's worship for a man could continue into his adult life. This is sadly displayed in Beaumont and Fletcher's *The Maid's Tragedy* (c.1611).

Melantius returns from the wars on Amintor's marriage day. He calls
Amintor his friend: 'wonder not that I call a man so young a friend'.
He remembers that

> When he was a boy,
> As oft as I return'd (as without boast)
> I brought home conquest, he would gaze upon me,
> And view me round, to find in what one limb
> The virtue lay to do those things he heard;
> Then would he wish to see my Sword, and feel
> The quickness of the edge, and in his hand
> Weigh it; he oft would make me smile at this

The man's sword in the boy's feeling hand is phallic. Melantius is surprised
to find that Amintor is not marrying Aspatia as he had expected but his
own sister Evadne. On the wedding night, Evadne reveals to Amintor that
she has been the king's mistress and means to continue so and that the king
has intended that her marriage should give a public cover to their affair.
Amintor tries to keep the truth from Melantius who tells him 'tis not like
a friend to hide your soul from me'. Once he knows the truth, Melantius
plans their revenge. He encourages Amintor: 'I warrant you, look up, wee'l
walk together, put thine arm here, all shall be well agen'; to which the other
answers: 'Thy love, O wretched, I thy love, Melantius; why I have nothing
else'. Evadne is persuaded to kill the king and then kills herself. The des-
erted Aspatia returns dressed as her own brother and fights Amintor who
kills her and then himself. As Amintor dies, Melantius holds him and says,
'oh thy arms are kinder to me than thy tongue' for Amintor can hardly
speak. His sister's death Melantius says was 'a thing to laugh at' compared to Amintor's, for in Amintor 'here was my sister, Father, Brother,
Son; all that I had'.[32]

In the plays of George Chapman, there can be found all the patterns
seen so far in Marvell, Jonson and Fletcher. There are men and their
pages, some of the boys foolish and some wise. There are boy actors.
There are girls (played by boys) who dress as boys and a man disguised
as a woman. There is the adult man who is the favourite or 'minion' of a
prince. There is the friendship between two men, one older one younger,
that had begun in the boyhood of the younger and is concluded when the
older promotes the marriage of his younger friend. In *Sir Giles Goosecap*,
Knight Momford and Clarence have been friends for twenty years and

shared a bed for ten, when presumably Clarence had been Momford's page. Clarence would have served until the end of adolescence in his early twenties and would at the play's time have been in his early thirties. At the play's end, Momford makes a marriage between Clarence and his niece Eugenia calling it 'a marriage made for virtue, only for virtue; my friend and my dear niece are man and wife'. This is a happier conclusion to a friendship than Beaumont and Fletcher presented in *The Maid's Tragedy*. But, there is a similarity in the expectation that when a boy grows to manhood, his older friend will promote the younger's marriage. This pattern perhaps explains why in Shakespeare's *The Merchant of Venice*, Antonio puts himself in so much danger to borrow money from Shylock so that he may promote the marriage to Portia of his younger friend Bassanio. Similarly, Shakespeare in his sonnets tells the youth he loves that he must marry and produce an heir: 'make thee another self for love of me, that beauty still may live in thine or thee' (no. 10), for then in after years, 'but were some child of yours alive that time, you should live twice, in it and in my rhyme' (no. 17).[33]

London sodomy, 1660–1700: Kynaston, Pepys, Rochester and Rigby

This repertory of early seventeenth-century plays disappeared from public view in the 1640s and the 1650s when the theatres were closed during the period of Puritan domination. With the restoration of Charles II, the theatres reopened and boy actors once again played women's roles. The most famous boy actor was Edward Kynaston. In 1660, Kynaston was seventeen years old. He played many of the roles that have been described. Samuel Pepys, who all his life was very responsive to adolescent male beauty, recorded the times he saw Kynaston act. In August 1660, it was in *The Loyal Subject* and he thought he 'made the loveliest lady that ever I saw in my life – only, her voice not very good'. After the play, Kynaston and one of the adult actors came and drank with Pepys and the two men he had gone with to the theatre, one of them a young military officer who knew the actors. In January, Pepys saw Kynaston in *Epicoene* and thought him both 'the prettiest woman in the whole house' and 'the handsomest man in the house'. At the end of the decade in 1669, Pepys tried again to see Kynaston, but the actor had been beaten by a bravo of Sir Charles Sedley's. Sedly was a rake who had been tried and fined for appearing naked in daylight on the balcony of a public house and 'acting all the postures of lust and buggery that could be imagined'. Kynaston by 1669 was playing adult roles. He was proud of resembling Sedley, had imitated him on the stage and then gone walking in St James' Park in the clothes he had worn for the role. For this Sedley punished him.[34]

It is apparent that Kynaston socialized with the men and women in his audience and that he enjoyed bringing his roles from the stage into real life. In his old age, he assured the young Colley Cibber that when he had been 'so beautiful a youth', the ladies of quality had 'prided themselves in taking him with them in their coaches to Hyde Park, in his Theatrical Habit, after the Play'. This confirms two points from the early seventeenth-century plays. Women were as attracted to these transvestite youths as were men. It also makes it likely that the boy actor Dickie Robinson from Jonson's *The Devil is an Ass* had in real life as in the play gone out with his male friends dressed as a woman. Kynaston seems to have had sex with at least one of his male admirers, the second Duke of Buckingham. One lampoon has the line 'and Kenaston's arse knows its own Buggerer' and another has Buckingham 'with Kenaston acting both Venus and Mars'. Buckingham was said by Lorenzo Magalotti, in his description of the court of Charles II, to enjoy unhealthy brothels of women and the 'most rascally lackeys' for sex. Buckingham had a very large penis, but Magalotti claimed that this had not stopped him from penetrating young males. As a consequence, a male dancer was not able to dance for some time, and a poor French lackey had to be put into a hospital and was later found in the street with his throat cut.[35]

Kynaston probably married at least once and possibly twice and by his first wife he may have had children, but the parish records may refer to someone else with the same name. The lampoons about Buckingham and Kynaston are from the 1670s when Kynaston was already in his thirties. If they are accurate, it would seem that Kynaston had grown into a married man who was sexually passive with other men. This is one of the usual developmental routes for a minority of males in systems in which most sexual relations between males occur between adults and adolescents. Kynaston would have been a boy who had not been able to change from the passive to the active role on achieving adult status. Another such man, the husband of Margaret Myler, turns up in the late fifteenth-century London records: he was said to be a 'woman' and to grab priests between their legs. (The discussion of Myler in the previous chapter does not fit him into this pattern.) The possible course of Kynaston's life from transvestite boy to passive man would then give a positive answer to the question raised by Lucio's experiences in Beaumont and Fletcher's *Love's Cure* (1606) whether transvestism in boyhood had permanent consequences in adult life. A single such man, Robert Chetwyn, was arrested among the thirteen people (all the rest are women) taken for public transvestism in London between 1554 and 1604. He was discharged and ordered to find a master to work for, which suggests that he was unemployed and probably living by prostitution. Kynaston and Chetwyn document both patterns of adult male deviance in the age-structured sexual system of relations between males in Renaissance London. Most boys would have changed from passive to active on achieving manhood. Those few boys who did not either grew into men who married women and had children but were secretly passive with other men or became men who left the world of the family and lived as transvestite prostitutes.[36]

Kynaston's life shows the reality of the references to the boy actor that turn up in plays. The diary of Samuel Pepys does the same for the pages and the boys of the lords and gentlemen in the plays. After Pepys in 1663 described Sir Charles Sedley displaying himself naked and acting out lust and buggery, he recorded that 'Sir J. Mannes and Mr. Batten both say that buggery is now almost grown as common among our gallants as in Italy, and the very pages of the town begin to complain of their masters for it'. Pepys then distanced himself from it all: 'But blessed be God, I do not to this day know what is the meaning of this sin, nor which is the agent nor which is the patient'. He seems to have passed by looking wistfully into the world of aristocratic gallantry. He may have put actual sodomy into that world, but the attraction to young male beauty on which that sodomy was founded, he certainly experienced.[37]

In his world, all men seemed to have a boy or a page. Pepys' tailor had a boy to send with his new clothes. When Pepys dined with the royal dukes he sat at the pages' table. His patron Lord Sandwich had a page called Loud. In December 1660, Pepys, who was twenty-seven years old, examined Loud and found 'him a very pretty boy and gone a great way in Latin'. The boy had inherited his mother's looks: when Pepys met her earlier in the day at dinner she 'seemed to have been a very pretty woman'. Pepys indulged the boy on another occasion and let him ride his horse. They twice slept together in the same bed at an inn. Two years later, he found Loud playing dice with Sandwich and Sandwich's brother-in-law – one of the 'pleasures and vanities' that Sandwich had forbidden before but had come to love. Pages like Loud who play dice, honestly and dishonestly, with their master and with others, were fixtures in the plays.[38]

During the ten years that Pepys kept his diary (1660–1669), he employed six adolescent males who lived with him, his wife and the maids.[39] Pepys does not record that he ever shared a bed with any of those boys as he had with Lord Sandwich's page. He certainly kissed and petted the maidservants and came to some grief with his wife in 1669 when she caught him with his hand in the 'cunny' of her companion, Deb Willet. Occasionally Pepys did share a bed with other adult men. Pepys' caution with his boys was probably the result of what he knew was possible. With Will Howe, another of Sandwich's servants, he seems nearly to have come to grief. Pepys had mixed feelings about Will Howe, who, in 1664, he could still describe as 'such a boy'. Four years before, they had shared a bed in Sandwich's house. Pepys said he 'did intend to lie' with Howe, 'but he and I fell to play with one another, so that I made him go to lie with' Mr. Shipley the steward. 'So I lay alone all night'. It is a compromising confession of the sort Pepys liked to make. It was safer to flirt with Dick Penn, his neighbour's son, as he lay in bed with his wife on Valentine's Day. Penn was 'a notable, stout, witty boy'. He came to the Pepys' bed 'to be my wife's valentine'. Pepys then tried to trick the boy: 'I had him brought to my side, thinking to have him kiss me, but he perceived me, and would not'.[40] Pepys' diary is full of the attention he paid to pretty boys and pretty young men. Pretty was also the usual term he used to describe the women he noticed. Among the younger boys, the palm went to one of the children of Christ's Hospital: 'one of the prettiest little boys, with the prettiest mouth, that ever I saw in life'. At fourteen, Lord Sandwich's second son was 'a pretty youth'. At fifteen, the King's bastard (soon to be Duke of Monmouth) was 'a most pretty sparke'. Pepys was dazzled by good-looking boys, women and men. But with the word 'pretty', he put the youths and women into the same category.[41]

The erotic ambience of the Restoration theatre eventually changed profoundly as boy actors were replaced by actresses who played the women's roles and even dressed as boys when the play required it. But sodomy was mentioned often enough in revivals of old plays and in the performance of new ones, and this can be seen in the plays associated with Lord Rochester. Rochester demonstrated in his letters and his poems his taste for boys, who were usually his servants and good musicians, able to sing to their master as do many of the pages in the plays. In 1677, he sent his friend Henry Savile in London a young French musician, James Paisible, who was twenty. He hoped the boy would be able to sing the king to sleep and signed himself 'un bougre lasse', a tired bugger. Two years later, he sent another young French servant, Jean-Baptiste de Belle-Fasse, to Savile in Paris. Jean-Baptiste was also able to sing. Rochester added that 'the greatest and gravest of this Court of both sexes have tasted his beauties', confirming the point in the plays that these young pages were desired by both men and women. In his poems, Rochester sang that 'there's a sweet, soft page of mine does the trick worth forty wenches' and shared the boy with his whore:

> Nor shall our love-fits, Chloris, be forgot
> When each the well-looked linkboy strove t'enjoy
> And the best kiss was the deciding lot
> Whether the boy fucked you, or I the boy.[42]

In the 1670s, Rochester revised John Fletcher's *Valentinian* which had been written in the second decade of the century. He removed the last act and added verses of his own to balance the play between the emperor Valentinian's rape of Lucina, the wife of Maximus, and his use of Lycias, one of Maximus' eunuchs. Rochester is responsible for the eunuch's story. Valentinian sends his servant Chilax for 'that sweet fac'd eunuch that sung in Maximus'es grove'. Chilax (in lines so shocking to the day that some manuscripts omit them) explains to himself that a boy's love is better than a woman's. Women always seek to satisfy their lust.

> But a dear Boyes disinterested flame,
> Gives pleasure, and for meer Love gathers Paine.

Boys, in other words, experience no pleasure in anal intercourse with a man, but endure it because they love the man. Lycias sees the emperor's summons as the making of his fortune and imagines himself a lamb or calf on Vesta's altar to 'bee burnt a senseless sacrifice'. When they meet, Valentinian says 'I must use the Lycias', and Lycias replies, 'I am the humble slave of Caesars will'. In the final scene, Lycias and the emperor meet their deaths to pay for Lucina's rape, but before they die, the emperor seated on couch by Lycias' side, tells him

> Oh let me presse those balmy lips all day,
> And bath my Love-scorch't Soule in thy moist kisses;
> Now by my joyes thou art all sweete and soft,
> And thou shalt be the Altar of my Love;

Upon thy Beautys hourly will I offer
And power out pleasure, a blest Sacrifice
To the deare Memory of my Lucina!

This is the most striking presentation in all these plays of a youth's sexual surrender to a man and a man's desire for absolute domination of a boy. With this force, Rochester dazzled his contemporaries, and they put him into their plays sometimes as a sodomite, sometimes not.[43]

By the end of the seventeenth century, the gallant of the earlier century who pursued boys had been transformed into the beau. Beau was a term that had come into use in the middle of 1680s to describe the man about town who imitated French manners, dressed elaborately, collected china, gossiped like a woman and was sexually interested in both boys and women. His interest in boys was in the usual way evaluated both positively and negatively. Those who condemned him drew on the early seventeenth-century examples of King James and the Earl of Castlehaven and the ancient examples of Nero and Sporus. The beau justified himself from the example of the French and Russian courts and Jesus' love of St John. The author of *Mundus Foppensis* (1691) excoriated the beaus and their clothes with the story of Nero and Sporus.

He then complained that men had taken to kissing each other (a French custom) and condemned them with the example of King James. He did not mention the court of the new king, William III, but others certainly did.[44]

It was the case of captain Rigby in 1698 that drew the greatest attention. He was the commander of a man-of-war. The naval fop or beau seems to have been a well-known type. Charles Shadwell in *The Fair Quaker of Deal* (1710) has a character called Mizen who is a 'sea-fop'. It is possible that Shadwell was inspired by Rigby's story, but he has left out Rigby's sodomy which may have been difficult to make comic. Rigby had like Mizen, however, been brought to heel by the Societies for the Reformation of Manners. These societies in the 1690s were the last instance of those urban-reforming religious societies that had appeared during the previous century. Like their early seventeenth-century Puritan predecessors, they went after the sexual frankness of the stage and pro-secuted swearing, prostitution and sodomy. For some playwrights, it became difficult to put sodomy on the stage. Jeremy Collier nonetheless attacked the stage in 1698 for promoting prostitution, drinking, gambling and unnatural sins. John Dennis answered that as to sodomy, it was 'either never mentioned' on the stage 'or mentioned with the last detestation'.[45]

On Guy Fawkes Day (5 November) which fell on a Saturday in 1698, William Minton went to see the fireworks in St James's Park. Minton was nineteen or midway through puberty. His voice had probably broken, but his beard had almost certainly not grown. In the crowd, Captain Rigby stood next to the boy. He took his hand and squeezed it and brought out his erect penis and put it in the boy's hand. He then kissed him and put his tongue into his mouth. The boy ran away. Rigby pursued. He got the boy to promise to meet him in two days' time. The boy told his master Charles Coates what had happened. Coates was a friend of the Rev. Thomas Bray, a principal member of the Societies for the Reformation of Manners. Bray took the lead in prosecuting Rigby writing that it 'cost him much trouble and charge, and exposed him to no small danger' but that the reformers wished to put 'a great check to an abomination ... that ... was grown so open and impudent'.[46]

The reformers made a plan to entrap Rigby. The constables would wait in the next room when Minton went to meet Rigby. Rigby arrived at four. Minton arrived at six. Rigby drank a toast to the boy. He took his hand, kissed him with his tongue in his mouth and pushed the boy's hand into Rigby's breeches. He told him 'he had raised his lust to the highest degree', to which the boy replied 'how can it be, a woman only was fit for that'. Rigby damned the women and said that they were 'all poxt' or venerally infected, 'I'll have nothing to do with them'. Rigby sat in the boy's lap, kissed him some more with his tongue in his mouth and asked 'if he should F[uck] him'. The boy replied 'how can that be' and Rigby replied 'I'll show you'.

At this point, Rigby attempted to explain to the boy the moral acceptability of what he was proposing that they do. First, he said that 'it's no more than was done in our Fore-fathers time'. The king of France did it (meaning either Henry III or Louis XIV's brother) and he had seen the Czar of Muscovy, that is Peter the Great, 'through a hole at sea, lye with Prince Alexander'. The Czar had 'made Alexander, a carpentar, a Prince for that purpose'. Rigby then 'further spake most blasphemous words'. The commentators on the case emphasized this blasphemy. Edward Harley told his father before the trial that Rigby was 'accused of most horrid blasphemy and sodomy'. The editor of *The Trial of Lord Castlehaven* (1699) declared 'you all know that Ri[g]by's other heinous crimes was accompanied with horrid blasphemy'. The clergyman who wrote *The Sodomites Shame and Doom* (1698) maintained that 'R[ig]by's prodigious lusts led him to unparallell'd blasphemies'. But what had Rigby said that was so shocking that no one would write it down? It almost certainly was that Jesus Christ had loved St John, the greatest of all possible justifications for sodomy and the only one that was blasphemous.[47]

Rigby now returned to his seduction. He kissed Minton several times more and took him in his arms. He wished that he could lay with the boy all night and exclaimed that his 'lust was provoked to that degree' that he had ejaculated in his breeches, 'but notwithstanding he could F[uck] him'. The boy doubted that could be done in the tavern room, but to show him otherwise, Rigby took him into a corner, put his hand into Minton's breeches and asked him pull them down. Minton would not but told Rigby that he 'might do what he pleased'. The boy must have been standing with his back to Rigby who pulled down the boy's breeches, lifted up his shirt and put his finger into 'Minton's Fundament' (or arse). Rigby now put his erect penis on the boy's arse, for Minton said that 'feeling something warm touch his skin, [he] put his hand behind him, and took hold of Rigby's privy member', declaring 'I have now discovered your base inclinations, I will expose you to the world, to put a stop to these crimes'. Minton made for the door. Rigby stopped him and drew his sword. Minton stamped his foot and cried 'Westminster' (the agreed signal). The constables came in and seized Rigby. He tried to bribe them but they took him to Lord Chief Justice, Sir Henry Colt, and charged him.[48]

Rigby's approach to the boy must have been ordinary enough. In the same month of November, Richard Kirby had tried to seduce the servant of his barber, a boy name Joseph Thomas. When the boy went down to the cellar to use the vault or toilet, Kirby followed him. As Thomas pulled up his breeches, Kirby took hold of Thomas' 'yard' or penis and rubbed it back and forth and then took the boy's hand and made him masturbate Kriby's own penis. Kirby took out a bottle of sack and a piece of maple biscuit and made the boy eat and drink. Kirby told Thomas to turn his face to the wall. When he refused, Kirby 'put a finger up [Thomas'] fundament and the nail of his finger under the foreskin of his yard' and advised him to 'go after lewd women'. Things went no further. On Easter Monday, Kirby came to the shop and invited Thomas for a drink. When the boy said he could not leave his master's shop, Kirby gave him two pence and sent him to get a pot of drink. As they drank in the shop (where presumably no one else was present), Kirby pulled Thomas to him, took out Thomas' yard and rubbed it and took out his own and made Thomas rub it. Kirby then masturbated himself until 'he spent his nature upon the boards' and rubbed it out with his foot. Kirby now took his penis again and this time put it under the boy's coat and between his legs 'and rubbed himself until he spent his seed into [Thomas'] breeches'. On Whitsun Kirby came a last time and asked the boy to go down to the cellar with him. When Thomas refused, Kirby said that he had wanted to go downstairs and feel Thomas' penis before his mistress came home. The boy made his complaint on the sixteenth of June.[49]

A few days before Rigby's trial, the Chief Justice received an anonymous letter offering to prove sodomy 'not only upon Rigby, but almost upon every body else'. The letter claimed that 'the City as well as the Court is full of such sparks and that they are all in all the offices'. The Chief Justice gave the letter to the Attorney General who showed it to the Archbishop of Canterbury and the Lord Chancellor, but they recognized the hand to be that of untrustworthy witness and decide not to pursue the charges. Rigby on the advice of his lawyers (to whom he had paid sixty guineas) tried to have the charges dismissed on a technicality. The judges ruled against him and found him guilty. They sentenced him to stand in the pillory on three separate days in Pall Mall, at Charing Cross, and at Temple Bar, from eleven to one o'clock. They fined him £1,000 and ordered him to find sureties for his good behaviour for seven years. James Vernon told the Duke of Shrewsbury that 'it is a smart [severe] sentence that some Beaux complain of, but much less would not have satisfied the Grave Reformers'. Vernon himself approved.[50] But Rigby had powerful friends. The novelist Daniel Defoe said that a paper defending him circulated after the trial. When he mounted the pillory in the Mall, he wore the fine clothes of a town beau and only stood beside the pillory without being required to put his head inside it. He was 'so attended with constables and beadles that nobody could throw anything at him'.[51]

Rigby and his friends had their public meeting places. The author of the *Sodomite' Shame and Doom* ominously intoned that 'your scandalous haunts are also known, and will (we hope) be visited by such as may bring your crime to just punishment'. Ned Ward found them at the Royal Exchange, where in the month following Rigby's trial, he 'jostled in among a parcel of swarthy buggerantoes, preternatural fornicators, as my friend called them, who would ogle a handsome young man with as much lust, as a true-bred English whoremaster would gaze upon a beautiful virgin'. It is tempting to label these meeting places a subculture and to imagine that one sees here the world of the adult effeminate sodomite whom Ward and others will describe in the next decade. But Ward also found on the exchange 'beaus, who I imagine, were paying a double price for linen, gloves, or sword-knots' to the pretty young milliners whom they hoped to pick up. Beaus still liked both women and boys. The man who picked up boys in Renaissance Florence also had had convenient places of rendezvous. Rigby and his fellow beaus belonged to that traditional world. There were no modern homosexuals to be found among them.[52]

Chapter 3

Modern Sodomy: The Origins of Homosexuality, 1700–1800

Randolph Trumbach

In the first decade of the eighteenth century, it became apparent that a profound transformation had occurred in the nature of sexual attraction in the societies of western Europe. A new kind of sodomite had appeared who differed entirely from the majority of Renaissance men whose sexual lives have been presented in the previous chapter. These new sodomites were the first European men who might reasonably be called 'homosexuals'. Homosexual and homosexuality were terms invented in the late nineteenth century to describe a mode of desire and behaviour that had first appeared nearly 200 years before in northwestern Europe, in England, France and the Dutch Republic. Modern sodomites were a numerical minority. The estimates made of the number of such men in twentieth-century western societies, whether in Germany at the beginning of the century, or for England, France and the United States in the 1990s, found that they were less than five and perhaps as little as 1 or 2 percent of the entire male population.[1] By contrast, sodomites in Renaissance Florence had comprised at least two-thirds if not all men in that city. In other societies outside Christian Europe that have organized sexual relations between males by differences in age, whether in ancient Rome or in the Middle East or in India in the twentieth century, the estimates of the number of males who engaged in such acts are similar to those for Florence, or to those for English monks at the time of the dissolution of the monasteries in the sixteenth century. From the early eighteenth century onwards, by contrast, sodomy between males came to be conceived of in western European societies as the behaviour of a minority. It is likely, however, that perhaps as many as a third of the men from what would later be described as the heterosexual majority continued to have sexual relations with this modern sodomitical minority.

The modern sodomite was not only part of a minority. He was despised for his effeminacy. The Renaissance sodomite had been disapproved of because his behaviour was immoral by the standard of Christian morality. But he was not despised. Indeed, he often was honoured by most men since he proved his masculine dominance by penetrating both boys and women. Modern sodomites or homosexuals were conceived to be men who really wanted to be women and took on many of the characteristics of women. They walked and spoke like women. They used women's names. They often dressed partly or entirely as women. But they did not desire women. Instead, they wished to have sexual relations entirely with males. Half of them still desired to have sexual relations with adolescents. But most adolescents no longer shared these desires, and their seduction therefore became extremely problematical. The other half of modern sodomites wished to have sexual relations with other adult men. They preferred men in their twenties and thirties. Men of these ages who shared these desires could be met in the illicit subcultures of larger cities, but these meeting places were often subject to invasion by the public authorities. Some of those who desired adult men preferred men from the heterosexual majority. It is likely that as many men as a third of such men had sexual contact with the modern sodomitical or homosexual minority. But these heterosexual men often blackmailed their sodomitical partners and sometimes subjected them to physical violence.

No one at the present moment has any satisfactory explanation as to why this transformation occurred. It brings sharply into focus the real limits on the power of historians to account for change. In the 1690s, England lived under one sexual system. By the first decade of the eighteenth century, England lived under a different system. The new system appeared simultaneously in northwestern Europe, in France, England and the Dutch Republic. These were the parts of Europe undergoing a vast transformation that is sometimes called modernization. A modern economy based on public credit, religious skepticism and the enlightenment, romantic marriage and the tender care of children are three examples of changes in other areas of life that can be coordinated with the appearance of the division of the world into a homosexual minority and a heterosexual majority. With that in mind, we can turn to the presentation of the evidence for the appearance of this new world of sexual relations.

The adult effeminate sodomite: life in the molly-houses

Thomas Baker's play, *Tunbridge-Walks, or The Yeoman of Kent* (1703), first establishes the appearance of the molly as the new exclusive effeminate sodomites were called in ordinary speech. Baker was probably a molly himself. It was claimed that in the character of Maiden, he drew his own picture. Maiden in the play was described as a 'nice fellow that values himself upon his effeminacies'. He was distinguished from Squib, who was a 'fluttery' or frivolous military fop. Maiden has many lady-like accomplishments, can sing, dance, play the guitar, do fancy work and dress a woman since he was once apprenticed to a milliner. But a 'gentleman took a fancy' to him and left him an estate. Maiden likes women's company but does not 'desire any private love-favours from 'em'. He admits that he has never had sex with a woman. When he was a boy, he 'loved mightily to play with girls and dress babies'. He and his friends, who are called beaus, meet together in his chambers in the Temple, where they 'play with fans and mimic the women, scream, 'hold up your tails', make curtsies, and call one another Madame'. He also says that he has gone to the theatre dressed as a woman. This is the first appearance of a gender role that will be described repeatedly during the course of the century in the imaginary and the legal sources. Some of the literary descriptions may possibly have drawn on each other. But, the corroboration in the legal sources from a great number of witnesses (many of whom were poor people without knowledge in all probability of the literary sources) that there were men who took women's names, were called 'she' and 'her' by all their acquaintance, screamed and called each other whore and madam and dressed in women's clothes, all make certain that what Baker presented to the general public eye, he had found in actual life.[2]

In 1707 and again in 1709, the Societies for the Reformation of Manners sent its agents into many of the principal meeting places of London's new effeminate sodomites. Some of their trials were printed, and they document the locations of activity and some of the kinds of men involved. But none of the trials explicitly show the new effeminacy of the molly (or passive adult sodomite) as the trials of the late 1720s eventually did. This effeminacy is found only in the comments of writers like Edward Ward and John Dunton. It is likely that this is so because this effeminacy and its rituals were displayed only in the relative security of the sodomitical tavern or molly-house, or in the private rooms of men like Thomas Baker's Maiden. The agents of the Societies in 1707 seem mainly to have gone into the more open meeting places. In 1709, they did attack the molly-houses, but the broadside describing the trials of that year is not very detailed. The evidence of what occurred in the molly-houses must have become widely known, and on the basis of it, Ward presumably wrote the account of the mollies' club that he published in 1709.

In 1707, the printed account of the trials said that seven men had been tried and found guilty of making a pass at one or more of the agents of the Societies. The men who were actually tried were part of a much larger group of those arrested. Lady Cowper knew of a list that was sold with the names of twenty-five sodomites in prison. These in turn were part of a still larger 'gang' or 'club' of forty-three according to John Dunton or of nearly a hundred according to *The Women-Haters Lamentation* (1707). All three of these sources agree that three of the accused men committed suicide rather than go through the shame of a trial, two by hanging themselves and the third with a razor. John Dunton said that the one who cut his throat was Jermain, the clerk of the church of St Dunstan's in the East. The *Lamentation* presented their pictures in a woodcut. Lady Cowper wrote that one of them died with a paper in his pocket showing his innocence. This raised the fear, she said, that many accusations were made by black-mailers. The cases, then, were widely talked about – but in what terms? The suicides of the three men are probably the best clue. When Pepys and others had gossiped about the sodomy of Sedley and Rochester, these gentlemen had not gone out and hanged themselves. The level of shame connected with sodomy had increased because the accusation now meant that one was exposed to the world as an effeminate molly and not a real man. Unnatural practices now brought with them (as the *Lamentation* said) unnatural ends. Sodomy was now tied to a deviant gender role.[3]

The broadside on the trials of 1709 is the first source to clearly mention the public houses in which sodomites met. A soldier called Skelthorp, who was executed for sodomy, had confessed the location of the houses. A footboy to a duke revealed another meeting place. A brandy shop in Jermyn Street near St James Park in London was one location, 'the person who kept the shop being one of the gang'. But the only evidence for what occurred inside these houses in 1709 comes from Ned Ward's account of the mollies' club. Ward wrote that the men in these houses called themselves mollies. The term becomes common enough as the century wears on, but Ward, again, is the only source for it in the first decade. Molly was a term originally used for female prostitutes. Its application to adult effeminate male sodomites was the beginning of a linguistic practice that has been maintained for three centuries in which many of the popular terms once used for female prostitutes were subsequently appropriated to categorize these men.

(Some later examples in English language usage: queen, punk, gay, faggot, fairy and fruit.) John Dunton did not use 'molly' but simply called these men he-whores and said there was a 'club' of them close to the Stocks Market. Two years before, either Ward or Dunton, the *Women-Haters Lamentation*, had said that these men formed a club and hated women, but it had not mentioned effeminacy nor compared the men to whores.[4]

Ward wrote that the men 'speak, walk, tattle, curtsy, cry, and scold' to mimic women. This was similar to Thomas Baker's description of Maiden. But Ward added that they did not omit 'the indecencies of lewd women' so that his men were bolder than Maiden. The mollies entertained themselves with the enactment 'of a groaning woman' (or a woman in labour) who was delivered of a 'jointed baby' or wooden doll. The man who played the mother was dressed in a 'woman's night-gown, sarsnet-hood, and nightrale': the man who was the country midwife wore a 'high crowned hat and an old beldam's pinner': and there was a nurse in a 'hussife's coif [housewife's dress]'. When the labour was done, the child was dressed, presented to its father and christened. A feast was laid, and the women sat and talked about their husbands and children. When the play was over, all these men had sex with one another. Ward protested that this profaned a holy sacrament as a diversion for profligates. He suggested that their sexual acts were those of men who were 'sunk into a state of devilism' and that their club was a 'diabolical society'. These libertines mocked true religion and worshipped the devil. It is a description that intriguingly ties them to the devil clubs of the male libertines who went with women that were described in this same decade. The mollies were certainly irreverent, but it seems unlikely that they were self-consciously libertine. Their mock groaning and christening was probably based on popular traditions that used such public enactments to express disapproval of various kinds of sexual irregularities, as has been seen in the previous chapter in the incident seven years later in 1716 in a rural Gloucestershire village of eighty inhabitants.[5]

It is apparent that both the villagers in Gloucestershire and the mollies in London saw sodomy as an inversion of sexual relations between men and women. When one male sodomized another, he treated him as men were supposed to treat women. The passive male indeed became a woman. But what did the London sodomites mean by their ceremony? It differed in a number of significant details from the rural one. In London, there were, of course, no female participants. The men played all the roles. In Gloucestershire, one man acted the midwife, but they sent actual women to sit with the lying-in woman and to talk to him as his gossips. In London, the men were the gossips. They enjoyed (as Maiden did in the play) the sociability of women's lives.

There is in the Gloucester story not much evidence or interest in male effeminacy. For the sodomites in London, it was the centre of their world. This makes it unlikely that concern about the molly's role had already made its way into rural Gloucestershire. It was instead that both groups of men drew on the satirical tradition of the charivari or public skit to make their points. The men in Gloucestershire wished to disapprove of a sexuality which was unnatural because it was not reproductive. It is more difficult to say what the mollies meant to satirize. Ward was certain that they wished to express their hatred for women. There was no doubt about that. But the mollies also liked women's ways, and that to them was the rub. Men were not supposed to like women's ways. They tolerated them. As Ward said, these were 'all the little vanities that custom has reconciled to the female sex'. The molly, therefore, could express his fondness for what he in part desired to be only by mocking it. He both loved and hated the female part of his role. He could indulge it in the privacy of the molly-house. But if his taste was exposed in public, his shame could be so intense that he might take his life.

In 1718, two years after the Gloucestershire groaning, Jonathan Wild, the leader of the thieves' underground, published an account of life inside the molly-house. It did not describe anything like the mock groaning, but it confirmed the effeminacy of speech and gesture, and it provided the first clear description of group transvestism. It was part of his controversy with Charles Hitchen, the corrupt Under Marshall of the City. Hitchen was a sodomite himself. In 1727, the Societies, who had long tried to prosecute Hitchen, successfully brought a case for attempted sodomy against him. Hitchen had frequently picked up soldiers and taken them to a public house where he would call for a private room. It had made one of the servants suspect that he was a sodomite. But Hitchen for years had been confident that no one would move against him. Accordingly, on a night in 1714, he had told Wild that he 'would introduce him to a company of he-whores'. Wild did not understand the word and 'asked if they were hermaphrodites: No ye fool, said the M[arsha]l, they are sodomites, such as deal with their sex instead of females'. The two men then went to a public house. Wild found that the men addressed Hitchen as 'Madam' and 'Ladyshi'. The men also called one another 'my dear', hugged and kissed, 'tickling and feeling each other as if they were a mixture of wanton males and females', that is, some took male roles and some the female. Their voices and their manner were effeminate. They were witty, 'some telling others that they ought to be whipped for not coming to school more frequently'. Wild did not describe any other ritual or any actual sexual acts.[6]

Hitchen, however, had not received the attention from some of the younger men that he expected, so he took his revenge. He arrested them when they held a ball. Hitchen explained that there was 'a noted house in Holborn to which [they] used to repair and dress themselves in women's apparel for the entertainment of others of the same inclinations in dancing and the like in imitation of the fair sex'. When the ball broke up, Hitchen arrested the men and took them to jail in their finery. The next day they appeared before the Lord Mayor still in their women's clothes. The Mayor ordered them to be taken through the streets in these clothes as part of their punishment. They were sentenced to the work-house and stayed there until one of them threatened to reveal some of his Hitchen's own adventures. Wild said that one of the young men found the public trial, parade and imprisonment 'so mortifying that he died a few days after his release'. It is apparent that a sodomite like Hitchen accepted that the men in the molly-house were equivalent to female whores; and to Wild's eye, it was the behaviour of whores and their male customers that these men imitated, and not the behaviour of respectable women.

The best evidence for life in the molly-house comes from the arrests and trials that the Societies for the Reformation of Manners inspired in 1726. In the last few months of 1725, a group of at least four agents of the Societies (Samuel Stevens, William Davison, Thomas Willis and Joseph Sellers) began to visit the molly-houses in order to gather evidence. They were led initially by a young sodomite named Mark (or Martin) Partridge who in the end did not appear in any of the actual trials, perhaps because his fellow sodomites had become suspicious of him before the investigation was completed. Partridge had quarrelled with another sodomite named William Harrington. In revenge, he had begun to inform against the entire world of his fellows. On one occasion, Partridge was nearly mobbed in a molly-house when some men called him a 'treacherous, blowing-up, mollying bitch, and swore they'd massacre anybody that should betray them'. Partridge was saved by the unsuspecting man who kept the molly-house who was six months later hanged for sodomy. In February 1726, Partridge bound himself to give evidence against eleven men and one woman for keeping molly-houses and against sixteen other men (including Charles Hitchen) for going to these houses and for 'acting sodomitical practices' there and elsewhere. The government intervened at some point early in 1726, and the prosecutions were directed by the Treasury Solicitor's deputy. The evidence of actual sodomy for which four men were condemned and three executed was in the end given by two young sodomites, Thomas Newton and Edward Courtney. They had been the passive partners and, for the sake of their evidence presumably, they were not tried themselves. However, a much larger number of men were arrested in 1726. There were at least (one of the rolls is decayed) twenty-one in the City and twenty-three in Westminster. Twelve of the men Partridge accused of sodomy do not seem to have been arrested. It makes for a total of fifty-six men charged or arrested for sodomy or sodomitical practices. In addition to the twelve people accused by Partridge of keeping molly-houses in Westminster, one more man was arrested on that charge. Three married couples and two men were also charged in the City with keeping molly-houses. Since two of the Westminster men kept a house together, it made a total of seventeen houses.[7]

The London Journal was therefore not much off when it reported in May 1726 that 'twenty houses have been discovered which entertained sodomitical clubs'. The paper added that 'these monsters' also met each other 'at what they call the markets': they were the Royal Exchange and the piazzas of Covent Garden, the Lincoln's Inn bog-houses, Moorfields and the south side of St James's Park. The first two were arcades of shops, the last two were public parks, in all of which one might saunter, catch an interested party's eye and consummate the act nearby. They were used as much by female whores and their male customers as by sodomites. This must have confirmed the public identification of sodomites with whores. Women were not likely, on the other hand, to be found lingering in men's toilets, but even there, the occasional whore was found with her man. The Societies, with the aid of disaffected sodomites, had laid open the topography of London's Sodom.[8]

The molly-houses came in different kinds. Most of them were alehouses. Some of them may have been open to the general public with a more private room or two at the back for mollies. This seems to have been the case for the houses that Thomas Orme and George Whitle kept. Whitle and his servants denied that his back rooms were used by mollies. He said that what one witness had seen were surgeons examining their patients. Margaret Clap and her husband kept a coffeehouse. In the manuscript records, the house is described a number of times as being John Clap's coffeehouse. But only Margaret was arrested, tried and sentenced to the pillory where she was treated severely by the mob. She protested at her trial that as she was a woman 'it cannot be thought that I would ever be concerned in such practices'. But Samuel Stevens, one of the undercover agents, said that she had appeared 'to be wonderfully pleased with' the obscene conversation that the men held in her presence. On a Sunday night (the busiest night of the week for the molly-houses), there had been from twelve to forty men in her house. At least two other houses were run by married couples. One of the husbands, Samuel Roper, was clearly a molly. He was charged with sodomy as well as with keeping a disorderly house. He was known as Plump Nelly. He died in prison awaiting trial. Two men, Robert Whale and York Horner, were mollies who together kept a house in King Street, Westminster. Whale was known as Margaret or Peggy and Horner was Pru. John Towleton who was Mary Magdalen and Thomas Mugg who was Judith also kept houses. But a molly-house could be a very modest affair. Thomas Wright kept two different rooms around Moorfields. He went out to fetch drink from alehouses, and the men 'allowed him a profit out of it'.9

The life inside a number of the molly-houses was described in 1726, confirming some of what had been described by Edward Ward in 1709 and Jonathan Wild in 1714. There was, however, no mock birth or groaning like those in Ward's description or the Gloucestershire case. It may simply have been that the agents of the Societies were not present on the night that it occurred in 1725. It probably continued to occur throughout the century. Certainly, Robert Holloway claimed that around 1790 in a house in Clement's Lane near the Strand, a group of men were arrested 'in the very act of giving caudle to their lying-in women [with] the new-born infants personated by large dolls'. What was described in 1726 were the effeminacy and the sexual flirtations and consummations. Three of the trials described Margaret Clap's house. It may have drawn the largest crowd. Thomas Newton, the thirty-year-old sodomite who led the agents to the house, said that Clap had beds in every room of the house for 'the more convenient entertainment of her customers'. Samuel Stevens saw men in a group of twenty or thirty, hugging and kissing and sitting in each other's laps in one room, 'and making love (as they called it) in a very indecent manner'. Couples then went into another room, and when they returned, they 'would tell what they had been doing, which, in their dialect, they called marrying'. Stevens said that William Griffin had kissed every-one around, and had then thrown his arms around Stevens' neck, and hugged and squeezed him, and tried to put his hands into his breeches. Stevens also described the men getting up to dance and making curtsies. They mimicked women's voices: 'O fie, sir! — Pray, sir — Dear, sir — Lord, how can you serve me so? — I swear I'll cry out — You're a wicked devil — and you're a bold face — Eh, ye little dear Toad! Come buss!'[10]

When Mark Partridge agreed to take Joseph Sellers to the house in Drury Lane, it was arranged that Sellers would pass as Partridge's 'husband', to 'prevent my being too far attacked by any of the company'. Martin Mackintosh – who like many of the men took a 'maiden' or woman's name: his was Orange Deb – came up to Sellers nonetheless and 'thrust his hand into my breeches and his tongue into my mouth'. He swore he would go forty miles to enjoy him and begged him 'to go backwards and let him'. When Sellers refused, Mackintosh offered to be passive to him instead, by pulling down his own breeches and trying to sit naked in Sellers' la Partridge, chased him off with a hot poker from the fire and 'threatened to run it into his arse'. (Samuel Stevens who was present confirmed this story.) Mackintosh had, like most of the men in the house, adopted some feminine characteristics, but in the sexual act, he was prepared to be either active or passive. It is likely that by 1726 such sexual versatility was widespread among all sodomites. Joseph Sellers and William Davison gave similar descriptions of the men in Thomas Wright's room for mollies near Moorfields after they were taken there by Mark Partridge. There was a fiddler for music and dancing and the singing of bawdy songs ('Come let us [fuck] finely'), which were accompanied with sexual gestures. There was a second smaller room with a bed where some of the eight men went to be 'married'. They sometimes closed the door, but they sometimes left it open, so that part of what occurred could be seen.[11]

The molly's interest in marriage is demonstrated by a final source from the 1720s. James Dalton, one of London's famous thieves who was hung in 1730, published in 1728 (or had published about him) an account of his robberies and his adventures among the whores and the sodomites. Dalton was introduced into the company of the sodomites by a man called Susannah or Sukey Haws. Haws claimed to Dalton that he was not a sodomite himself but only associated with them so that he could blackmail them, especially 'those that were not established in clubs'. But Dalton was sceptical and called Haws 'a persecutor of the party he falls in with and a traitor to both sexes'. Haws took Dalton into at least three clubs or molly-houses, and Dalton described two others as well. All of the men in these houses took women's names 'in order to be concealed',

Dalton thought. The houses clearly provided a measure of safety. Haws
blackmailed men who did not use the houses but picked men up in the
street. Two fishmen from Billingsgate, Nursh Ashcroft and Fish Hannah,
told Dalton that he was 'encroaching upon their property' in Susan Haws
and suggested that they should meet to discuss the matter at a noted
molly-house near Billingsgate because 'they were not willing to expose
themselves in the street'.

Inside the molly-house, the men enacted their rituals and had sex.
Dalton said the sex was too astonishing and shocking to describe. But he
told of two different ceremonies, neither of which he actually seems to
have seen himself. One of them was the now familiar mock groaning or
delivery. One man was placed in a chair and the others attended with
napkins and a basin of water. Susan Guzzle, a gentleman's servant, was
the midwife, who brought forth a 'jointed baby' or wooden doll from
under the chair that the man in labour sat on. Dalton said that men also
gave birth to a pair of bellows and to a Cheshire cheese. Sukey Haws told
Dalton of the other ceremony which was a marriage. Moll Irons had
married another molly who was a butcher. Two other butchers stood
as bridesmaids. One was called Miss Kitten and the other the Princess
Seraphina. The Princess (or another man who used the name) will shortly
be described as a real enough transvestite from an Old Bailey trial in
1732. The marriages probably continued throughout the century. Robert
Holloway described a man in the first decade of the nineteenth century
who had 'married a little catamite called Miss Reed, according to the
rites of the Vere-street church' – the church being actually a molly-house.
This husband took his male wife home to live with the female wife he
already had, passing the boy off as 'a young man who wished to board
and lodge in a decent family'.

Dalton concluded his account of the mollies by quoting a song that
Moll Irons sang in the mollies' club. In the song, the mollies contrasted
themselves with the fops who liked women. They praised the Turks and
the Jews because they took 'all liberty' in sex 'before or behind'. They
pointed out that Achilles had Patroclus and Jove, Ganymede. And consequently they asked 'why should we then be daunted when both gods and
men approve the pleasant deed'. It was an appeal from the restrictions of
England and its Christian culture, to the wider world, both ancient
and modern. The song provided a libertine justification for an otherwise
despised life and served, no doubt, the same purpose as did the ceremonial
inversions of birth and marriage. Dalton is, of course, a source written to

entertain, and its information is therefore not entirely trustworthy. But there is a consistency with all the stories from the other sources. The group's assertion of its liberty and human dignity in this song also fits with the voice of the sodomite William Brown who, when he was arrested for 'taking out his privy member and putting it into [Thomas Newton's] hand', declared that he 'did it because I thought I knew him, and I think there is no crime in making what use I please of my own body'. In Moorfields, a man's sense of property began with his property in himself. A molly retained that sense. Neither the individual molly nor his underworld was without defences in the face of a dominant hostile world. They moved back and forth between that hostile world and their own. They belonged to both worlds. And they drew their defences from the larger world in which most of them in daily life seem to have passed undetected.[12]

The difficult question to answer is to what extent a molly became effeminate because of his role. What men did in the molly-houses was not necessarily what they did in the streets or at home or at work. It is likely that most mollies were able to put on and discard their effeminacy at will. They at least could do so for the public eye. But in their own minds, it is more likely they felt themselves part man, part woman. It was not uncommon for a molly once he was arrested to turn out to be a married man with children. It is not possible to be more precise than that since there is no information about most of the men who appear only once and fleetingly in the criminal records. There is more information on the eight men whose trials for sodomy in 1726 were printed. Six of them were or had been married, two were single. Five of the married men had had children. Two of them were widowers, one of whom was about to remarry. One of the fathers hoped that the 'world would not be so unjust as to upbraid his poor children with his unfortunate death'. It was said of Patrick Malcolm and William Brown as a point in their favour that each of these married men preferred the company of women to that of men. But this could have been ambiguous evidence, since a man like Maiden in Thomas Baker's play liked women's company but had no sexual interest in them. It was also Brown who had said that he thought he was free to use his body as he wished. George Kedger, one of the single men tried, brought two women to swear that 'he loved a girl too well to be concerned in other affairs'. Only Thomas Wright of all the eight men tried admitted at his execution that he had followed 'these abominable courses', though he said that some of Thomas Newton's evidence was perjured. But when Wright attempted at his trial to save his life, he was able to get the two women who lived above his room to come and swear that while they had heard music and merry-making from below, they had never known of any sodomitical practices and that Wright himself behaved 'like a sober man and was a very good Churchman'.[13]

From the early eighteenth century on, it was suggested that men who were sodomites congregated in the various trades that dealt with women's hair and clothes, presumably because they could there both display an interest in such things and have license to behave with an elegance that verged on effeminacy. Thomas Baker in *The Female Tatler* in 1709 described the assistants in the millinery shops on Ludgate Hill as the 'sweetest, fairest, nicest, dished out creatures; and by their elegant address and soft speeches, you would guess them to be Italians' – when Italian was synonymous with sodomite. Two generations later, Fanny Burney imagined Evelina's visit to similar shops. She found the mercers even more 'entertaining' than the clothes. They seemed 'so finical, so affected', and they 'recommended caps and ribbons with an air of so much importance, that I wished to ask them how long they had left off wearing them!' In the 1790s, it was even claimed that such men took away legitimate work from poor girls who were left with the options of becoming servants or prostitutes. To Mary Hays, these men were 'delicate, contemptible beings', and a 'she-he gentry'. To Priscilla Wakefield, they were 'a brood of effeminate beings in the garb of men' who ought to exchange 'such frivolous avocations for something more worthy of the masculine character'.[14]

Most sodomites, however, were employed in a wide range of occupations in which it is unlikely that they could have displayed any marked effeminacy. From the printed trials and the manuscript criminal records, it is possible to recover the occupations of thirty-one men in the four years from 1726 to 1729. Two were perriwigmakers and one each a tailor and a wiredrawer, all of whom might have worked on women's clothes. But among the rest, there were servants (three); yeomen (three) and gentlemen (four) (both of these last two were vague categories); carpenters (two) and a cabinetmaker; two clothworkers; a milkman, a grocer and a coalseller. The largest category (7) were men who ran public houses and who were classified variously as a cook, a fruiterer, an alehousekeeper, a vintner or as victuallers. At least three of these certainly kept molly-houses, and the other four may have also. It may have been that molly-house keepers, many of whom used women's names and were sodomites, were some of the most publicly known mollies and were therefore very likely to become the targets of denunciations.

Most mollies must have passed for most of their lives as husbands and fathers or as single men who liked women. Most of them were usually employed in jobs where they could show nothing of their sexual tastes. It was only in the molly-house that they came alive. There they could be outrageous, kissing and groping each other, dancing and singing bawdy songs, lisping like women, sometimes dressing like women, getting married or giving birth like women, using women's names. James Dalton said that mollies used women's names to hide their identities in the molly-houses. But it is as likely that they took these 'maiden' names not so much to hide one identity as to take on another. The names in fact were sometimes partly composed of their actual family names. William Gent was Mademoiselle Gent and Thomas Wareham was Miss Wareham. (Thomas Baker possibly had called his molly *Maiden* because of this custom.) These maiden names were probably the piece of effeminacy that was most widely practiced. It is apparent that dressing in women's clothes was much less frequent and widespread. The humiliation of exposure that arrest, trial and standing in the pillory brought to these men must therefore have been devastating. The families of some men stood by them and bailed them when they were arrested. William Buck was bailed by John Buck and Thomas Buck: the entire family were carpenters and clogmakers. Edward Lance was bailed by William Lance and Benjamin Lance: two of them were cordwainers. John Derwin was bailed by his father. Some sodomites who were fathers steadfastly denied their crime even after conviction, probably to protect their children. But most poor men cannot be followed after their trials.[15]

It was probably impossible for some men to hide their effeminacy in public even though it would have been to their benefit to do so. That they could not is probably an indication that they had internalized the molly's role so deeply that they enacted it involuntarily. It is difficult to prove this since the trials did not give descriptions of the way men looked, or spoke, or moved. It is likely, though, that many of the men who were blackmailed for sodomy had laid themselves open to their tormentors by displaying what were taken for tell-tale signs of effeminacy. One case may serve to make the point. John Potter charged that two foot soldiers had tried to extort money from him by saying that they would otherwise swear that he was a sodomite and would have him hanged. Potter was probably effeminate. He made fashionable wigs for men, one of the trades that sometimes attracted effeminate men. One of Potter's former employers who was a barber said that he had heard one of the two soldiers say that 'he did not know whether John Potter was a man or a woman'. Potter said that the two men had invited him into a private room in an inn. Although he wanted to go home, one of them 'unbuttoned my breeches and used me very unhandsomely', by which he probably meant some kind of active poking at his backside. They asked him if he had any money. He had only three halfpence in his pocket. They 'damned their souls' and said they wanted money. Potter was allowed to leave. But if he was effeminate, it did not mean that he was to be intimidated. He returned with a warrant and a constable. It is apparent that the soldiers tried to brush the matter off. The constable spent two and a half hours trying to get the three men to make the argument up. Potter was not to be satisfied. The case came to court. The soldiers appeared in their regimentals. Their sergeants swore to their good characters. They were acquitted. It is likely that the court had not been able to take John Potter seriously. Neither had the soldiers. Potter's effeminacy had brought him to this pass. If his effeminacy had been more at his conscious command, the soldiers very likely would never have invited him into their private room.[16]

There were a few men who lived the effeminate life fully and consciously. They dressed in the public street in women's clothes for a great deal of their time. They were referred to by all their acquaintances, male and female, as she and her. They took women's names. They were usually involved in prostitution. Sometimes they were prostitutes for men who were seeking other men. But sometimes it was for men who were seeking women. These men who acted out most fully the molly's role literally became whores. It is the final demonstration that the molly was a man who had become a he-whore. John Stevens was a waterman by trade. This was a laborious business that required 'great strength and a robust constitution' in order to 'ply in small boats upon the River Thames'. His neighbours complained in 1729 that Stevens was a nuisance who disturbed the peace by 'going about in woman's apparel in a very impudent and insolent manner, insulting the neighborhood'. In this case, effeminacy was combined with great physical strength: his effeminacy revealed the state of Stevens' mind not his body. Stevens, like James Dalton's male friend Sukey Haws, probably blackmailed his customers. Certainly, Thomas Foster said that Stevens had threatened to swear sodomy against him.[17]

John Cooper was the Princess Seraphina. In 1732, he accused Thomas Gordon of forcing him in Chelsea Fields at the point of a knife to exchange clothes with him and to give him a ring that he wore. Gordon told Cooper that if he charged him with robbery, he would say that Cooper had given him the clothes so that he could bugger Gordon. A crowd whom Cooper asked for help refused because Gordon told them that '[he] was a molly;' one man even said that Cooper should be hanged and that he would have nothing to do with him. What is clear from the two conflicting stories is that the two men had drunk together in the early morning and had then gone into Chelsea Fields where the exchange or the robbery of the clothes had occurred. It is also apparent that that morning Cooper was dressed in men's clothes of good quality. At the trial, however, a number of women testified that Cooper was known as the Princess Seraphina, dressed often in women's clothes, and made his living in part from sodomitical prostitution.

Margaret Holder said that Kett Sanford and Cooper often came 'with such sort of people' to the night cellar that she kept. Cooper was 'one of the runners that carries messages between gentlemen in that way'. 'Why', she said, 'he's one of them as you call molly culls, he gets his bread that way; to my certain knowledge, he has got many a crown under some gentlemen, for going of sodomiting errands'. But it was Jane Jones, a Drury Lane washerwoman, who identified Cooper as the Princess Seraphina. She had gone next door for a pint of beer to the Two Sugar Loaves that Mary Poplet kept. Seeing Cooper, she had said, 'There's the Princess Seraphina. So I looked at her [sic] … ' At this point, the Court intervened, and it was explained that Cooper went by that name. Mary Poplet then gave her evidence and spoke of the Princess alternatively as she and he, him and her. Poplet testified to Cooper's transvestism: 'I have seen him [sic] several times in women's clothes, she [sic] commonly used to wear a white gown and a scarlet cloak with her hair frizzled and curled all around her forehead; and then she would so flutter her fan and make such fine curtsies that you would not have known her from a woman'. Poplet added that the Princess took great delight in balls and masquerades. She and another woman agreed that the Princess sometimes worked as a nurse. Poplet said that 'Her Highness' lived with a man and his wife in Eagle court in the Strand. Cooper called the man his master because he had served as nurse when the couple were undergoing a salivation or cure for venereal disease. But Poplet said that 'the Princess is rather Mr. Tull's friend than his domestic servant'. She added that 'I never heard she had any other name than the Princess Seraphina'. A final woman testified that she and the Princess had discussed the loan of women's clothes. These women all came from the Drury Lane world where it is apparent that the worlds of male and female prostitution lived together. In it, the molly who was sometimes active and sometimes passive, was an accepted feature. But given a choice between an 'honest man' like Gordon and a molly like the Princess, these women took Gordon's part. Even in this underworld, the Princess and her like received only a limited toleration. Gordon, of course, was acquitted of robbery.[18]

Later in the century, transvestite males who were unambiguously prostitutes turn up. When John Gill was arrested in 1764 at eleven o'clock on a Tuesday night, he was having sex with a man in a coach in the Strand (one of the standard locales for female prostitution). It is not certain that his customer was a molly or that he knew that Gill was a man. Gill was known in his neighbourhood as Miss Beasly and had been dressed in earrings and a bracelet, women's satin shoes and white silk stockings and an outside petticoat trimmed with silver lace when he was arrested. Later in the same year, the constables on a Monday night cleared the streets around Covent Garden of twenty-two female prostitutes, as they thought. But it turned out that two of the prostitutes were men dressed in women's clothes. It would be intriguing to know whether the sexual partners of these male prostitutes, or the women with whom they walked the streets, knew the anatomical identity of these men beneath their women's clothes. It is likely that the women knew but not the male customers. Male transformation had gone as far as it was possible to go. But whereas in other cultures with a male transvestite role, the individuals who undertake it are sometimes classified as wives or concubines, in eighteenth-century London, the men who so transformed themselves were always whores. The molly was a he-whore.[19]

The men so far described very usually had sex with other adult men, though some of the young prostitutes in the trials were adolescents. But until 1750, if a man was found with a boy in a large city, it is not always possible to say whether he was a traditional pederast, a man like those discussed in the last chapter who liked boys and women, or a modern sodomite who liked only boys. Sailors in their ships at sea might of course be either, and even at the end of the century, the traditional system, in which men might retain their masculinity and have sex with both men and women, seems to have survived in England in rural areas like Somerset.[20] But if gender formation could be significantly different in rural than in urban areas, it makes it hard to explain why adult sodomites would flee the countryside to pursue their new identities in the relative anonymity of a large city's sexual subculture. The English records did not note the ages of men arrested for sodomy, but the French ones did. These records for Paris seem to tell the story of a gradual and eventual complete change from the old system to the new over the course of the eighteenth century. Out of 65 cases between 1697 and 1718, only one in 1706 involved young men who took women's names and married each other: all the rest were for relations between boys and men who were either priests or aristocrats. Between 1724 and 1750, only a third of the men arrested were priests or aristocrats, but many were still looking for younger passive partners. But by the 1780s, the majority were poor, unmarried men in their twenties and thirties who were having sex with each other and who displayed various degrees of effeminacy. A public sexual subculture composed mainly of men in their twenties and thirties who had sex with each other had made its appearance. The figures for Paris a century later show the same thing. From this, it is apparent that in the modern sexual system, the preference was for men in their twenties and thirties, whereas in the traditional pederastical system, all adult men from their twenties to their sixties together had pursued adolescents who were between fifteen and nineteen.[21]

Adult sodomites and adolescent boys: sex outside the subculture

It was nonetheless the case that in the modern sexual system after 1700, a substantial number of sodomites (that is males who desired only males) continued to be attracted mainly to adolescent boys. At the beginning of the twentieth century, the sexologist Magnus Hirschfeld estimated that 45 percent of homosexual men sought post-pubertal boys and another 5 percent boys who had not reached puberty. George Chauncey found in early twentieth-century New York that at least 40 percent of the sodomy cases prosecuted were of men who pursued adolescents.[22] It is therefore likely that the number of men in eighteenth-century London who pursued boys rather than men would similarly have been about 45 percent of all sodomites. These boys would have been pursued outside the subculture in which usually men in their twenties and thirties had sexual relations with each other. Modern sodomites whose preference was for adolescent males turn up in the eighteenth-century London cases for sodomitical assault in which males of a variety of ages complained of the sexual advances of another male.

It is probably useful to take up first and separately what must have been the cases of physically prepubescent boys. There were not many of them. In fact, between 1730 and 1830, only five of seventy cases before the Old Bailey involved boys younger than fourteen which was the age of legal consent for boys.[23] These were the kind of boys Michael Levi pursued. Levi was a young man whom his fellow Jews thought to be a virtuous and sober fellow who was religious and kept the Sabbath. He lived in Holborn and had a stall under an alehouse called the Baptist's Head. As he shut up his stall one night, he asked Benjamin Tailor, twelve years old and the son of a tailor who lived forty yards away, to help him carry up his boxes to the room he had in the alehouse. Once they were in the room, Levi locked the door, unbuttoned the boy's breeches, threw him face down on the bed and entered the boy for a quarter of an hour. The boy was hurt and cried out. He told one of his playfellows what had happened; this boy told his father, who told another boy's father, who told the injured boy's father. The father spoke to his son and assured him that he need not be ashamed or afraid to tell the truth. This all took a week, at which point other boys started to come forward. Thomas Lambard said that the same thing had happened to him two months before. He was a school fellow of Tailor's and fourteen years old. But he seems to have had no understanding of semen and said that 'when he got up he thought the prisoner had pissed on him'. A third boy, Samuel Tidmarsh, who was thirteen, had had his encounter with Levi a year before. When questioned, Benjamin Tailor said that he had not spoken sooner because he was ashamed to, but that he thought at the time that what Levi did was wrong. Apparently, Levi had made his way through a network of boys who lived in the same neighbourhood, but the boys initially seemed to have kept their startling experiences to themselves. They apparently had not masturbated since they did not know what semen was. None of them seems to have returned of their own accord to repeat the experience with Levi. The fathers of these boys and Levi were of similar social standing, though Levi's Jewishness would have made him to some degree different. But Levi did not have any authority over these boys; he does not seem to have given them any money, and it was apparently friendly and neighbourly interaction that allowed him to have access to them.[24]

Isaac Broderick, a schoolmaster, did use his authority over the boys in the school he taught for the Coopers' Company. Broderick had been educated at Trinity College and had a reputation for being pious and regular. But within a fortnight of being in the school, he sent eleven-year-old William Han upstairs, lowered the boy's breeches and put his member between his thighs. William claimed that Broderick did the same to four other boys. William's father, who was accustomed to questioning his son about his day at school, at first took his dislike of his new master to mean that he had been whipped. But after the boy's mother examined him, the story came out. Edward Calley, who was ten, said that the master had taken down his breeches and 'felt all about my body, gave me a gentle stroke or two, and bid me not cry out, he would not hurt me'. Calley told his bedfellow, but not his grandfather, because he was afraid that it would get back to the schoolmaster and that the master would beat him. But when Edward's grandfather questioned him, the boy knew what kind of man his master was: 'the boy replied his master had served him as the two men had served one another that stood in the pillory'. A ten-year-old, in other words, might have had little or no experience of sex and even not realize what masturbation or semen was. But he would know from the life of the streets what an effeminate sodomite was and realize that sexual interaction with him was forbidden. The schoolmaster in this case, unlike Levi, had not been violent, because he did not intend to penetrate the boys. But the nature of his authority over them may, in a quite different way, have had a greater effect on their minds.[25]

Relations between men and the boys past puberty whom they either met in the street at night or by sharing a bed covered a wide spectrum of possibilities, depending on whether or not a boy shared a man's sodomitical desires. A boy like seventeen-year-old William Tailor did not share these feelings, but he accepted Richard Spencer's offer of a drink. After some salacious conversation and a few kisses, he went for the constable and had Spencer arrested. John Holloway also allowed Henry Wolf to treat him and consented to being fellated once in a public toilet. But when Wolf tried to turn this into a steady friendship, Holloway brought two friends along, and together they chased Wolf in the street shouting that he was a sodomite and managed to have him arrested. Boys who probably became sodomites could be altogether more willing. John Meeson in the course of a day's encounter drank several times with John Dicks, and after he became drunk, Dicks sodomized him. But Meeson insisted that he was not 'sensible enough to know' whether this had happened – he had, in other words, been too drunk. The second of these boys, Joseph Churchill, tried to be affectionate with Charles Horn who rejected him and forced him to share a bed with two Portuguese sailors. One of these sailors then buggered young Churchill in the night. But in court, Churchill's behaviour towards Horn was used against him to suggest that he was a sodomite, and the sailor escaped punishment. The third boy, William Curtis, shared a bed with John Ashford who eventually sodomized him frequently. Curtis then left the house and moved into a circle of sodomites, some of whom he blackmailed and then denounced to the magistrate. The first two of these five boys would not tolerate any sustained interaction with a sodomite. The third boy when drunk enough could have sex with a man. The last two boys were almost certainly sodomites themselves. One of them was attracted to a boy of twenty near his own age, but his effeminacy allowed a sailor (who was probably accustomed to having sex with boys on ship when there were no women) to use him brutally. The fifth boy, though a sodomite himself, exploited the older men who were his companions. But none of the men in these cases had any sort of sustained relationship with the adolescents they had attempted to seduce.[26]

In those cases where such a relationship did exist, and especially when the adult man had authority over the boy, the boy's psychological reaction could be quite intense. There are two cases to consider. In the first, Charles Bradbury, a Methodist minister, sustained a relationship for several months with James Hearne, a fourteen-year-old, whom he moved into his lodgings. Bradbury also had a relationship with another boy in his congregation, and the three on some occasions had sex together. Hearne eventually had an attack of conscience and denounced Bradbury after the minister foolishly preached on Sodom and Gomorrah. But at the trial, Hearne broke down weeping and declared that Bradbury was innocent. He 'wished he had never been born and was sorry he had charged a person who was his best friend'. 'Best friend' was what sons called their fathers, and it seems likely that the confusion of roles in Bradbury, who was pastor, father and lover all at once, had put the boy under great pressure. Bradbury was acquitted of the charges.[27]

In the second case, Robert Thistlethwayte, the Warden of Wadham College, sent for William French to come to his lodgings on Saturday afternoon after evening prayer. French for two years had been an undergraduate in the college. Thistlethwayte had had sex with at least one of the male college servants, and he unsuccessfully on other occasions had tried to seduce the college butler and the barber as they waited on him. The servant with whom he succeeded served the Rev. John Swinton who was a fellow of the college and William French's tutor. It was noted that Thistlethwayte and Swinton had become good friends after Swinton had made a trip to Italy, where (it was implied) Swinton had learned to indulge his taste for males. Swinton was later accused of sodomizing a young, retarded college servant, but he successfully defended himself because the boy's evidence was confused. Thistlethwayte did not survive the charge of a young gentleman like French that he had made a sodomitical pass at him on that Saturday afternoon in his lodgings. But it was as much French's strong emotional reaction to the encounter as his social class that made his charges stick. After his interview with the warden, French was 'very much disordered' at the dinner table, and later to the surprise of the friend with whom he spent the evening he 'was taken very sick and vomited ... he afterwards sat down and behaved during the rest of the night as if he had been distracted, calling the warden the worst of scoundrels and villains'. He eventually told his friends, and they helped him to prosecute Thistlethwayte who resigned his posts and fled abroad where he lived until his death. In all of this, French carefully avoided his tutor Swinton who he must have come to realize shared Thistlethwayte's attraction to him. But Swinton, by wisely limiting his advances to the young servants, survived the scandal. French, however, was not able to cope with sexual advances or interest of two older dominant men of his own social class; the advances that the butler or the barber had managed to fend off, reduced him to vomiting.[28]

Most of the sex that occurred on British naval vessels over the course of the eighteenth and the early nineteenth centuries seems to have been structured by differences in age. Between 1706 and 1809, in fourteen of seventeen cases an adult man had sex with a boy sixteen or younger, and most of the boys seemed to have been twelve or thirteen. In only three of the cases was the encounter between two adults. Some boys clearly did not know what semen was and said that the man had 'pissed in his arse' or that 'it was the same as if he was making water'. The sex involved was usually anal, but one man made the boy fellate him also.[29]

The situation on board the ship the *Africaine* in 1816 was more complicated. Some adult men were passive with other men, some men were both active and passive, and some men had relations with boys and with men. The *Africaine* was in fact known as a 'man-fucking shi'. James Cooper was both active and passive with Raphael Seraco. Emmanuel Cross did it both with William Dane and with a fourteen-year-old boy, and Raphaelo Treake did it with two boys and with several men. One of the English midshipmen accused the two principal witnesses of being sodomites, and by this he probably meant that they were effeminate sodomites of the modern kind. But one of these men was a black Spaniard from Santo Domingo and the other a Portuguese sailor from Madeira, and it is likely that for them sodomy with a boy did not exclude a sexual interest in women. Indeed, it is possible that the heightened sexual life of the ship was produced by the interaction between (heterosexual) men, adult sodomites and boys from England, and Mediterranean sailors who in the traditional way liked both boys and women. The English officer, W. L. Crutchly, not only had a boy whom he penetrated and who masturbated him; he was also charged and convicted of embracing and kissing another man. Men's kissing had in England in the course of the eighteenth century come to be taken as a sure sign of effeminate sodomy. The same was true in the Netherlands, and Dutch sailors who had kissed each other aboard ship were punished much more severely.[30]

It follows from this that in ships at sea, there were three different sexual categories of males: heterosexual men, boys, and adult effeminate sodomites. The boys were the most complicated category: some were prepubescent and some had entered puberty. Most boys would eventually become heterosexual and a few homosexual, but these realizations would not necessarily have been arrived at during their time at sea. From the *Africaine* case, it is apparent that ships witnessed a complicated set of relations with heterosexual men having sexual relations structured by age with both heterosexual adults and boys, and relations with homosexual men structured by their effeminacy. It is therefore likely that while after 1700 a substantial minority of homosexual men structured their sexual relationships with males by differences in age, in ships at sea, heterosexual men were very likely to use differences in age to establish sexual dominance.

Sodomites and other men: the drunken mate and the blackmailing soldier

In the early stages of the modern homosexual/heterosexual system, there frequently was sexual interaction between men who were sodomites and those who were not. Historians and anthropologists have found this to be so well into the twentieth century. There was a substantial amount of such interaction in early twentieth-century London and New York. But it has been in Latin America that the most extensive activity has been documented. In the 1970s and 1980s when the modern system was only a hundred years old in Mexico, it was probably the case that as many as

30 percent of young Mexican males had sexual contact with the exclusively homosexual minority of 5 percent or less. This began to change only in the 1990s. This pattern was also found elsewhere in Latin America, in Costa Rica and Peru, for instance. Such a statistical measure cannot be made for eighteenth-century London, but it is likely that as many as one-third of the men in London in that century had sexual contact with sodomites.[31]

There were at least two kinds of contact between adult sodomites and other adult men who were not sodomites. They met either while drinking in a public house or as they urinated together at a 'pissing post' or sat next to each other in a 'bog house' or public toilet. These contacts must often have been by mutual consent, but the sources tend to describe only those which went awry. Male prostitution was the other means for making sexual contact. Transvestite homosexual prostitutes (who have already been described) had sex both with other sodomites and with men who were not sodomites. It is not easy to say whether a sodomite's heterosexual partner knew that he was having sex with another man. These transvestite males sometimes blackmailed their customers. When the cases came to court, the victim occasionally claimed not to be a sodomite himself, and this may or may not have been true. Soldiers were the other kind of male prostitute who engaged in blackmail. The adolescent male prostitutes (like the telegraph boys), who turn up easily enough in nineteenth-century sources, are not so conspicuous in the eighteenth century, but a number of the blackmailing soldiers were certainly late adolescents. The cases do not usually stress their prostitution, but it is very likely that this was the means by which contact between the blackmailer and his victim had often been made.

In most of the complaints made to the eighteenth-century magistrates that a man had tried to seduce another male, it is often not possible to tell which were made by late adolescents and which by adult males. These complaints make up the bulk of the manuscript materials on sodomy in the quarter-sessions' rolls. In contrast, the printed trials and the newspapers deal more often either with the seduction of adolescents or with raids on the molly-houses in which adult sodomites had consensual sodomy with each other. The attempted seductions recorded in the manuscripts usually took the form of quite open lunges made at another man's privates while drinking together in a public house; but they were sometimes also made in a pubic latrine or in the street. Sometimes more than a lunge was made; actions that became complicated and took long enough seem to imply some degree of initial interested consent which eventually changed to anger or alarm. But sometimes after the charge was made, it was withdrawn, after the two drinking companions decided to forget the matter. William Green in 1788 charged that Thomas Impey had attempted an unnatural crime when they were drinking together. But the next day, Green refused to maintain his charge and said that he had been drunk and could not recall the matter. The magistrate had no choice but to discharge Impey: so he fined Green five shillings for being drunk by his own confession. Similarly, Peter Campbell charged that Francis Philpott had touched him several times in Catherine Street and unbuttoned his breeches in Fleet Market; but since they had then agreed to go together to have a drink in a public house in Fleet Street, the magistrate dismissed the matter.[32]

The most elaborate attempted seduction that I have found occurred in 1761 when John Lowther and John Bushnell followed each other from one pissing post to another through several neighbourhoods. Lowther remained ever hopeful that Bushnell would comply with his desires. Bushnell was intrigued enough to see how the matter would end and had decided to lure the other man on with the intention of eventually charging him with sodomy. Bushnell began by saying that 'John Lowther came up to me and brushed on my elbow … stared me full in the face, and then crossed the way into Pope's-Head-Alley, and turned to the wall to make water … I then went past him, and looking back, observed the defendant looking after me'. Lowther now followed Bushnell to a courtyard 'and turned himself against the wall as if going to make water'. Lowther stayed in that position for a little time and then turned towards Bushnell. He had unbuttoned the flap of his breeches and 'shook his private parts at me, making a great panting noise much like a person out of breath with running'. Lowther then buttoned up and walked on to a second courtyard, where he again stood against the wall to pee, took out his penis, shook it at Bushnell and panted loudly. When Lowther did this ritual a third time in a third courtyard, he came closer to Bushnell, put his head on the other man's shoulder and stared him in the face as though he meant to kiss him. The two men continued their way through the courtyards. All told, Lowther stopped to pee, shook his penis and panted at Bushnell, eight times as they walked through a series of eight courtyards. After he 'made water the eighth time', Lowther came closer, took his penis in his hand and rubbed it against Bushnell's waistcoat. He then tried to take Bushnell's hand; but Bushnell drew back his hand. So Lowther caught Bushnell by the thigh and squeezed his penis through his breeches for a minute. Lowther then pushed his hand into Bushnell's breeches. He could only get four fingers in; so with his free hand he tried to unbutton Bushnell's breeches, but he could get only one button partly undone. All this while, Lowther's own breeches were undone and his penis hanging out. Bushnell now thought Lowther had gone quite far enough. He seized him by the collar and called for help to his friend who had followed them by prearrangement. Lowther struggled free and ran. But the two men pursued him, crying out 'Stop, Sodomite'. He was soon caught. When he came to trial, his neighbours said they had all known Lowther's reputation as a sodomite. He was fined £20, imprisoned for three months and sentenced to stand in the pillory near his own house.[33]

Over the course of the century, some men who were not sodomites were successfully blackmailed, and this raises a series of interesting questions. Why did men who were not sodomites pay blackmailers? Would it be possible to blackmail a heterosexual man today by claiming that he would otherwise be charged with committing or attempting to commit a homosexual act? If this is unlikely today, why was it possible in the eighteenth century? Were the markers of sodomy less clear then than they are now? Were the blackmailers themselves always able to tell the difference between a man who was a sodomite and one who was not? Why were some heterosexual men so timid once they were challenged? How did the public's reaction differ from today's? But it is apparent that from the moment that the first mass arrests of sodomites were made in 1707, they brought with them blackmail attempts on some considerable scale.

Soldiers appeared more frequently as blackmailers than any other group of men, especially during times of war when there would have been many of them passing through London. Their role as blackmailers may have been the result of being young underpaid men stationed in London with not enough to do. But it is also likely that soldiers in their uniforms were frequently solicited for sex by sodomites. Soldiers were therefore better informed about the sodomite's world in London than were most poor men. It may have been easy to turn from prostitution to blackmail; blackmail was probably more financially rewarding than prostitution; and it was certainly less threatening to a young man's masculine self-image. Soldiers blackmailed as lone operators, in pairs and in gangs. Some blackmailing soldiers became professional robbers.[34] Groups of soldiers seem to have acted together as blackmail gangs. The presence of these gangs in St James's Park was of long standing.[35] In the middle of the century, in a single year in 1759, there was a rash of these attacks on men in the park. London was then probably full of soldiers because of the war in progress. There was a barracks close to the park, and some soldiers were familiar with sodomites as sexual customers. John Fielding therefore had to commit to Newgate several individuals who had charged supposedly innocent men in the park with sodomy as a means of robbing them.[36]

The blackmailing soldier in the park in the story of George Hadley in 1778 vividly shows how the fear of being exposed as a sodomite left men paralysed. Hadley was approached by Robert Harold in the general vicinity of the Park. Hadley, who must have stared at Harold, said that he thought at first sight that he recognized some old soldier with whom he had served in India. After this exchange of glances, Harold told Hadley that he 'must have something' from him. The peremptory tone apparently made Hadley hostile, and he told him that he would give him nothing. But when Hadley tried to resume his walk, Harold went around behind him, took him by the collar and said, 'God d[am]n your blood, you shall not escape in this manner'. Hadley then let go of Hadley's collar and with his right hand seized Hadley's left hand and forced it down his great coat. Under the coat, Harold's penis was exposed and he touched Hadley's hand to it. At that moment, with his hand on a strange man's penis, Hadley said, 'that the idea of resistance entirely forsook me'. A mere robbery he would have resisted, he added, but this left him without the ability to resist. Harold then said to him, 'god damn your blood, you shall not escape so. There; there, you want to make an attempt on me. I will have justice'. Hadley now understood Harold's 'entire scheme' and was desperate that no one else should observe what was occurring. 'Be quiet', he said to Harold; 'I see what it is you want, it is not justice, it is money'. Harold now looked carefully around himself and replied, 'it is so; come, make me a present – I am a very needy man'. Hadley drew Harold aside and gave him what money he had. Hadley chose the spot so that they would not be observed 'for I was more afraid of [...] than he seemed to be at that time'. Harold, however, demanded five guineas more. Hadley agreed to meet him later and to pay the sum to him. He said he believed that if he had had a hundred guineas in his pocked at that moment, he would have given them to Harold.

Hadley thought of going to a lawyer at this point, but instead he met Harold a second time and gave him five guineas. As he did so he told Harold, 'Sir, this is a wretched way of getting money, and I am a wretched fool for giving it to you, but as I have been a fool in the first instance,

I cannot help it, and must pay for my folly'. Hadley saw Harold a third time seven days later. But by then he had gathered up courage to talk to an attorney and some friends. They advised him to have Harold arrested, which he did with the help of two constables. This story, like all the others, raises the question whether Hadley was in fact a sodomite. A detail of his initial encounter with Harold suggests that he was. He testified that when he saw Harold, he stared at him. To the court, he claimed this was because he recognized an old soldier. But it is possible that this stare had been one of sexual interest and that Harold had recognized this. Harold was evidently prepared for such an eventuality in the place where he encountered Hadley: it may have been a pick up spot for sodomites. Harold had come wearing a great coat and had his genitals exposed beneath it. Hadley's only recourse was to publicly insist that he was not a sodomite and that he was instead a man terrified of the consequences of the charge. 'My fear', he said, 'was of my character'.[37]

In a final case from the 1790s of blackmail by a soldier in the Park, a flirtatious comment by an ostensibly heterosexual man was interpreted in the most offensive way. Sir John Buchanan Riddle and a male friend were on their way into the park about quarter to ten in the evening on 19 June to see the fireworks. Riddle said that he was following a woman (almost certainly a prostitute) whom he thought he knew. But just before entering the park, Riddle stopped to talk to some other prostitutes who were looking out a window. Riddle was clearly excited by the bustle and the women. At the entrance to the park, Thomas Davis, a twenty-two-year-old guardsman, stood on duty as the sentinel. In his expansive state of mind, Riddle turned to Davis and said (according to Riddle's friend), 'soldier, I suppose you would have no objection to do something to these girls'. But instead of joining in the banter, Davis interpreted Riddle's remark as a sexual advance to himself and asked Riddle how dare he propose such a thing. Riddle was infuriated and boxed Davis down. Another man came to the soldier's aid. Davis now threatened Riddle with his musket and bayonet and demanded a present. Riddle said that Davis also claimed in front of what must have been a growing audience that Riddle had asked the soldier if he 'wished to know a girl, and if his p[rivate] p[arts] stood'. Riddle had then opened the flap of his breeches and taken hold of his testicles.

Riddle now became very uneasy lest anyone he knew should pass by, see the altercatione and put the worst possible interpretation on it. He therefore gave Davis a few shillings. But when Davis demanded more, Riddle decided that they should all go to the guardhouse. There the version

that the two gentlemen told was given credence over the soldier's. Davis
was brought to trial, found guilty and sentenced to death. Whatever Riddle
said to the guardsman raises two possibilities. It may have been common
for sodomites to make sexual approaches to soldiers in the park by opening with some speculation about the young man's prowess with women.
Riddle's question and his evident state of excitement may therefore have
misled Davis as to what was occurring. Riddle's question does, however,
open the possibility that it was not unusual for an older heterosexual male
like Riddle to enjoy the sexual good looks of a younger man like Davis,
provided that he could hide this from himself by supposing that what
he felt was the excitement of a mutual interest in women that he shared
with the younger man. The blackmail cases therefore open to us not only
the interactions of the sodomitical minority and the heterosexual majority
but may also bring to light the covert sexual interaction between men
in the majority who were supposed to be exclusively heterosexual in
their desires.[38]

Chapter 4

Secrets, Crimes and Diseases, 1800–1914

H. G. Cocks

Nineteenth-century Britain appears at first glance to be a place of repression and terrible punishment for homosexuals. The fall of Oscar Wilde, tried and imprisoned in 1895 for acts of 'gross indecency', would seem to represent the typical fate of the Victorian homosexual. Wilde, once the most famous writer of his day, was first scorned by his own society, then put to degrading and physically wearing punishment in Reading gaol and was finally forced into exile where he died, a broken man. In spite of his celebrity, Wilde's fate is typical in many ways. The nineteenth century witnessed an unprecedented rise in the numbers of men punished for simply having sex with each other. Never before in the history of Britain had so many men been arrested, convicted, imprisoned, pilloried and even executed for homosexual offences. The structures of criminal justice which policed homosexuality which were established in this crucial period were to endure until at least 1967. Same-sex desire was criminalized in new ways and policed more vigilantly than ever before. Sodomy remained a capital offence until 1861. This process of punishment was reflected in an entire vocabulary of moral opprobrium. A homosexual act was *the* 'unnatural crime', it was a 'nameless', 'abominable' or 'infamous' offence, not even named in the press, but represented instead by a series of asterisks or dashes. It was 'so unnatural as even to appear incredible'.[1] All these euphemisms were supposed to render same-sex desire silent, unseen and unknowable. It was, as Wilde's lover Lord Alfred Douglas put it so famously in 1891, 'the love that dare not speak its name'.[2]

However, even though the nineteenth century saw the rise of moral policing and punishment on a new scale, and the attempt to erase same-sex desire even from language itself, there were also signs of hope and life. In spite of the heavy punishments meted out by the courts, subcultures of sex remained a pervasive feature of urban life, not only in the capital. It was clearly possible-if risky-to-evade the law. In the course of the century, several places in London, in particular, became notorious as sites of cruising and assignation. The Royal Parks at night, West End music halls and theatres, along with many different streets across the capital famed for all kinds of prostitution, became known as places where men in search of sex could meet. Molly houses continued to exist in the capital until well into the 1820s, while new institutions arose to replace them, including the fancy dress, or drag ball. New languages arose to be used by men who met for sex. A new style of slang developed, later called Polari, or Parlare, and adapted from criminal argot.[3] For instance, the use of 'drag' to refer to wearing women's clothes was new in the 1860s, while 'Mary-Anne', 'Margery' or 'poof' might be used by men to describe themselves or their friends. Homosexual pornography was available, if you could afford it.

In addition to these widespread but mainly metropolitan networks of association, intellectuals, artists and writers began to make subtle inroads into Victorian prejudices and silences. Some men found refuge right at the heart of mainstream culture. In the controversial Anglo-Catholic Oxford Movement, effeminate young men seemed to find refuge. Similarly, the beginnings of a modern gay movement can be discerned in three overlapping areas of British culture. The first of these was the artistic movement known as aestheticism which began in the 1880s. Its key tenets, although not openly homosexual, nevertheless rejected Victorian bourgeois ideals like duty and morality. Instead aestheticism replaced the notion that art should perform some moral function with a love of art for art's sake, a passion for intense feeling and an embrace of classical Greece, including its subtly homoerotic ideals of beauty. In addition to the aesthetic revival of Hellenism, scientific enquiries into the nature of sexuality began to be made from the 1880s onwards, partly in an effort to combat England's harsh laws and to try and make a case for the legitimacy of same-sex desire.

Scientific enquiries into various kinds of 'perversion' had begun on the continent, and many of these ideas began to gain some currency in Britain in the 1890s. These enquiries had begun in the 1860s with the invention by a German doctor, Karl Heinrich Ulrichs, of a system of classifying the various types of same-sex desire, or Uranism as he called it. An attempt to overturn the harsh German laws against homosexual acts led another German, Karl-Maria Kertbeny, to coin the term 'homosexual' in 1869. By the 1890s, British writers who wished to make a case for the legitimacy of homosexuality had taken up some of these ideas, the most important one being that homosexuality was somehow innate or congenital and was not, as popularly supposed, merely a symptom of moral degradation or wickedness. Homosexual writers like John Addington Symonds and Edward Carpenter borrowed this idea and mixed it with indigenous traditions of Hellenism, socialism and masculine comradeship to produce a powerful argument in favour not only of the normality of homosexual desire, but of its social usefulness as well.

From these sources, scientific justification seemed to be forthcoming for the view that homosexuality was an ineradicable aspect of the personality or physiology. It therefore followed that enforcing laws against it was both inhuman and pointless. Before the Wilde trial, secret societies formed, devoted to the aim of using these arguments to ultimately overthrow English laws against homosexual behaviour. Writers like Carpenter began to publish subtle books containing careful arguments for the acceptance of homosexuality. Across the country, homosexual men found in these and other books a new way of understanding themselves. In these small efforts, we can see the beginning of Britain's movement for gay rights and some of the first public attempts to articulate a homosexual identity. Albeit in a tentative way, by 1914 homosexuality was forcing itself on the political and cultural agenda.

The law

Between 1806, when reliable figures begin, and 1900, 8,921 men were indicted for sodomy, gross indecency or other 'unnatural misdemeanours' in England and Wales. Ninety men per year were, on average, indicted for homosexual offences in this period. About a third as many again were arrested and their cases considered by magistrates. Most of the men convicted were imprisoned, but between 1806 and 1861, when the death penalty for sodomy was finally abolished, 404 men were sentenced to death. Fifty-six were executed, and the remainder were either imprisoned or transported to Australia for life. Two such men, James Pratt and John Smith, were the last to be executed in Britain for sodomy on 27 November 1835.

The fateful association of Pratt and Smith had begun when they met at a run-down boarding house in Southwark, on the south bank of the river Thames, on 31 August 1835. They were poor men, both married. Pratt was a groom in the service of a south London gentleman, and Smith was also a servant. At the house in Southwark, they were seen having sex either because they were heedless of observation or because the shabbiness of the house meant that they could get no privacy. They were discovered and arrested, it is not known by whom, and committed to Newgate prison. Their trial followed on 21 September. Although they and their wives sent petitions to the Home Office trying to save them from the gallows, and their case was heard by the privy council, all appeals were rejected. Smith, it was reported, went to his death with 'a firm step', but Pratt 'needed support to the last moment'. They were dispatched together, before a crowd which was said to have been 'excessive, but exceedingly decorous'.[4]

Pratt and Smith were hanged despite the appeals of their families, and even in the face of the strong objections of magistrate who had considered their case. Even those who had to enforce these laws felt decidedly ambivalent about them. Although homosexual behaviour had been illegal since the sixteenth century, the law was hardly enforced at all before the 1720s. It was only after about 1780 that the numbers of men arrested for homosexual offences began to rocket. This expansion in criminal justice occurred almost by accident. In general, there was no sustained witch-hunt against identifiable groups of 'sodomites', but instead a series of sporadic efforts at policing cities and individual behaviour. The rising level of arrest was due mostly to changes in the structure of criminal justice which were not necessarily intended to police homosexual behaviour, but instead were directed at more ordinary offences such as theft, violence or political sedition. However, the effect of these changes overall was to make policing far more visible and efficient, and to make the courts more accessible to ordinary people. In spite of this apparent lack of a coordinated policy, it was nevertheless the case that between about 1780 and 1840 laws were adapted so that they could be used against all kinds of homosexual behaviour. The criminal law began to cast a long shadow over all kinds of masculine intimacy.

By the eighteenth century, it was possible to prosecute all kinds of homosexual acts using the sixteenth-century laws against sodomy in spite of the fact that these statutes appeared to only criminalize one kind of sexual act. In English law, any attempt to commit a crime counted as a crime in itself. Hence, all homosexual acts were deemed to be 'attempts' to commit sodomy and were therefore crimes in themselves. It is difficult to date the specific emergence of this rule as it applied to cases of sodomy, but it was in place by at least 1699.[5] As a consequence, any kind of touching or even invitation to a homosexual act was a crime. Men could be prosecuted for a variety of common law offences – so called because they were established by the courts through the process of precedent rather than enacted by Parliament – which together were grouped under the general rubric of 'unnatural offences'. In legal terms, this category comprised sodomy (which also included bestiality – about a quarter of indictments), indecent assault (any touch or sexual act ostensibly committed without the other's consent), indecent exposure with the intention of committing the crime (exposing one's private parts for this intention), invitations to commit the crime ('inciting and soliciting'), 'suffering and permitting' someone else to have sex with you or even 'meeting together' for the purpose of committing a homosexual act.[6] Men walking about looking for sex or prostituting themselves could also be arrested under the Vagrancy Acts as 'disorderly persons' or 'rogues and vagabonds'. In general usage, 'sodomy' was not an exact term and did not merely refer to a specific sexual act. Rather, it described the whole range of homosexual behaviour, sexual or otherwise, which belonged, as one Regency pamphlet put it, to 'the ancient lechers of Sodom and Gomorrah'.[7] This Biblical idiom was as commonplace in the nineteenth century as it had been in previous ones. It implied that 'sodomites' shared both the practices and the fate of the inhabitants of that mythical city and that 'sodomy' represented all that was terrible, nameless and immoral about them.

This bewildering variety of offences and definitions attracted an equally varied set of punishments. Until 1861, sodomy was a capital offence. Although no executions took place after the deaths of Pratt and Smith in 1835, those 348 men whose sentences were commuted from capital punishment between 1806 and 1861 were either imprisoned or transported for life.[8] Men convicted of homosexual offences could meet death or serious injury in other ways, however. Until 1818, a man convicted of any of these crimes could be put in the pillory. His feet and hands were placed in the stocks so that he was immobile, and he would be exposed for a certain time to the anger of the mob who would pelt him with rotten fruit, dead animals, excrement, pieces of wood, rocks and stones. The pillory could be, in effect, a public stoning, involving serious injury or even death. In 1810, a group of men arrested at the White Swan molly house in Clerkenwell were subject to this particular punishment. Not only did they have to stand in the pillory, but they were also pelted with refuse and stones while being transported there in an open cart. When they were finally exhibited to the mob, 'upwards of 50 women were permitted to stand in the ring' in front of them, from where they 'assailed them incessantly with mud, dead cats, rotten eggs, potatoes, and buckets filled with blood, offal, and dung'. Two other men were rendered 'almost insensible' by the blows 'rained down upon them'.[9]

The reform of criminal justice that took place in the 1820s ensured that such primitive punishments were replaced with prison terms. For indecent assault, the usual length of sentence before and after 1861 was two years, although sentences could be as short as a few months. Inciting or soliciting the offence, or meeting together were customarily punished in the same way, with sentences ranging from six months to two years. When the death penalty was abolished it was replaced by terms of penal servitude (prison including hard labour) of between ten years and life, depending on the circumstances. The penalties for indecent assault were set as prison terms of between three months and two years.

A further change in the law followed in 1885, when the Liberal MP and journalist Henry Labouchere introduced a clause to the Criminal Law Amendment Act of that year. Labouchere's amendment, as it came to be known, stated that 'any male person, who, in public or private, commits ... any act of gross indecency with another male person, shall be guilty of a misdemeanour' and punishable by up to two years in prison.[10] What gross indecency actually meant in law was never specified in the legislation, but the courts seem to have merely added it to existing offences and used it to describe consenting acts which fell short of sodomy. This is how it was applied in the trial of Oscar Wilde, at any rate.

Although Labouchere presented his amendment as revolutionary, we have seen that it was not MPs like Labouchere who made the law, but judges, whose myriad decisions when facing the everyday question of how to police and prosecute homosexual acts, together made up a body of precedent and legal practice. This haphazard process, in which rules of evidence and procedure were as much honoured in the breach as the observance, ensured that the criminal law was a very flexible instrument. By interpreting homosexual acts in a broad sense as 'attempts' to commit sodomy, the courts could use the seemingly archaic laws against sodomy dating back to 1533 to do almost anything.

A 'nameless offence'?

In many ways, the presence of homosexuality in early nineteenth-century British culture was paradoxical. Homosexual behaviour was subject to the law in new ways, and men were arrested for these relatively new offences in ever-greater numbers. In this respect, it was more visible than ever. As a result of the legal process sodomy, the crime not to be named, had to be discussed. Its paradoxical status as an open secret therefore became unbearable at the beginning of the nineteenth century, and much of the anxiety that swirled around it centred on this paradoxical need to both name and erase it. Sodomy had a dual character in this respect. It was frequently assumed that it was so unnatural as to exist outside of human experience, but it was also thought that discussing it, or admitting its existence, might mean that its perverse attractions might be advertised to the unwary or to those like the young or the poor who were not morally self-possessed. The general view of those in authority was that in order to protect public morals sodomy should remain nameless, or at least should not be discussed more than was necessary.

As we saw in previous chapters, this imperative to silence sodomy was deeply embedded in English legal and cultural tradition and could be traced all the way back to St Paul. The eighteenth-century jurist Sir William Blackstone noted with approval that 'the delicacy of English law ... treats [sodomy], in its very indictments, as a crime not to be named'.[11] In these terms, rising numbers of prosecutions at the end of the eighteenth century presented a particular difficulty and encouraged judges and jurists to argue even more vehemently for the virtues of silence. One judge, when presiding over a series of sodomy trials in 1806, 'lamented that such a subject should come before the public as it must do, and above all, that the untaught and unsuspecting minds of youth should be liable to be tainted by hearing such horrid facts'.[12] The press concurred and tended not to describe such cases as sodomy, but instead to use euphemistic terms such as 'revolting', 'infamous' or 'unnatural' to refer to them. Before the 1880s, newspaper accounts also tended to blank out the key evidence with asterisks, dashes or with the statement that the evidence was, of course, 'unfit for publication'.

Indeed, in some cases, the judiciary feared that prosecuting large numbers of people for these offences would, in itself, harm public morals by showing that homosexuality was quite common. The Lord Chief Justice Lord Ellenborough, commenting on the same series of nine sodomy trials at Lancaster in 1806, feared that the cases threatened to show that a 'widely extended ... conspiracy against nature exists in point of fact' knowledge that might prove the 'generality and notoriety of the crime'. This in itself was dangerous, since it threatened to show that homosexual behaviour was not unusual or unknown. It would, he said, 'diminish much of the abhorrence which it is to be wished should always belong to it'. Sodomy should not even be discussed, he argued, because it might become a general practice: 'A mischievous curiosity is by the very description of the subject excited in vicious and depraved minds', the Lord Chief Justice suggested, which had led, 'in some ascertained instances, to the commission of the crime by persons who otherwise would never have thought of it'.[13]

These prohibitions and judicial attitudes clearly had some effect, especially in preventing a wider debate on the abolition of the death penalty and the necessity of harsh penalties and criminal sanctions. One magistrate who was against the death penalty for sodomy wrote in 1835 that the capital nature of the crime was only sustained by the 'difficulty of finding any one hardy enough to undertake, what might be represented as, the defence of such a crime'.[14] Similarly, another judge lamented the fact that the punishments for homosexual acts were archaic and disproportionate to the offence but complained that the main problem was that 'there is no one to take the matter up'.[15]

Although the judiciary was inclined to keep arrests reasonably low in order to silence sodomy, it was nevertheless the case that the criminal process itself generated an enormous amount of publicity and demonstrated by default that 'unnatural practices' were not necessarily as unimaginable as might be assumed. Rising numbers of arrests in the early nineteenth century inevitably attracted public attention, partly because of the nature of the arraignment process. Those arrested by constables or the police – around fifty men or more per year in London by 1830 – usually had to pass through at least one court hearing before magistrates, to determine whether there was enough evidence to send them for trial in a higher court. The theatre of the magistrates' court therefore pro-vided public and press with a regular diet of shocking and sensational entertainment. Thousands of people would gather in the streets around the court to hear the case against anyone of standing, and even more mundane crimes were open to public inspection.[16] The magistrates' court was, one reporter commented, an irresistible attraction, 'particularly for the lower classes'.[17] The volume of cases was small in relation to the total number of all crimes, but was nevertheless unprecedented and attracted comment to that effect. In 1825, the London *Times* complained that the magistrates at Union Hall in Lambeth were again being forced to occupy themselves considering 'one of those revolting and unnatural cases, so many of which have recently been heard at the different police offices in town'.[18] By 1830, when sixty-one men were put before magistrates in London, these courts were considering more than one homosexual offence each week.[19]

The cases which received the most publicity were those involving upper-class men. The arrest of gentlemen was comparatively rare, but always attracted the most attention partly because of the recurring popular suspicion that the poor were coerced by laws which the rich were able to escape by virtue of their wealth. Bishops, MPs, peers of the realm, civil servants and military officers were all caught in the grip of the law in the nineteenth century. Percy Jocelyn, the Irish Anglican Bishop of Clogher, was one such man arrested, in 1822. He had been caught in the back room of a tavern in St James's with a soldier named Morelley, much to the delight of his anti-clerical critics, who nicknamed him the 'Arse-Bishop'.[20] It was not only the newspapers who exposed the Jocelyn case. His arrest also provided ammunition to radical printers and pamphleteers. Instead of the boasted ignorance which English legal tradition was intended to maintain, a wide reading public was informed in the greatest detail about the crimes of men like Percy Jocelyn. As the victim of one of these pamphlets put it, 'the circumstance [of the case] very soon got sent all over London' and 'at length the names of the parties concerned were soon spread about in every direction'. Pamphlets like these detailing the crimes of 'sodomites' were estimated to sell as many as 20,000 throughout the Britain and its Empire.[21] As a result, Jocelyn's name was 'in the mouth of the meanest little boy' not long after his arrest.[22]

Arresting men like Jocelyn also publicized the continued existence of a street subculture and advertised the locations in which you might meet other men for sex. Molly houses continued to be reported into the 1820s, while the parks at night rapidly became notorious, not only for the cover they provided for illicit intimacy, but also because they contained a garrison of soldiers on permanent duty as sentries who also ran a sideline in prostitution and blackmail. Certain streets in the West End and in the narrow, winding thoroughfares of the City became equally infamous. Public urinals became dangerous sites of assignation and also blackmail for the unwary. Later, certain institutions such as the music hall, theatre or the fancy dress ball became the locations of homosexual desire. As far as we can tell from reported cases, over half of all offences took place in public, either in the street, parks, pubs, theatres or urinals.[23]

The most famous molly house of the Regency period was the White Swan in Vere Street, Clerkenwell. Until it was raided in July 1810, this tavern hosted regular gatherings during which a mixed clientele of mollies, soldiers, servants and working men kept alive long-standing molly rituals such as mock marriages and female personas. There was also said to be a permanent staff of prostitutes. The members of this 'Vere Street Coterie' were rumoured to be not only working men but also wealthy gentlemen and even men of more noble rank. After his arrest, James Cook, the White Swan's landlord, promised to make 'a disclosure of the transactions for which he, and the others were convicted, with the names and rank in life of a great number of persons implicated; not only at his own house, but at many others', but his offer was mysteriously rejected by the authorities.[24] Three similar molly houses, the Barley Mow off the Strand, the Rose and Crown in St Martin's Lane near Soho and the Bull Inn also in the Strand, were suppressed in 1825, 1827 and 1830 respectively. At the Barley Mow, it became known that on certain days an evening of music and dancing known as a 'free and easy' was held at which soldiers and effeminate men mixed. It was reported that on Sundays and Mondays 'scenes of the most horrible kind took place'.[25] While the Rose and Crown was said to be mainly frequented by soldiers, two of the Bull Inn's customers were said to have 'excited the greatest disgust' when placed in the dock at Bow Street magistrates' court, since they had 'paint on their cheeks, with their hair curled in drop ringlets such as women wear'.[26]

Accounts like this fixed the image of certain West End streets and taverns as places where men might meet for sex. The areas surrounding the theatres in Drury Lane and Covent Garden, just to the north of the Strand, were equally dangerous and inviting. Around this area, 'swarms of lads who carry on the infamous occupation of *catamites*' were said in the 1820s to 'infest the streets at night' under the noses of the police.[27] Places and practices like this were even marked out in certain guides to the city. *The Yokel's Preceptor* (c.1840) offered to point out the dangers of the West End to unsuspecting country boys, but also must have inadvertently advertised their attractions. The area around Soho and Covent Garden was so thronged with 'Margeries' and 'Pooffs', the Preceptor's anonymous author proclaimed, that it had become necessary to post bills in the windows of various taverns 'cautioning the public to Beware of Sods!'. There were certain ways of spotting them, the guide went on. They were 'generally to be known by their effeminate air, their fashionable dress, etc', and when they saw someone they liked, they would 'place their fingers in a peculiar manner underneath the tails of their coats, and wag them about – the method of giving the office'.[28] Similar dangers lurked at picture shops in the Strand where paintings and prints were exhibited in the windows. A crowd was attracted by the display, and the casual brush of bodies could be used either to make someone's acquaintance or to practice blackmail. One man arrested at a picture shop in 1842 was reported to belong to a 'gang of an infamous character' and to have made his living by soliciting and blackmailing for about fifteen years.[29]

The parks were perhaps the most notorious metropolitan location for homosexual activity. They were nominally closed at sunset, but it was still possible to gain access, with the result that all sorts of homeless people and criminals frequented them. One reporter described the denizens of the parks as 'hordes of half-dressed, filthy men and women' who were 'no doubt concocting midnight robberies'.[30] The royal parks were also sporadically policed, and so it was relatively easy to avoid detection. The frequency with which the soldiers who stood on sentry duty in the parks appeared in the courts also suggests that they were easily available to be picked up.[31] In one brief two-month campaign in 1830, two policemen arrested nineteen men for homosexual offences in Hyde Park.[32] Even in 1912, moral campaigners continued to complain that 'indecency, sexual intercourse and sodomy are being constantly carried on in various parts of Hyde Park especially after dark'.[33]

Certain public urinals also gained a reputation as sites of sex via the publicity they gained from the courts and press. Many of these were in the West End of London and continued to be sites of assignation until well into the twentieth century.[34] One of the most notorious in the 1840s was in Orange Street, behind the National Gallery in Trafalgar Square. A nearby barracks seems to have provided a ready supply of soldiers willing to accept all kinds of invitations. One of these men, William Malt, a private in the Grenadier Guards, was arrested in November 1842 for unspecified 'indecent practices' committed in the toilet with a civilian. The policeman who arrested them testified that they had been 'most barefacedly committing the act with which he charged them'. Police constable Harvey told the court that these 'filthy practices' were not only frequent, but were also organized. It was, he said, 'exceedingly difficult to detect the offenders in these acts, as they kept persons on the watch'.[35] By the 1860s and 1870s, groups of men had become known to the courts for 'following persons who entered those places [urinals in the West End] and attempting to extort money by certain threats'. One barrister confidently asserted in 1871 that 'it was becoming altogether dangerous to go into one of those places at all'.[36]

While public spaces remained popular places for meeting men in nineteenth-century cities, private gatherings were equally significant. In 1806, it was discovered that a group of sodomites had formed their own association similar to freemasonry. These men, who were from various social classes across the north west of England, met in a village called Great Sankey in Cheshire, not far from Warrington and just to the south west of Liverpool. There they kept a house and appointed a housekeeper specifically to cater for their little society. On Monday and Friday evening they pretended, it was said, 'to hold a kind of Masonic lodge …' at which they 'accosted each other with the title 'Brother' '![37] Many of the working men involved had originally met each other in the taverns and public spaces of Manchester, Liverpool and Warrington. In Manchester, men would advertise their sexual interest by standing against the wall of the Exchange building in the town centre as if 'making water'. According to a witness who frequented the Exchange, anyone who 'wanted to be connected with people of that sort … might go and stand near them and put their hands behind them', upon which the men 'would put their yards [penises] into their hands'.[38] The arrest of the group, in which artisans, labourers and servants mixed with lawyers, gentlemen and merchants, showed that widespread networks of private as well as public association existed across the north of England.

In the capital, a successor of the tavern 'free and easy', which had evolved from the eighteenth-century molly house, was the commercial fancy dress ball, which appears to have become popular from the 1850s onwards. These balls often took place in theatres and were not specifically homosexual, but provided a useful justification for going in drag. In one case at least the fancy dress ball was used as an elaborate cover for a sort of club or private society whose purpose it was to organize similar events for men across the north of England. This fact was revealed in October 1880 when a drag ball in Manchester was raided by the police. The revellers had rented the Temperance Hall in Hulme, a working-class district of the city, by pretending to be organizing a function for the Manchester Pawnbrokers' Association. In order to ensure secrecy, they covered the windows with black paper and employed a blind accordionist to provide the music. The man who led the raid, Detective Jerome Caminada, told the magistrates that he had learned of these things in 1876, when he had received a tip-off about another such event. On that occasion, he had been unable to act, but this time he had gathered a combined force of police constables and local working men. Before mounting the raid, the detective climbed onto a neighbouring roof so that he could see over the paper which covered the windows. There, he later told the court, he had seen a mixed group of 47 men, some smart and some shabby, half of whom were dressed as various male historical figures, and the other half dressed as women. Especially to the fore, and later depicted on the front page of the *Illustrated Police News*, were Henry VIII and Anne Boleyn, next to Romeo and Juliet. From his vantage point, Caminada saw 'a sort of dance to very quick time, which my experiences has taught me is called the 'can-can' ' and in which 'the men in female attire took a prominent part'. From time to time, Caminada reported, men left the hall, passing into an ante-room in which unspecified indecencies took place. He could, he said, 'hear the persons 'squealing' and talking loudly in feminine voices, which they all affected'.

From his contact, he had learned that the way to gain admittance was to give the password 'Sister' in an effeminate voice. On the night in question, he had approached the door, which was opened a crack by a man dressed as a nun. Caminada gave the password in a falsetto whisper upon which he and his gang burst into the Hall. They arrested everyone present and carted them off, still in their fancy dress, to the magistrates' court in the city centre. It was discovered that the organizers of the ball in Hulme were not all from Manchester, but apparently formed 'a sort of private society' devoted to arranging such events 'in different parts of the country' including Leeds and Nottingham.[39] Although this fact suggested that wider investigations might take place, the magistrates proved peculiarly reluctant to pursue the matter further. The case was a difficult one and threatened to drag the city's name through the mud. The defence argued successfully that the defendants had been foolish, but not criminal, and the threat of scandal made the magistrates blanch. The defence suggested that the police were asking them to say 'that in this city-not in Turkey or Bulgaria or some places where these odious practices were common-but in Manchester this vice … was practiced and solicited'.[40] Instead of investigating the affair right to the bottom, all the defendants were bound over and released.

The criminal process, then, by default illustrated the patterns and processes of sodomite life. Its locations were highlighted, its practices were described, and the men who participated in it were subject to scrutiny. Far from concealing anything, prosecuting homosexual offences merely drew attention to the fact that this was far from a 'nameless' or unknown phenomenon. The fears of Lord Ellenborough, that arresting large numbers of men for these crimes might advertise its appeal, clearly reflected a fear that anyone might become a sodomite merely by hearing about it. Although it was almost impossible to refer to 'unnatural' crimes in polite society, or even to make any kind of argument for the repeal of harsh laws against them, they were a continuous and disruptive presence throughout nineteenth-century British culture. It was not difficult to find out about these things. Even the respectable press such as the *Times* or the *Morning Chronicle* would report court cases at great length, often over several days, while an acute observer of London's West End could hardly fail to notice 'swarms of lads' who plied their trade outside the theatres and music halls, or the uncomfortable atmosphere in the crowd outside a picture shop.

Drag and effeminacy

Can we know how such 'lads', or the revellers at the Manchester drag ball, thought of themselves? How did they and others perceive their own identity? How did they understand their lives and their desires? Historians have spent a lot of time arguing about when the 'modern homosexual' emerged. That is, when did homosexual behaviour come to define the homosexual as a particular type of person or as someone whose inner psychology and physiology matched the nature of his desire? When did homosexuality come to be seen as a kind of inner 'femininity' matched by outward displays of effeminate behaviour? In this and in the previous chapter, we saw that in eighteenth-century British cities, there were groups of men who adopted feminine habits and deportment as a sign of their desire. However, the question remains whether this was how they were universally understood. And if it was the case that sodomy was merely the preserve of a particular group, how could it be assumed that anyone might succumb to its charms simply by hearing of its existence? Moreover, was the 'modern homosexual' only one type, only one way of being to which all those who felt same-sex desire conformed?

It was certainly the case that being effeminate, and being known as a 'Margery' or a 'puff', was a common style among sodomites at their balls or free and easies in the nineteenth century as in the eighteenth century. As we have seen, there were supposed to be certain ways of knowing a sodomite simply by looking at him. A judge, on seeing the appearance of one Henry Whayman in his court in 1851, told him that 'his attitude, his dress, his singularly effeminate manner, the peculiarity of his style of headdress and his general bearing [were] quite sufficient to indicate the sort of person he was'. Another man, a member of a blackmail gang, told his colleagues that a potential victim was an 'old *puff*' because you could 'see sodomy printed on his face'.[41]

Moreover, dressing as a woman in the sense of trying to pass as one, was a sufficiently common phenomenon to attract the attention of the press. The word 'drag', meaning wearing women's clothes, was first coined publicly in the 1860s, and at that time it did not only take place within the relatively safe confines of the fancy dress ball. In British cities throughout the nineteenth century, men were arrested and imprisoned for wearing women's clothes in the street. Some of these men were prostitutes, some claimed to be doing it 'for a lark', while others were, like those arrested in Manchester, poised awkwardly between street life, the stage and respectable society. Jerome Caminada, the Manchester detective, felt that several of the revellers at Hulme in 1880, some of whom were 'shabby and unkempt', may have been prostitutes.[42] He informed the court that, 'in society, there existed a class of men, almost unknown to many gentlemen, who prowl about the streets almost to the same extent as unfortunate women'. Some of the prisoners in the case, he affirmed, 'belong to that class, as he could prove'. One of them, named Parkinson, was a professional female impersonator with a theatre troupe named Tute's Minstrels but, it seemed, was also linked to the world of prostitution. Caminada claimed that he had 'heard him address men in a female voice in the streets', thereby heavily implying his connection to this world of 'unfortunates'.[43]

Parkinson was far from alone. In London, the cross-dresser was a regular feature of the police court. In general, such men were judged to be 'rogues and vagabonds' who were behaving indecently in a public place. This made them subject to the vagrancy laws, and to fines and prison terms of up to three months. However, such men occasionally gained a wider audience. One of the most sensational trials of the century involved two of the most famous cross-dressers in Victorian Britain. Frederick Park and Ernest Boulton were from respectable backgrounds, Park being the son of a judge and Boulton the son of a suburban clerk, but both were shown to have lived at the centre of a group of men who dressed, and in some cases, lived, as women. Their alleged crime was 'conspiring' with others, both known and unknown, to commit sodomy.

Boulton and Park's antics were first revealed to a wider public in April 1870 when they were arrested leaving the Strand theatre in London's West End. That evening they had left their lodgings in St Pancras, where they kept an entire wardrobe of dresses, jewellery and wigs. There, they had transformed themselves into their customary female personas: Boulton was 'Stella' and Park was 'Fanny'. At the magistrates' hearings which followed, and at the trial in May 1871, it emerged that Boulton and Park had made a pastime of wandering about the West End in drag. They were not alone in this. Press reports of the case refer mysteriously to 'certain young men, who, for years past, have been in the habit of visiting places of public resort in feminine attire'.[44] Boulton and Park also appeared as women on the stage during a series of charity concerts in Essex and Scarborough in 1868. For all Boulton's later notoriety, he was clearly something of a minor celebrity.

The police, however, perceived a more sinister side to Fanny and Stella's behaviour. Boulton, it was revealed, was also the paramour of Lord Arthur Clinton, the son of the fourth Duke of Newcastle, a former cabinet minister. Indeed, he and Boulton had taken rooms in Southampton Street near the Strand where they lived, apparently as man and wife. In addition, Boulton and Park's wanderings in the West End at night looked suspiciously like prostitution. They were seen accosting men, and it was rumoured that Park had sought treatment at Charing Cross hospital for a venereal disease. When they were arrested, both men had been given a medical examination at Bow Street police office which seemed to indicate that they were in the habit of committing sodomy. The circle of guilt expanded as far as Edinburgh where the American consul, John Safford Fisk, was found to be in possession of a number of love letters and photographs from Boulton. Louis Hurt, another of Fanny and Stella's paramours, was also arrested and charged with conspiring with them to commit sodomy.

The police strongly suspected Fanny and Stella of being prostitutes. They appeared to have few means of support, but nevertheless kept up two addresses. Their wanderings in the West End also mimicked the activities of female prostitutes. They had been ejected from the Alhambra theatre more than twenty times and also thrown out of the fashionable Burlington Arcade several times for 'chirruping' at men. For Fanny and Stella, much of this appears to have been a game. Sometimes they went to these places dressed as women, and at other times they dressed in men's clothes but did themselves up so that they looked like women dressed as men. On the night they were arrested, Boulton and Park had caused a sensation at the Strand theatre. They strolled about as though they owned the place, winking at men in the stalls from their box, lighting their cigarettes from the gas lamps and captivating a young swell named Hugh Mundell who spent most of the fateful evening with them.

The evidence against them seemed overwhelming. The love letters exchanged with Fisk and Hurt spoke in camp tones of 'my darling Ernie' and of Boulton crying on the train having been separated from his love. Hurt had written to Boulton that he was 'rather sorry to hear of you going about in 'drag' so much' and offered to send him money so he would not do it.[45] Another letter, from Fisk, spoke of Boulton 'living in drag'. Fisk's letters promised that 'I love and dream of you' and that 'I am yours'.[46] Letters exchanged by Park and Lord Arthur, on the other hand, spoke of the 'matrimonial squabbles' between Boulton and his lover. A maid who worked for Lord Arthur and Boulton at their Southampton Street rooms testified that Boulton often wore dresses even at home and that there was only one bed in the flat for both men. She had heard Lord Arthur addressing Boulton 'more as a lady than as a man'.[47]

However, in their defence, Boulton and Park and their barristers presented drag as something completely ordinary and familiar in middle-class Victorian society. It was no more than a fascination with private theatricals taken to foolish lengths. It was certainly the case that their stage performances, especially Boulton's opposite Lord Arthur in a play called *The Morning Call* in Scarborough in 1868, had attracted rave reviews and public adoration. Local high society also took a keen interest in what later seemed to the police to be an 'unnatural' spectacle. A photographer from the town who had sold thousands of cartes de visite of Boulton and Park that summer told the court that Boulton's act had been attended by 'the very best that we have in town at that time of year', including ladies. He had sold photographs of Boulton 'as fast as we could print them'.[48] In addition, during their charity tour of Essex in 1869, Boulton and Park had attracted enormous interest and been invited into people's homes 'in character' as women. At Romford, the show had even been sponsored by a local clergyman and a Baronet. They had also attended the Oxford–Cambridge Boat Race in women's clothes and been seen at high-class fancy dress events at London hotels. They were, it seemed, welcomed as puzzling, but not unpleasing freaks of nature. Boulton was even invited to go fox hunting in women's clothes.

The trial lasted a week and ended with still more sensation when all four men were acquitted of conspiring to commit sodomy with each other. How had it happened? There seemed to be overwhelming evidence against them, and the courts had shown themselves quite keen on punishing homosexual behaviour. Had the courts, police and British society as a whole understood what Boulton and Park were? To modern eyes they, especially Boulton, seem to be transvestites or drag queens. However, at the time, these ways of understanding cross-dressing had not developed, and instead the police assumed that they were effeminate sodomites. But a large amount of ambiguity remained. What about those people who saw them on stage, or at social events in high society dressed as women? Did they also see them as sodomites? The ambiguities of the case show that the connection between effeminate behaviour and sodomy was not necessarily made in a universal way, even in 1870. To be effeminate at this point did not necessarily mean you were a sodomite, or vice versa. As we have seen, this connection was made easily in many contexts associated with low life and prostitution. However, there were other ways of understanding what it was to be a 'sodomite'.

Effeminacy seems to have been particularly associated with low life and lower-class men, especially prostitutes. In addition, it was a style adopted primarily by working men. As we have seen, the clientele of the Georgian molly house was diverse, but appeared to be drawn mainly from artisanal trades or domestic service. One of the painted, powdered and wigged young men who frequented the White Swan in 1810 and who went by the name of Pretty Harriet was a butcher. Another, known as Lady Godiva, was a waiter, while others were servants, blacksmiths, bargemen and coal-heavers.[49] This association of effeminacy and class seems to have persisted throughout the century. Many of those identified as taking the women's part in Manchester in 1880 came from lower-class occupations such as domestic service. On the other hand, upper-class men like Boulton and Park's paramours Louis Hurt, Johh Fisk and Lord Arthur Clinton, not to mention the various soldiers who danced with men at free and easies or drag balls, were not regarded as effeminate, but were nevertheless suspected of 'unnatural crimes'. There were also a variety of ways to describe sodomites, not all of which registered the clarity which was later assigned to the term homosexual. The various names used to describe sodomites, such as Mary Anne, Margery or poof, probably referred in the nineteenth century to a prostitute, but may have had other applications. In some cases, a sodomite was associated specifically with the act which the name seemed to describe. However, it was also assumed that a sodomite might also be someone who, because of his low station in life, had turned to selling himself and blackmail simply to make a living. By the mid-twentieth century, this kind of man was called 'trade' or rough trade – terms which were also revealed by the Boulton and Park affair to be current in the 1860s.[50] In this respect, being a sodomite was nothing to do with having a sexual identity in our terms, but was merely a sort of sexual opportunism.

So even though there were established ways of understanding effeminacy as a sign of sodomy, some ambiguity about their association remained. As I will explain below, it was only in the 1890s that the connection between an inner 'inversion' of gender and sexual preference became thoroughly established as part of public discourse on the matter. In the mid-century, and even up to the 1870s, it remained the case that there were a variety of ways in which 'unnatural desires' could be understood and that these were refracted through the prism of class. However, effeminacy and related questions of 'perversion' had a much wider relevance in mid-Victorian Britain than simply describing sexual ambiguity.

Effeminacy, religion and national identity

Effeminacy was not only relevant to discussions of sodomites, but the question of what it meant also went to the heart of Victorian conceptions of national identity and religion. This is clear when we consider the history of the Oxford Movement and Anglo-Catholicism, both seen as deviations from true religion in an age when Christianity was taken immensely seriously. The Oxford Movement, so called because it began at Oxford University, was a reform group within the Anglican Church of England which had its heyday between about 1830 and 1860, and which was devoted to reviving the Church by returning it to its ancient roots. This reform agenda was based on moving the protestant Anglican Church nearer to the Catholic Church from which it had been split by the Reformation. The Oxford Movement saw this as returning the Church to its proper course. To their critics, though, the movement seemed to be perverting the true religion of England and turning it towards Rome. This trend was extremely controversial in a period when anti-Catholicism was still a pervasive feature of British culture, bound up as it was with fear of Catholic Irish immigrants. However, its critics also saw in the Oxford Movement a form of effeminacy, which though not necessarily associated with homosexuality did nevertheless contain the hint of perverse sexuality. In some instances, protestant critics of Anglo-Catholicism did accuse it of being explicitly immoral and sexually dangerous.

The Oxford Movement, also known as the Tractarians from their controversial series of pamphlets entitled *Tracts for the Times*, had a varied set of aims. Their primary goal was to try and move the Anglican and Roman Catholic Churches closer together. This effort focused on liturgy and ritual, which they proposed to alter in the direction of Catholic practices, hence their other name, Anglo-Catholics. The proposed reforms of Anglican ritual incorporated particular high church practices normally associated with Catholic liturgy such as rich ornamentation, elaborate vestments, Latin mass, decorated altars, celibacy and monasticism. Many of the leaders of the Oxford Movement, including its most prominent figure John Henry Newman, set up their own monastic institutions where men would gather to study.

Although these distinctions of ritual can appear arcane to modern eyes, at the time they went right to the heart of national identity. In nineteenth-century Britain, the Anglican Church was regarded as a pillar of the constitution; to weaken one was to attack the other. Attacks on the Church of England at this time were particularly problematic because it was an era when the constitution was being altered by the extension of the franchise, in 1832 and again in 1867. Catholic immigrants from Ireland complicated the picture still further and were met by a virulent anti-Catholicism, especially in northern cities. Therefore, the Oxford Movement was seen not only as dabbling in specific spiritual matters, but also weakening the social and national fabric by undermining religious faith.

The principal critic of the Oxford Movement was the Anglican clergyman and writer Charles Kingsley. In 1851, he launched a famous assault on the Tractarians and singled out their leader John Henry Newman in particular. In a series of articles, Kingsley hinted that the Tractarians' perversity was not only religious, but also seemed unmanly and even unnatural. 'In all that school', Kingsley wrote, 'there is an element of foppery ... a fastidious, maundering, die-away effeminacy, which is mistaken for purity and refinement'.[51] Some historians see Kingsley's assault on Newman as an assault on the sexuality of the Tractarians.[52] By invoking their effeminacy, Kingsley appears to be attacking their barely hidden homosexuality. It has to be said that the Oxford Movement did seem to provide a refuge for serious-minded and celibate young men who were attracted perhaps by the lush sensuality of high Anglican ritual and the atmosphere of virginal purity which pervaded the Tractarian monasteries. One of these institutions near Norwich, run by the self-styled Father Ignatius, was in fact the subject of a homosexual scandal. Of its leaders, Newman and others were well known for intimate friendships with other men. Commentators at the time remarked on the attraction of Tractarian ritual for 'sentimental ladies and womanish men-youths of a lachrymose turn of mind'.[53]

Was the Oxford Movement then some kind of religiously sanctioned homosexual association that threatened to undermine the English Church from within? Some anti-Catholic pamphlets did in fact make this link. One of these pamphlets, which was generally anti-Catholic rather than merely anti-Tractarian, was published repeatedly in Britain from 1836 onwards. *The Confessional Unmasked: Showing the Depravity of the Romish Priesthood* ... complained specifically that Catholic priests were undermining the English family and spreading sexual indecency via the practice of confession. The anonymous author complained that priests taking confession were able to ask men and women about the intimate details of their sex lives and feelings on the pretence of questioning them about whether they had committed any sins. The consequence was, the pamphlet declared, that the priest was morally suspicious and a threat to young women as well as men. Although he claimed to be 'pure as an angel', he was in fact 'more corrupt than a Sodomite ... the slave of the most debasing sensuality', guilty of 'exposing the nakedness and perverting the faculties of those who put themselves under his influence'.[54]

However, although rabid anti-Catholic propaganda specifically stated that priests and their works were sexually suspicious, attacks on the Oxford Movement were less precise. Kingsley's assault on Newman shows us that effeminacy was not necessarily a telling sign of homosexuality at that time. Instead of attacking Newman for hiding an unnatural passion, Kingsley's assault was directed in a more general sense against the Tractarians' celibacy. It was this, rather than any specific evidence of sodomy, that aroused protestant ire. In particular, Kingsley argued that the Oxford Movement was a dogmatic withdrawal from the world into matters spiritual and celibate. For him, religion should be about engaging with the world and its problems. In addition, Kingsley saw celibacy as a perversion of natural sexuality. In his own life and theology, he saw marriage, and especially marital sexuality, as a kind of spiritual union. Celibacy for Kingsley was the most perverse feature of the Oxford Movement and one that matched its attempt to pervert true religion. In addition, some of the more rabid critics of Anglo-Catholicism did not see the movement as homosexual at all, but as embodying a particularly troubling heterosexual menace. Through the process of confession, Anglo-Catholic priests were said to be corrupting the innocence of young women, playing on their fears of sexual immorality and thereby providing the means by which they might usurp the proper authority of English fathers. In this perverse fashion, effeminacy could even mean a sort of heterosexual excess that threatened the good order of the English family.

Even though the Kingsley–Newman controversy was not specifically about homosexuality, it showed that questions of perversity, and effeminacy were germane to ideas of religion and national identity. The controversy over the Oxford Movement reinforced the fact that these matters were central to British culture at this time. It also demonstrated that in spite of its association with mollies, prostitutes and urban low life, effeminacy might not mean homosexual desire. In fact, it might mean excessive *heterosexual* passion. Nevertheless, just as the criminal law ensured that sodomy and sodomites were a continuous cultural presence, questions of effeminacy which dominated the debate over Anglicanism in the mid-century showed that masculinity and perversity were never far from the centre of national culture.

Scandal and politics in the 1880s

During the course of the 1880s, it became more obvious than ever that homosexuality was a matter of national and imperial interest. In that decade, two major scandals unfolded in Dublin in 1883 and in London in 1889. The first of these developed when several Crown officials were accused in the Irish nationalist press of being involved with male prostitutes and of covering up the affair. The second, known as the Cleveland Street scandal, followed the discovery of a male brothel in central London which was frequented by Telegraph messengers and members of the aristocracy. Once again, the government were accused of covering up the facts and of trying to ensure that the rich could escape. In many ways, these scandals had their precursors in the many thousands of criminal cases which had preceded them. What was different about these affairs, though, was that they spread into the political mainstream, caused questions to be asked in parliament and generally threatened to disrupt the smooth running of English politics. Another difference with earlier, more short-lived scandals was the nature of journalism. By the 1880s, the 'new journalism' had pioneered a more populist style involving sensational revelations, banner headlines, private investigation and the use of scandal to both make political points and sell papers. By using these tactics, the new journalism completely revolutionized the politics of scandal. Homosexuality was shown to matter as a political and national issue.

The first of these scandals began in Dublin in 1883. The chief protagonist was William O'Brien, an Irish nationalist politician and editor of the newspaper *United Ireland.* Men like O'Brien had been agitating for Irish independence from Britain since the Act of Union which had joined the two countries in 1801. The first objective of the nationalist cause, which in 1883 was led by Charles Stuart Parnell and a clutch of Irish MPs at Westminster, was Home Rule. This would involve autonomy from the British parliament, but Ireland would remain within the Empire. In addition to this political strategy, which involved forming alliances in parliament and trying to hold the balance of power between the parties at Westminster, there were a number of other strands to Irish nationalism. One of its strands was agrarian protest against unfair rents and evictions of tenants from their farms. This often took the form of rent strikes, boycotts and violent confrontation with land-lords and farmers. Occasionally, these outbreaks would result in the intimidation and even murder of landlords or farmers thought to be collaborating with unjust landlords. These periodic confrontations were known to the English press as 'agrarian outrages'. At the beginning of 1883, Parnell and O'Brien were arrested for alleged complicity in this kind of nationalist violence, in particular the murder by a republican splinter group of the Chief Secretary of Ireland (the second most important British official in Ireland) and his deputy in a Dublin park in 1882. They were soon released, but the struggle against British rule was at a low ebb when O'Brien discovered the allegations of sodomy against important British officials. This gave the nationalist movement a new focus and a new way to continue the struggle for Home Rule. In parti-cular, O'Brien tried to find the entire British administration guilty by association and to discredit the way in which agrarian outrages had been investigated and their perpetrators prosecuted by the government. Only the gang of wretches who made up the Dublin government and who were obviously immoral in every way, he said, could have produced the unjust and oppressive laws that were governing Ireland.

O'Brien had heard that James Ellis French, the head of the detective division of the Dublin Police, Gustavus Cornwall, the secretary of the

Irish post office, and Corry Connelan, the Inspector-General of prisons, were all associated with a group of young men 'of a disreputable class', perhaps prostitutes, whom they met regularly in a private house in the city.[55] Together, the details amounted, O'Brien claimed, to 'a criminal confederacy which for its extent and atrocity almost staggered belief'.[56] O'Brien's accusations against the three men were intended to provoke them into suing his newspaper, thereby allowing him to put a series of detailed allegations against the corrupt nature of British rule into the public domain. He got his wish, as French at length served a libel write against *United Ireland* in November 1883. However, French suddenly fell ill with 'softening of the brain' and various neurotic symptoms including paralysis in his legs. His fitness to plead was the subject of several enquiries by doctors, who ended up repeatedly applying electric currents to the unfortunate man's legs in order to see if he really was paralysed. While this quasi-judicial torture went on, French's case against *United Ireland* was thrown out the following June.

The outcome of the French case deprived the nationalists of their show trial, but this did not prevent O'Brien turning to his next target, Gustavus Cornwall. O'Brien employed a disgraced English detective by the name of Meiklejohn who, in the course of two weeks, O'Brien later recalled, had amassed enough evidence to bring criminal cases against Cornwall and his cronies. By July, the jury had found for O'Brien in the libel case brought by Cornwall, and the latter was arrested, along with French and a Dublin merchant named James Pillar. Three young Mary Annes named Patrick Molloy, Michael M'Grane and Clark Cooper were also arrested and shared the charge of conspiring to commit sodomy with the British officials. Two more Dubliners who kept the house in the city where they all met were also arrested. The scandal spread to London via a captain in the Dublin Fusiliers who had contacts in the English capital, two of whom, an army doctor and a private in the Grenadier Guards, were also apprehended. The entire group was charged with conspiring to commit sodomy and with specific homosexual acts.

In the end, French was tried three times because of uncertainty over his sanity and the disagreements of the jury. He was finally found guilty in December 1884, having suffered a public and judicial pillorying lasting more than a year. Cornwall was tried for sodomy in July 1884 and was acquitted, much to the disgust of the nationalists, who thought that the trial had been fixed. O'Brien and his allies made much of the contrast between the enthusiastic pursuit of nationalist agitators or agrarian protesters by the Dublin authorities, and their inability to bring Cornwall and French to justice. For the nationalists, the Cornwall case epitomized the entire corrupt system of British authority in Ireland. The British had set up an extensive system of informers in order to prosecute political dissidence and, according to O'Brien, had packed juries with their supporters in order to achieve favourable verdicts on flimsy evidence. One of O'Brien's parliamentary allies told the House of Commons in November that the jury in the Cornwall case had only returned a not guilty verdict because 'sufficient evidence had not been brought forward by the Crown'.[57] The jury was, he said, packed with Freemasons who were there to acquit their fellow Mason. In both the French and Cornwall cases, O'Brien argued, the standards by which British justice operated in Ireland had been exposed. He would, he told the House of Commons, 'ask any fair-minded man whether the whole result of these trials could be contemplated without shame by Englishmen'.[58]

O'Brien's tactics helped the Home Rule party at Westminster harass the Liberal government. In addition, the campaign demonstrated to the government the power of the Irish bloc in Parliament. The affair seemed to the nationalists to show how partial the administration of justice in Ireland really was. More importantly for the history of homosexuality, however, was that the scandal showed that mainstream politicians were prepared to break their silence and use such scandals as a political weapon. The press, in the form of O'Brien's *United Ireland*, were also willing to name the crime and exploit its political importance in new ways.

The Cleveland Street scandal

Five years later, similar charges of cover-up and vices in high places rocked the Tory government and its supporters in England. The affair began in the unlikely environment of the postal sorting office at Mount Pleasant in central London. This office, the largest in London, sent out an army of youthful, uniformed messengers to deliver telegrams throughout the city. By the 1880s, these youths, some as young as 14, were notorious for the fact that their principal sideline was prostitution. When one of them, Charles Swinscow, was discovered to have the suspiciously large sum of eighteen shillings in his possession, alarm bells began to ring. On being questioned about the money, Swinscow admitted that another Telegraph boy named Alfred Newlove had persuaded him to go to a house in

Cleveland Street, just north of Soho, in order to have sex with men for money. The house, at number 19, was run by two men, Charles Hammond and the self-styled 'Reverend' George Veck. Its clients, according to Swinscow, were army officers, businessmen and aristocrats, among them Lord Euston and Lord Arthur Somerset, the latter an equerry to the Prince of Wales and son of the Duke of Beaufort. That was not all, as some of the boys hinted that Prince Albert Victor, known as 'Eddy', the son of the Prince of Wales and second in line to the throne, was also one of Hammond's customers.

The police hoped to use the Telegraph boys as their principal source of evidence and accordingly interviewed them several times and promised them lower sentences. One of the key witnesses, Lord Arthur's alleged favourite Algnernon Allies, was taken from his parents' home in Sudbury and kept at a pub at Houndsditch in the East End of London for the entire duration of the cases. The police also took the Telegraph boys to Piccadilly to see if they could see any of the aristocrats involved as they emerged from their clubs. Lord Arthur was positively identified on one of these jaunts but was not arrested and instead fled to France. The first trials, of Newlove and Veck, took place in September, and the witnesses in the case were again taken to Pall Mall on missions of identification. In November, Ernest Parke, the editor of the populist evening paper the *North London Press*, published an article suggesting that Lord Euston had been one of the habitués of number 19. He assumed that the peer had fled the country, but in fact Euston was still in Britain and sued Parke and his paper for libel.

At the trial in December and January, Parke's witnesses failed to properly identify Euston, and the editor's main witnesses were treated as pariahs by the court. One witness tried to identify Euston by the way he walked, which proved laughably inconclusive, while the peer himself claimed that he had in fact gone to the house, but not to have sex with the telegraph boys. Instead, he claimed that the had been walking in Piccadilly circus when he had been accosted by a young man who had given him a card bearing the address in Cleveland Street and which promised *poses plastiques* – the Victorian term for a female strip show. Euston said that he had then gone to the house in order to see this admittedly indecent, but wholly natural display, and had left in a hurry when he realized what sort of place it was. The other factor which weakened Parke's case was the fact that his star witness was a self-confessed Mary Anne named John Saul who had been connected at one remove with the earlier scandal in Dublin.

His testimony in the libel case caused a sensation. When asked if he saw anyone in the court who had been at the house, Saul deliberated for one dramatic moment before pointing out Lord Euston. He had, he said, met him in Piccadilly and had 'picked him up, just as I might have picked any other gentleman up'. They had then gone to number 19. However, although the detail of Saul's earlier statement to the police suggests he was probably telling the truth, his status as a prostitute destroyed his credibility as Parke's chief witness. He admitted having earned his trade as a male prostitute since at least 1879, a fact which led the judge to declare that it was difficult to imagine 'a more melancholy spectacle or a more loathsome object' than Saul.[59]

Among Parke's chief supporters was the Liberal journalist Henry Labouchere, he of the infamous amendment which in 1885 had added the crime of 'gross indecency' to the statute book. Labouchere was the key figure in the case. It was he who made Cleveland Street into a major political scandal on the model supplied by his Irish parliamentary allies five years previously. From his record, it might appear that Labouchere was a classic homophobe, but instead he was something of a bohemian who kept a mistress and also his distance from the more censorious moral campaigners of the period. He was the editor of a muck-raking newspaper called Truth, and also a radical Liberal MP known for his democratic and populist leanings. A major part of Labouchere's politics was the detestation of aristocratic privilege and the social injustice which went with it. All through the 1880s, it had been his intention to try and turn the Liberal party in a more populist direction by stressing its detestation of the aristocracy and building links with radical clubs and Irish nationalist MPs. Cleveland Street provided Labouchere with the opportunity to secure all of these aims at once. This political opportunism was the reason why Labouchere took up Parke's defence with such zeal. The government, he alleged, had tried to cover up the connections between aristocracy, royal family and brothel to Parke's detriment. Furthermore, they had warned Lord Arthur to flee the country before finally, with the greatest lethargy, instituting proceedings against him. They had perpetrated this cover-up, Labouchere said, in order to protect the Tory government and the reactionary aristocracy which supported it. The only way to get the bottom of it, he argued, was through a proper parliamentary enquiry.

An uproarious session of parliament at the beginning of February 1890 saw this demand rejected and Labouchere suspended from the House of Commons for unparliamentary behaviour. The scandal had reached its high point and began to die down after that. Was Prince Albert Victor involved and was Labouchere right to say there had been a cover-up? No conclusive evidence of the former has ever come to light. Of the latter, it is certainly true that the Prince of Wales (later King Edward VII) sent two emissaries to see the Prime Minister, Lord Salisbury in October 1889 to find out if Lord Arthur Somerset was to be charged. Labouchere alleged that they then went to see Somerset and told him to flee. The Prince's men of course denied this, saying that Somerset had already left by the time they had gone to search him out. Recent research suggests that the slowness of the government in issuing warrants for Somerset's arrest can be explained by the fact that historically the Home Office had been extremely reluctant to proceed with cases on the unsupported evidence of low-class 'accomplices' such as the telegraph boys or John Saul. The Lord Chancellor, Lord Halsbury, argued at the time that such evidence was extremely unreliable and not likely to ensure the success of any prosecutions. So was there a cover-up or was the scandal caused merely by procedural delays and governmental confusion? It is certainly the case that the criminal law tended to work in favour of the wealthy in the nineteenth century and that the vast majority of those punished for homosexual offences were poor. Also, Halsbury's remarks probably conceal unspoken assumptions about the need to protect the political and social order from unruly and disreputable accusations. Behind these bland statements, there probably lurks an attempt to protect Britain's ruling class, but in truth, it is difficult to prove anything specific beyond the circumstantial evidence.

What is more important is the way in which both the Dublin and the Cleveland Street scandals publicized the existence of homosexual subcultures and made them into a matter for mainstream politics. Both affairs showed that homosexuality was never very far from the political agenda. In addition, these events showed that a variety of homosexual types existed. The scandals of the 1880s demonstrated that British culture at the end of the nineteenth century had begun to be increasingly interested in 'perversion', whether in legal or medical terms.

Sexology

Part of the response to the scandalous events of the 1880s was a growing interest in sexual behaviour and its social significance. Prompted in part by the arrest of men for sexual offences, a variety of enquiries began into the nature of sexually 'perverse' behaviour. Of course, this new awareness of the 'abnormal' also inevitably led to new ideas of what 'normality' was. These enquiries began on the continent, when, instead of merely cataloguing physical signs of illicit sex, police doctors gradually became interested in the psychology of offenders and began to build up a map of their different characteristics. Sexology was a term first used in an American text of 1902 to describe these varied investigations into the sexual impulse.[60] However, this effort at classification had begun in the 1860s, when the German writer Karl-Heinrich Ulrichs began to describe the different types of homosexuality, or Uranism as he called it, as a way of arguing for its social acceptance. Ulrichs identified three major categories, lesbians ('urninds'), homosexual men ('urnings') and bisexuals ('uranodionings'), with several intermediate categories in between. These notions focused on the idea of the homosexual as a particular type of person with characteristics determined by his desire, psychology and physiology. By the 1880s, these two lines of enquiry had generated a whole new set of terms for sexual behaviour. Paedophilia, exhibitionism, sadism and even sexual perversion itself were all coined between 1877 and 1890, while 'homosexual', a mixture of Latin and Greek that had originated in German in 1869, entered the English language in 1891.[61]

Sexology had a dual character. On the one hand, an apparatus of treatment developed around the perverted, accompanied, as Robert Nye puts it, by a 'small army of medical and legal specialists devoted to studying, curing or punishing them'.[62] On the other, more liberal writers like the Australian doctor Henry Havelock Ellis employed the methods of sexology in order to show that perversity of all kinds was merely one aspect of human sexuality and should be judged accordingly. Sexologists like Ellis and his followers tended to think of sexual behaviour, and hence homosexuality, as inherent to the personality, as something inborn and congenital, either physiologically or psychologically. The typical method employed by sexologists to show that this was true was the study of individual case histories. In this way, homosexual desires and characteristics could be traced right back to childhood. One consequence of thinking in this way was the popularization of the idea that 'true' homosexuals were a particular type of persons with specific characteristics that developed from a kind of inner effeminacy.

These ideas and methods were taken up by a few writers in Britain and adapted to local needs and traditions. Havelock Ellis, and men of letters such as John Addington Symonds and Edward Carpenter, helped to spread the ideas of continental sexology during the 1890s and in doing so provided a powerful new vocabulary for those seeking to legitimize homosexuality. The prevailing view of Victorian society was that homosexual acts were merely the result of moral wickedness or degradation and should therefore be curtailed through deterrent punishment. To argue the contrary, as Ellis did, was little short of revolutionary. He suggested that true homosexuality – as opposed to merely situational perversion which might occur in prison or other places where usual sexual outlets were unavailable – was simply a harmless physical variation, a bit like colour-blindness, and no more worthy of blame. Ellis' masterwork *Sexual Inversion* (1896), on which he worked with Symonds until the latter's death in 1894, was the first British attempt to synthesize biological, anthropological and psychological knowledge on the subject. Ellis understood homosexuality as a 'congenital' condition, which he labelled sexual inversion. It was the result of a mysterious physical or psychological state: the true 'invert' had a female soul in a male body. For lesbians, the reverse was the case. Gender characteristics, according to this way of thinking, therefore aligned with sexual preference. The male invert was, above all, defined by small and subtle signs of feminine physiology, such as rounded hips and buttocks.[63] However, others who took up Ellis' ideas went further, arguing that even minute features of the personality would be determined by the fact of inversion. The homosexual would, it was said, be unable to whistle, have a particular feel for embroidery, 'be passionately fond of children and animals' or would have an intense love of the colour green.[64]

This idea, of the inherent effeminacy of the invert, was not new. As we have seen, it was traditionally associated with men of low status who gathered in the free and easies, molly houses and drag balls of Georgian and Victorian cities. What was different about the sexologists' version of homosexuality was that it was placed in a much larger scheme of understanding sexuality and the self. Over the next hundred years, ideas originally associated with sexology were gradually taken up by influential institutions like the law, medicine and the state. Furthermore, all this thinking and writing about perverse sexuality also implied a rethinking of what was normal. After sexology, sexuality of all kinds began to be understood as the key to understanding the entire personality. It was increasingly suggested that the mysteries of consciousness could be best understood by scrutinising a person's desires from childhood onwards. Hence, a whole panoply of techniques to do this were born which were to have tremendous influence on the lives of individual men and women in the twentieth century. These ranged from legal and medical investigations to psychoanalysis and psychiatry, the nostrums of which were eventually distilled into more everyday forms like marriage counselling, child psychology or an array of psychological tests which were then spread abroad by print and television media.

The idea of inherent inversion as the explanation of homosexual behaviour also applied in a much more general sense than before, to men of all classes. Inversion might, it was thought subsequently, be lurking unknown within one's body or mind. In his book *The Intersexes* (1909), which was influenced by Ellis as well as Ulrichs and Edward Carpenter, Xavier Mayne (the pseudonym of American writer Edward Prime-Stevenson) went so far as to produce a questionnaire which would tell you the answer to the question, 'Am I at all Uranian?'[65] One way of doing this was to check your physiology for signs of femininity. Were your bones and joints large or small, was your chest broad or narrow, was your wrist flat or round, were your fingers pointed or blunt, your skin soft or rough, your body 'odorific' or neutral smelling, could you whistle and sing easily and naturally?[66]

For the socialist Edward Carpenter, homosexual men and women made up a third or 'intermediate' sex in between men and women. This meant that inverts shared some of the characteristics of both, and, Carpenter suggested, gave them a whole range of the beneficial characteristics usually confined to one gender. Inverts, it was argued, had more acute sensibilities, mixing as they did women's intuitive faculties with masculine rationality. This, fact, along with their freedom from family life, made this intermediate sex not only more likely to be involved in socially useful work but also more open-minded and progressive. In Carpenter's terms, homosexuals were the bearers of the future, a sign of the evolutionary progression of the human race into a higher sphere and emphatically not representative of societal degeneration.[67] This capacity for higher perception and acute sensibility, along with their inherently progressive outlook meant, Carpenter argued, that homosexuals were in fact likely to be more useful to society than 'normal' men and women.

While sexology of this kind was developing, there were other stirrings of protest against Victorian morality. One of these came from the writer and poet George Ives, who used the inspiration provided by Carpenter to begin a secret society devoted to setting 'all loves free'.[68] The society, which began in the mid-1890s, was called the Order of Chaeronea, after the battle of the same name in 338 BC when the Theban Band, a Greek force made up entirely of friends and lovers, was slaughtered by the Macedonians. The membership was small, and the society remained devoted to discussion and mutual support rather than active campaigning. However, it did attract a number of writers and intellectuals such as the designer C. R. Ashbee and probably the poet A. E. Housman.

The existence of Ives' Order of Chaeronea demonstrates the confluence of certain sources of opposition to the prevailing morality of the period. On the one hand, Ives and his ilk were inspired by the eclectic sexology of Edward Carpenter, with its mixture of continental systems of classification and British traditions of socialist and masculine comradeship. On the other, the very name of the society indicated its reverence for the comradeship and purity of ancient Greece. Furthermore, the society contained several writers and poets who had been influenced by the ethos of aestheticism. Together, these trends represented the beginnings of a challenge to the moral order, and the embryonic origins of gay liberation. However, these hopes were to be dashed in 1895 by the trial and conviction of Oscar Wilde.

Oscar Wilde and aestheticism

The most famous victim of Labouchere's Amendment was the playwright Oscar Wilde. His fall had all the hallmarks of a tragedy that was all the more terrible for being largely self-inflicted. It has to be said, moreover, that Wilde, the most famous playwright of his day, fell victim to hubris. The entirety of his art was devoted to inverting conventional morality and satirizing the inane comforts of received wisdom. His first trial often seemed at times to be providing Wilde with merely another opportunity for flouting convention. Wilde's eloquence from the witness box showed him triumphant in the face of the highest test of his life and art. However, the jury judged him by the more prosaic standards of criminal evidence, and he was at length sent to prison for two years. The effect of Wilde's conviction on British life is difficult to gauge, but it did have undeniable and specific effects. It threw a shadow not only over homosexuality, but also over more ordinary kinds of masculine intimacy. Literature and art were similarly forced to shy away from the overly intimate, effusive and romantic style that had characterized late-Victorian letters. The case also made it much easier to associate the florid and rather effeminate style of aesthetes like Wilde with homosexual acts. The idea of the homosexual as a type, something which was beginning to be publicized by sexology, had therefore gained a more solid outline.

Wilde was born in 1854 into an Irish gentry family. His education was littered with prizes, culminating in a scholarship to Magdalen College, Oxford, in 1874. There, he came across two ideas that were to inform not only his own work, but which also nourished men like George Ives, Edward Carpenter and John Addington Symonds. Oxford education was, at that time, still based around the classics, Latin and Greek. In the intense single-sex environment of the Oxford college, young men like Symonds and Wilde studied the major classical authors, including those like Plato who wrote enthusiastically of love between men. For educated Englishmen, ancient Greece was a key point of reference and informed not only their views of intimate life, but also coloured their vision of society and politics. Right at the heart of British culture, in its major universities, a reverence for classical authors was not only encouraged, it was an indispensable guide to life. For Wilde, Symonds and others, the Greek spirit in which poets and philosophers wrote approvingly of homosexual love became a crucial resource.

Wilde was also touched by the spirit of aestheticism, a philosophy associated with another of his Oxford mentors, the art historian and critic Walter Pater. Aestheticism represented a revolt against the dominant tone of Victorian art and letters which stressed moral seriousness and social purpose. Against this, Pater drew inspiration from the glories of ancient Greece. A central theme in Pater's thought was the art and sculpture of the European Renaissance, in which he found a spirit of which ancient Greece was the truest ancestor. In Greece, as in the Renaissance, a true ideal of beauty had reigned, and Pater encouraged his students to give it life once more. Instead of seeing art embodying a moral purpose, its sole raison d'etre should be to worship beauty. It was no coincidence that Pater found this spirit most often expressed in the exquisite marble sculpture of the Greeks, a form which exalted the beauty of the male body. Pater's philosophy was also, however, a manifesto for modern living, and one that Wilde took to its frequently illogical conclusion. We should live life, Pater said, as a series of intense moments in which we endeavour to become conscious of beauty and passion. 'To burn always with this hard, gemlike flame', Pater insisted, 'to maintain this ecstasy, is success in life'.[69] It was in this seeking of experience that one would be most able to imitate the Greek spirit of beauty.

Aestheticism and Hellenism provided a potent combination for men like Wilde. In the 1890s, the beginnings of an intellectual movement which drew on several sources and acted as a counterweight to a century of persecution had begun to emerge. It was Wilde's misfortune, and ours, that he found the Greek principles of beauty embodied in the all too human form of Lord Alfred Douglas, son of the Marquess of Queensbury. Wilde and Douglas had met in 1891 and had a short-lived affair. Wilde remained somewhat inexplicably devoted to a man who happily ran up debts all over London in his suitor's name and who petulantly denounced the author when he failed to get his way. Danger arrived when Douglas' father, a bluff sporting aristocrat who had invented the modern rules of boxing, discovered some passionate letters sent to Wilde by his son and, determined to 'protect' him, stalked the author through London's clubland before finally tracking him down at the Albemarle Club in February 1895. There, he left his card for Wilde and scrawled a fateful and misspelled insult on the back. 'To Oscar Wilde', it read, 'posing Somdomite'.[70]

Wilde, convinced that he could face down the Marquess and the philistine British public beyond him, sued for libel. However, Queensbury had amassed a substantial collection of evidence against his prosecutor, one that would eventually bring him down. Further suspicion was cast over Wilde's art, especially his novel *The Picture of Dorian Gray* (1890), by Queensbury's barrister Sir Edward Carson. Dorian was a beautiful young man who escaped blame for his dissolute life and nameless crimes because the portrait in his attic magically bore all the scars of his infamous double life. The implication was that Wilde's life imitated his decadent art.

Wilde's prosecution failed, and he was faced with a criminal trial on the evidence of his former companions. This time, it was not his art, but Lord Alfred's, which was at issue. To taint Wilde by association, the prosecution dug up an old Oxford University magazine from 1891 in which Douglas had published a poem called 'Two Loves', one of which was 'the love that dare not speak its name'. What, Wilde was asked, did it mean? His response, bright with frustration, drew a burst of applause from the court. 'The love that dare not speak its name', he said, was imbued with the spirit of the Greeks and the Renaissance. It was

> such a great affection of an elder for a younger man as there was between David and Jonathan, such as Plato made the very basis of his

philosophy, and such as you find in the sonnets of Michaelangelo and Shakespeare. It is that deep, spiritual affection that is as pure as it is perfect ... It is in this century misunderstood, so much misunderstood that it may be described as the "Love that dare not speak its name," and on account of it I am placed where I am now. It is beautiful, it is fine, it is the noblest form of affection. There is nothing unnatural about it. It is intellectual, and it repeatedly exists between an elder and a younger man, when the elder man has intellect, and the younger man has all the joy, hope and glamour of life before him. That it should be so the world does not understand. The world mocks at it and sometimes puts one in the pillory for it.[71]

It was a resonant performance that moved one sympathetic listener to observe that Wilde had 'never had so great a triumph'.[72] Yet in spite of Wilde's oration, the jury found it difficult to reconcile these high-flown sentiments with the stories of stained sheets in hotel bedrooms and champagne with 'renters' at the Savoy and at Kettner's restaurant in Soho. Although they could not agree at this trial, Wilde was subjected to the ordeal of yet another prosecution, and 'the High Priest of the Decadents' was finally convicted of gross indecency on 25 May 1895 and sentenced to two years in prison.[73]

In the short term, Wilde's opponents gloried in the defeat of 'the aesthetic cult'. His conviction also lent substance to the nebulous idea of the homosexual by providing a figure around which such notions could coalesce. Wilde's name had become, as he put it, 'a synonym for folly'.[74] By 1913, the title character of E. M. Forster's homosexual novel *Maurice* could be easily understood when he described himself as an 'unspeakable of the Oscar Wilde sort'.[75] The case also led to some speculation, informed and ignorant, about the nature of homosexual desire. Max Nordau's assault on modern morality *Degeneration* (second edition 1894) had depicted Wilde as a prime example of an aesthetic sexual degenerate, a theory that has now gained a wider currency. Wilde himself also tried to make use of the theories of sexology. His appeal to the Home Office for a reduction in his sentence in 1896 tried opportunistically to employ the language of sexological research to mitigate his punishment. His crimes, Wilde stated, were more the result of the kind of 'sexual madness' described by eminent criminologists than anything else and were as such 'diseases to be cured by a physician, rather than crimes to be punished by a judge'.[76] As well as being used in these desperate attempts at exculpation, sexology was also gaining a wider audience. In the years leading up to 1914, the sexology of Ellis and Carpenter gradually became a key resource for those radical voices looking to explain or understand homosexuality. A few organizations took up the challenge of providing a morally neutral language to describe same-sex desire. By 1913, the British Society for the Study of Sex Psychology (BSSSP) had been established with Edward Carpenter as president.

Although in the eyes of his detractors Wilde became a symbol of all that was wrong with the febrile 'naughty nineties', his life and work nevertheless became a reference point for homosexual men in the years following the case. Early lonely hearts advertisements, a form which developed in Britain in the years leading up to World War I, show that Wilde's aesthetic style continued to be a major influence on gay life. These ads, although written in a coded language, advertised their sexual interest by reference to a homosexual canon of writers which included Wilde, Carpenter, Ellis and others. The men who placed them also described themselves as quasi-aesthetic types who also had the special characteristics of Carpenter's intermediate sex. One was an 'idealist', who was 'artistic, [and a] firm believer in [Edward] Carpenter's books'. 'Iolaus', who showed his allegiance to the same author by naming himself after one of his works, was 'intensely musical', of a 'peculiar temperament' and had been 'looking for many years for [a] tall, manly Hercules'.[77] Another advertiser described himself as a virtual aesthetic archetype. He was, he wrote to a friend contacted through such a 'companionship' ad, 'very fond of artistic surroundings, beautiful colours in furniture and curtains and softly shaded lamps and all those beautiful things which appeal to the refined tastes of an artistic mind' namely, 'Flowers, perfume, colour and beautiful scenery'. He was also careful to advertise love of particular homophile authors including Edward Carpenter, Walt Whitman and the poet Rupert Brooke. There was, he wrote, 'nothing that I could not give to a friend who loved me'.[78] The effeminate homosexual, hitherto someone confined to a particular class fraction and to a bracket of low urban life, had become an aspirational archetype.

By 1914, the homosexual type had taken on a more solid outline. He had been defined more clearly by the twin effects of scandal and science as a separate type of person. For many writers, sexologists, doctors, journalists and much of the public at large, the homosexual was increasingly seen to have a special panoply of characteristics. He had his own language, physiology, personal history, manner, dress and voice, to name but a few. Wilde's case helped this process by linking his flamboyant aesthetic personality with homosexual desire, while sexology also stressed the connection between gender and sexuality. For the sexologists, homosexuality was a form of gender 'inversion' that resulted from a congenital 'anomaly'. The 'modern homosexual', it seemed, was decidedly effeminate. This was not necessarily a new idea, although in the past, the relationship between effeminacy and homosexuality had been a more complex one. The century had started with two virtually contradictory ideas of what homosexual behaviour was. On the one hand, homosexual acts did belong to a particular group of people – the effeminate mollies who occupied a particular place on the social spectrum. On the other, however, it was frequently assumed that it was possible, simply through becoming aware of sodomy, that men might fall for its charms and become sodomites. This confusion was reinforced by the masculine working men, or 'trade', who were willing to have sex with effeminate sodomites. Same-sex desire was uncertainly related to effeminacy, and the entire picture was complicated by class. In general, the association of homosexual sex and effeminacy was greatest when it applied to lower-class men or prostitutes, two groups that were often indistinguishable in this context. What was new about the idea of the effeminate homosexual in 1900 was that the combined forces of journalism and science had given it a much more general applicability. Moreover, homosexuality was now seen not as a 'deviation' from the normal, but as its polar opposite. It could now hardly be considered without an examination of its obverse: heterosexuality. If 'abnormality' was to be more clearly defined, then so was 'normality'. By 1914, there were a whole new series of ways to measure one's own desire, personality and physiology against a standard of 'normality' and to investigate whether any hint of perversity lurked within one's psyche.

For homosexual men, these ideas were not necessarily negative. An idea that homosexuality meant refinement, delicate taste and a feeling for music and art was available to gay men of whatever class as a means of understanding themselves. They could also draw on the Carpenterian idea that they represented a higher stage of evolution and therefore had more acute faculties and intellects than most people. They were, Carpenter said, more suited to social reform. These ideas not only provided comfort and a sense of identity, but also created the basis of resistance to Victorian morality. Using ideas like Hellenism, aestheticism and sexology, an embryonic movement for gay liberation could take root.

For much of the century, it had been assumed that homosexuality was 'nameless' and unknown and was kept in check by repressive laws. However, we have seen that in spite of these draconian measures, it remained a constant presence in British life, persistently intruding into mainstream politics and culture. It had its own forms of life and entertainment, language and culture which survived persecution and damnation. Homosexuality was also present in debates on religion, national identity and empire, the city and its morality, science, evolution and law. Although it seemed at the end of the century that the homosexual was a separate species, it continued to be the case that gay life was a major component of British life. An emerging movement against persecution and damnation was beginning to develop, and the stage was set for the campaigns and debates of the twentieth century.

Chapter 5

Queer Conflicts: Love, Sex and War, 1914–1967

Matt Cook

In the first months of the Great War, Robert Ross, Oscar Wilde's close friend and literary executor, sued the playwright's former lover Lord Alfred Douglas for libel. Douglas, now married (though separated) and with a son, had sent Ross a letter accusing him of being a 'filthy bugger' and 'notorious sodomite'. Ross abandoned the case after a number of courtroom revelations – including his friendship with an amateur actor who 'paint[ed] and powder[ed] his face' and his attendance at a New Year's Eve party in 1911 where 'twenty or thirty men had danced together'.[1] Not content with this victory, Douglas published a poem, *The Rossiad*, which dwelt on the danger of men like Ross to the nation. 'Two filthy fogs blot out thy light', he wrote, 'the German and the Sodomite'.[2]

This connection between sodomy, Germany and treachery was made repeatedly during the war. In 1916, the Irish Nationalist Sir Roger Casement was hung for his part in a plan to allow a German submarine to land in Ireland. His diary detailing his homosexual adventuring in London, Dublin and the Belgium Congo (where he had worked to bring Belgian atrocities to light) was produced to curtail sympathy and expedite his death sentence. Two years later, the independent MP Noel Pemberton Billing alleged that the Germans had a book of 47,000 British men and women – 'privy councilors, youths of the chorus, wives of cabinet ministers, dancing girls, even Cabinet Ministers themselves' – who were open to blackmail by the enemy on account of their sexual deviance. The Germans were apparently using homosexual perversity as surely as guns and grenades to conquer Britain. Like Douglas before him, Billing exposed the moral laxity of the ruling elite and the protection they supposedly gave to each other in their pursuit of sexual pleasure. On the streets around Piccadilly, meanwhile, the *World* newspaper found 'painted and perfumed travesties of men openly leer[ing] at the passer-by'. 'Certain bars and restaurants are meeting places for these creatures', it went on, adding that it was 'lamentable to know that their victims or accomplices are largely drawn from the ranks of the British Army'. 'Abnormal vice' was apparently 'rampant'[3] – part of what one of Billing's supporters called 'the German system here in London'.[4]

Those involved in this fresh outbreak of depravity were putting Britain's moral reputation and the whole war effort in jeopardy, whilst 'our boys' were dying in France and Belgium. As the previous chapters have shown, sodomy had frequently been identified as a foreign vice before and at times of national crisis was made to seem positively unpatriotic. And yet whilst these men were demonized collectively and suspected of forming a conspiratorial 'co-fraternity of nastiness',[5] closer examination exposes the plurality of queer experience. This chapter considers the period 1914–1967 and looks at the ways in which war, urban scenes, class, love and domesticity, and the law and the press could differentiate as well as connect queer lives. It looks too at the post-World War II debate about the homosexual 'problem', the passage of the 1967 Sexual Offences Act and the parallel (and related) shift towards a more universal understanding of what sex between two men 'meant'.

Wartime intimacies

World War I
There was no clear or convenient division between the 'leering creatures' in Piccadilly and our national heroes, as the *World* sensationally observed. Soldiers on leave in the capital might have sex with other men, attend all-male parties or drink at the Criterion in Piccadilly or the cave of the Golden Calf off Regents Street. Such behaviour was seen to work to the detriment of the war effort. On the front, meanwhile, intense bonds formed between soldiers were often celebrated in photos of embraces and kisses in the news-papers or acknowledged in letters and other wartime writing.[6] Lieutenant Frank Cocker wrote to his fiancée, Evelyn, about his stolen kiss with another soldier, for example:

> I felt an arm round my neck, and the dear lad kissed me once – 'that's from Evelyn' he said; then he kissed me again and said 'that's from your mother'. I returned his tender salute and said 'that's from me'.[7]

Such attachments and affections filter through the poetry of Wilfred Owen and Siegfried Sassoon, and the autobiographies of men like Eric Hiscock. Hiscock refers to the solace of chaste physical and emotional closeness on the front as well as to the sex sought by some soldiers; one man had attempted to unbutton his flies on a train heading for Dunkirk and demobilization.[8]

There is nothing to say that Cocker, 'Jock' or the man on the train would have identified themselves as having a distinctive homosexual identity in the way Ross, Sassoon and Owen did. Jock and his pal could be 'normal' men and still be physically intimate with other men at this time and especially in the context of warfare and devastating personal loss. Cocker told his fiancée about the kiss he shared with his comrade and did not see it compromising their relationship or his masculinity. Such closeness could indeed be memorialized as part of the story of national heroism: the war memorial in Battersea Park depicts members of the 24th Infantry Division tenderly holding hands; 10,865 of their number had been lost during the War. That an alternative gloss could be put on wartime intimacies is nevertheless suggested by the soldier who felt the need to insist that there was 'nothing sodomitical in these friendships'.[9] For those who had not experienced life on the front, such physical and emotional closeness might be understood rather differently. Context could be highly significant in understanding love, affection or indeed desire for another man.

The same was true of drag – a staple of troop entertainment in both wars. In these shows, performers were often obviously male, but there were also sometimes more genuine attempts to pass as female. A play was often made on the performers' attractiveness to the all-male audiences. This, in the context of barracks and the front, was all good clean fun and did not necessarily impugn the sexual reputation of the performers or audience. One paper in 1917, for example, advertised the charms of Private Carpenter: 'one of the latest and most successful additions to our gallery of false women'.[10] The *Mirror* in 1918 carried a photo of two soldiers – one in drag – dancing; the byline read: 'Courtship duet: good practice for both of the boys'.[11] After the war, military drag troops toured the country. When the civilian Robert Courthard masqueraded as a woman in Gateshead in 1915 and the labour exchange official Victor Wilson did the same around the streets of Edinburgh three years later, however, their frocks and make-up were key to the cases laid out against them in court.[12] Just after the war, the *Empire News* was 'sickened by the number of men paraders who ape women in voice, dress and manners' along the promenade at Brighton.[13] Drag in the forces did not need to compromise the manliness and presumed 'normality' of those involved;

undertaken by civilians and 'male harpies' in the streets of Gateshead, Edinburgh and Brighton, however, it suggested a dangerous perversion – part (supposedly) of a wider outbreak of immorality during the war years in which women succumbed to 'khaki fever' and lesbian 'ecstasies' and (civilian) men leapt into each other's embraces.[14]

World War II

Though the newspaper response was overblown and sometimes hysterical, it is perhaps not surprising that the wars opened up new erotic opportunities. People were on the move: troops travelled between the major cities; nurses, doctors, farm workers, intelligence staff, civil servants and conscientious objectors drafted into noncombative duties found themselves posted to work away from home. There was the scope for new friendships: 'let's face it', recalls Frith Banbury of World War II, 'people were in different circumstances, away from their families so the what-will-the-neighbors-say factor didn't come into it'.[15] 'The war', observed Stephen, 'led to a sort of breaking down of old inhibitions and customs and family ties'.[16] John Beardsmore recalls many men having affairs with other servicemen during World War II and then marrying postwar – sometimes becoming godfather to each other's children.[17] Overtly queer men could find themselves relatively accepted in the services, meanwhile. John, who served in the army in World War II, found the attitude of his comrades 'protective': 'They used to send me up like mad. But if a stranger did it he used to be kicked to death [...] I was a sort of Evelyn Home to the boys you know, comfort for the troops. They didn't confess their homosexuality to me, but they 'used' me sexually occasionally'.[18] John's peers 'sent him up' to mark out his difference from them. Thus pigeonholed, the social and sexual connections they also had with him were less potentially compromising. Freddy, a former London chorus boy, had a similar role in the navy. He had the job of relaying messages from the captain to the rest of the ship. 'At moments of high drama he sometimes diffused the tension by camping it up, so when the captain issued orders to open fire, he simply repeated 'open fire dear' which would crack up the troops. [...] He was immensely popular on the ship'.[19] Freddy was a kind of mascot, and the interviewee who related this story clearly saw himself to be in a different category, even though he himself identified as homosexual.

Whilst such campery could be tolerated and enjoyed in the forces, sex between men still led to court martials, and these continued and increased during the war years – rising from 48 in 1939 to 324 in 1944/1945.[20] Men in higher ranks had to be especially cautious.[21] The military authorities took homosexuality seriously, and reports were commissioned on the behaviour of homosexual soldiers. One observed that the homosexual recruit was 'less resistant to trauma and demonstrated excessive grief for comrades-in-arms'. Another noted that the military homosexual needed 'to dominate the male group, obtain love, respect and acknowledgment for his prowess. He must lead, cannot be led, and finds it intolerable to be in the passive position of obeying'. Over a third of the cases of homosexuality, the report went on, 'had fascist leanings' and constituted a 'foreign body within the social macrocosm'.[22] By World War II, this kind of psychological and psychoanalytic explanation and analysis had become more common as we will see later. In this case, it was used to underscore familiar stereotypes of queer treachery and to make draw an implicit analogy between the 'passive position' in the forces and in homosexual sex.

On the home front in World War II, the blackouts in major cities provided cover for casual sex. John describes a sexually charged atmosphere in London and 'a great deal more fumbling than ever'.[23] Quentin Crisp recalls asking an 'invisible passer-by' where he was, whereupon the man 'kissed me on the lips, told me I was in Newport Street and walked on'.[24] Gerard Dogherty remembers leaving the Fitzroy Tavern just north of Oxford Street on the first night of the Blitz, meeting a 'barrow boy' and spending the night having sex in a first-class carriage stranded in Charing Cross station: 'it was most exciting with the bombs dropping and the glass shattering and I thought this is the way to spend the first night of the Blitz: in the arms of a barrow boy in a railway carriage'.[25] Roy remembers Edinburgh being 'full of sailors' who were 'quite easy; quite quite easy. The place was as if the world had gone mad because it was so easy'.[26] Barry meanwhile describes trips from Brighton to Portsmouth during the war: 'the navy was famously sensible about [homosexuality]': 'they were friendly, pleasant, amusing, ready to talk, some of them were ready for sex'.[27] Each of these men testifies to a sense of living in the moments – death could have been imminent for each of them, and this necessarily changed the way they and many others responded to sexual possibility.

The influx of foreign troops exposed British men to different sexual attitudes; many experienced the sexual ease of some of the American GIs arriving after 1941. Trevor Thomas described the American homosexual scene before the war 'as rather more open, even then',[28] and John recalls that the 'introduction of American queens [to Britain] changed a lot of homosexual people's attitude towards sex'. 'The Americans were much more inventive'. The American's presence also had an economic impact. 'I think the rates [for rent boys] were £1, in those early days. But the Americans ruined the market; it went up to $10'.[29] Quentin Crisp nevertheless waxed lyrical about the availability of north American soldiers:

> It was the liberality of their natures that was so marvelous. Never in the history of sex was so much offered to so many by so few. At the first gesture of acceptance from a stranger, words of love began to ooze from their lips, sexuality from their bodies and pound notes from their pockets like juice from a peeled peach. [...] While the GIs were around I lived almost every moment that I spent out of doors in a state of exhilaration.[30]

Queer 'scenes'

London

Crisp attests to London's permissiveness during World War II – the city was, he says, like a massive double bed – but he also describes a visible and vibrant subculture in the city in the interwar years. Freddy's camp confidence on board ship may in part have come from his experience of that scene as a West End chorus boy. The *World* had observed 'painted and perfumes travesties of men' around Piccadilly in 1916, and after the war the *Sunday Express* spotted 'our new decadents [...] at Covent Garden [opera house], at the Alhambra [theatre in Leicester Square], wherever [the ballet dancer] Dighileff had his seasons'. 'Rouge and powder are known to this co-fraternity of nastiness', the paper added.[31]

Norman and Roy describe finding men standing around in the circle at the Empire Theatre in Leicester Square and at the nearby Prince of Wales theatre.[32] Gregory used to go to the London galleries to meet other men, preferring these and the numerous 'tremendous' cottages (public toilets) around the city to the bars, clubs and theatres which he associated with a particular 'style' of man.[33] As 'Paul Pry' observed in *For Your Convenience* (1937), a thinly veiled cottaging guide, public toilets often developed a distinctive reputation. School teacher Bernard Williams recalls: 'If you wanted a piece of rough you'd look round the cottages in Covent Garden. [...] On the other hand, if you wanted the theatrical trade you'd do some of the cottages round the back of Jermyn Street or if you did the cottage at Waterloo Station you'd have a good class of trade there, dear'.[34] Hyde Park was still notorious for guardsmen rent, and most open spaces in the city had a cruising area. The canal towpath at Putney was well known, and the opening of the Hampstead tube (later the Northern Line) in 1907 made the heath more accessible and also encouraged more people to move to the area.

There was a lively pub culture throughout the period, and like the cottages, different places catered for differing queer punters. The Running Horse in Shepherds Market was popular with a cross-section of men and women. Stephen was a senior civil servant and remembers visiting the pub after dining at his nearby Mayfair club: 'I met several of the waiters from the club there who were off duty [and] they used to tease one a bit'.[35] When the pub was placed under police surveillance in 1936, the more respectable drinkers like Stephen were not identified. The police report instead referred to the 'two youths in the bar [who] had their hair waved and their faces and lips made up'. One of these men had 'screamed in an effeminate way when touched', whilst in another part of the bar, 'two young men were kissing the ear of another man'. There were also 'three women of masculine appearance. [...] Their hair was cut short in manly fashion, and they wore costumes of collars and ties and no hats'.[36] The pub clearly welcomed queer men *and* women, indicating some cross-over of lesbian and gay 'scenes' in the city. Roy in fact remembers seeing Radclyffe Hall drinking at the Running Horse before the publication of *The Well of Loneliness* (1928).[37]

In Fitrovia, just north of Oxford Street, there was a cluster of pubs – the Bricklayers Arms, the Wheatsheaf, the Marquis of Granby and the Fitzroy Tavern – which if not quite as queer as the Running Horse or the Cavour in Leicester Square were bohemian enough to accommodate 'the fringe of the gay worlds'.[38] Michael remembers the Fitzroy as a bohemian hang-out, with gay men, lesbians, actors, artists, uniformed soldiers and sailors, and sometimes a kilted pianist.[39] At other bars, the clientele would change at particular times: the Criterion at Piccadilly Circus was empty of 'respectable characters' by mid-evening and by 10 p.m. 'the great ornate hall had been filled [...] with well-behaved male trash'.[40] Across the Circus, Lyons Corner House had a particular section which waiting staff reserved for queer clientele.[41] Quentin Crisp describes sitting with his friends at the

Chat Noir – or Black Cat – coffee shop in Old Compton Street 'night after loveless night [...] buying each other cups of tea, combing each other's hair and trying on each other's lipsticks'.[42] In the 1930s, the Caravan Club and Billies Club in Soho were popular with a similar crowd, and there were queer dances and parties. Two were exposed within weeks of each other in 1933 – one in Holland Park Avenue organized 'Lady Austin' for his 'camp boys' and the other in Baker Street.[43] The *News of the World* tied itself up in euphemism describing the clientele at the latter: 'about 10 per cent were women, and women of a particular class, not prostitutes, but another sort of woman. The remaining 90 per cent were men, men of a class well known to the public in London, men who speak to each other endearingly and dress effeminately'. One man 'wore only his pyjama trousers' for the event.[44] On a much larger scale, Lady Malcolm's Servant Ball and the Chelsea Arts Ball, both held annually at the Royal Albert Hall in the 1920s and 1930s, became key dates in the queer calendar, though this was not the intention of the organizers!

If queer men had a visible presence in the West End, they were also necessarily aware that tolerance was highly contingent. Effeminacy could be entertaining but at other times was seen to be embarrassing or compromising. After years of turning a blind eye, organizers of Lady Malcolm's Servants Ball forbade cross-dressing men in 1935: 'NO MAN IMPERSONATING A WOMAN [...] WILL BE ADMITTED', the ticket read. Terry Gardener was asked to leave Lyons Corner House on account of his effeminacy,[45] and Crisp was repeatedly barred from the Corner House and the Wheatsheaf in Fitzrovia. 'My friends protested hotly to the landlord [about the ban] but he coolly pointed out that he could not have a license and me'.[46] The police raided pubs and made arrests throughout the period, though they were pretty unsystematic and unpredictable; queens and homosexuals never knew quite when the police would act. The Running Horse had a reputation for years before it was placed under surveillance, for example.

London's queers were not necessarily passive in the face of the law. Three men arrested after dressing up at home in Fitzroy Place in 1927 as Salome and other 'exotic' figures protested their prosecution on the grounds that 'a man could what he liked in his own house'.[47] When police told the court that George Morgan had only been wearing a cape and a belt at the Holland Park Avenue party of 1933, Morgan pointed out that he was also wearing 'brocade slips' and added that 'surely in a free country we can do what we like. I am afraid', he went on, 'a few will suffer yet before these things are made legal'.[48] Sentencing the twenty-seven men prosecuted in the case – to terms of up to twenty months in prison – the judge observed that 'the peculiarity of sex perverts is that not only do they not think they are wrong, but that they are right and they regard any kind of interference as an infringement of individual liberty. They glory in their shame. Sometimes they are blatant about it'.[49] Certainly, many men were prepared to stand up to attacks and abuse in court and beyond. Crisp's friends had 'protested loudly' to the landlord of the Wheatsheaf when he was barred, and Terry Gardiner recalls the tongue lashing he gave people who shouted abuse at him. 'What goes up my fucking arse won't give you a headache', he remembers telling one man.[50]

After World War II, the historian Matt Houlbrook argues, London's scene became less 'blatant' and the flamboyant queens began to disappear from the streets. A growing emphasis on domesticity and family life, rising prosperity, changing work patterns and a burgeoning youth culture affected the dynamics of the queer subculture. Though there was no coordinated witch-hunt, arrests did go up, and many queer men felt more fearful and cautious than before as we will see later. In this sense, the discreet, staid and respectable private members clubs of the 1950s like the A & B (the Arts and Battledress) and the Rockingham (the so-called 'poof's Athenaeum') might be seen to be representative of this new era.

These were by no means the only bars, however, and the Fitzroy continued to be popular, as did the Salisbury in St Martin's Lane and the Golden Lion (famed for rent) in Soho.[51] The opportunities for sex also continued plentiful. At the YMCA in Great Russell Street, trunks were forbidden well into the 1950s on grounds of hygiene: 'you can imagine', recalls Bernard Dobson, 'a lot of people who were gay were members of the YMCA. It was easy to pick people up'.[52] Scandal brought trunks and attendants to the Y, but there was no such supervision at the infamous Biograph Cinema in Victoria which became known post-World War II as the 'Biogrope'. More exclusively, Turkish Baths – and especially those in Jermyn Street, Edgware Road and under the Imperial Hotel in Russell Square – provided plenty of scope for homosexual contact.[53] The Jermyn Street baths had been on the queer map since before World War I and in the 1950s Michael remembers customers at Edgware Road giving the attendants hefty tips so that they would ignore the discreet night-time goings on.[54]

Burgeoning youth culture of the 1960s brought back some of the pre-war flamboyance. Illegal 'bars' run by recent Afro-Caribbean immigrants often welcomed younger lesbians and gay men. 'They were in houses; they were usually run by black people who were sympathetic to lesbian and gay people who didn't have a place to go', recalls Calare Andrews.[55] Michael remembers going to an all-black gay house party in Notting Hill the early 1960s.[56] Le Duce in Soho had opened, a bar which Peter Burton describes as 'a watershed between the more discreet drinking clubs of the 40s and 50s and the super club' of the 1970s.[57] It was the dance floors, music and drugs (especially dope and speed) which made the difference. Le Duce played Motown, whilst at the nearby Kandy Lounge, police reported men doing the twist together. Le Gigolo in the Kings Road also had a dance space downstairs – though when Robert visited in the early 1960s he discovered 'not so much a dance but more of an orgy': 'The further one got sucked into the heaving mass of bodies, the more overt the sexual activity became. [...] One had to literally fight one's way out. I developed a way of simplifying my exit. I would say 'excuse me, I'm going to throw up!' and the crowd would part like the Red Sea!'[58]

Outside London

Although London was the most notorious centre of queer life in Britain and is the city for which we have most oral history and other evidence, smaller cities and towns also had their own queer sex and social scenes. In the bar of a town's main hotel, Alan Horsfall recalls, you could often meet other men socially 'with less hassle' than elsewhere.[59] The bigger provincial cities had established venues. In 1925, for example, the 45 Café in Liverpool's Hanover Street was exposed after PC Plank visited 'powdered, painted and wearing horn rimmed spectacles'. He found men in make-up and with painted fingernails and calling each other 'dear'.[60] Around the same time, Trevor Thomas recalls private parties in the city. These were not necessarily safer than the more public venues, however, and one group he went to regularly was raided, and the members were arrested and imprisoned. The policeman testified to what he had seen through the key hole and to one of the participants calling out in delight: 'my, that's a whopper!'[61]

In 1930s Cambridge, Sam would organize private dances and drag shows. 'They used to call me Lady May Cambridge. They said Lady May's putting on another do, and they all used to come down [from London]. Of course we had a wonderful time'.[62] Men would also travel to Brighton and Blackpool throughout the period, and both towns had queer pubs and fairly permissive places to stay. Just after World War II, a boarding house used by 'men of a particular type' was exposed in Blackpool; visitors had come from Preston, Lancaster and as far away as London and Plymouth.[63] The *Empire News* had drawn attention to the 'nancy' types on Brighton's promenade in 1924, and the town's reputation endured. James remembers the draw of post-World War II Brighton: 'Everybody would go there. Queans [sic] from all over England. Brighton was probably the most outrageous place in the country'. 'Brighton's gay now but it was very very gay then', recalled Sandie.[64] Whereas most towns and cities outside London had one or two bars and clubs at most, in Brighton there were several in the 1950s and 1960s: Reginas, Club 42, the Golden Fleece, the Spotted Dog, the Quadrant, the 'classy' Argyle Hotel and the Greyhound were amongst the most popular. At the latter, you had to cross through the straight bar to get to the gay bar upstairs. 'I can't tell you how much courage it took to walk from that bar, to go up those stairs because what you were actually doing, in front of all those people was saying, 'I'm one of them' '.[65]

The Sussex Arts Ball at the Brighton Aquarium had the same kind of notoriety as the larger annual London events at the Royal Albert Hall.[66] 'We used to say that a certain number of queans [sic] used to spend the whole summer sitting on the men's beach sewing sequins on the gowns'.[67] There were also frequent parties: 'it was unusual for seven days to go by without a party somewhere', recalls John.[68]

Ian Christie talks of parties being a mainstay postwar scene in Edinburgh too. On a Friday and Saturday, he and his friends would meet at Crawfords café in Frederick Street before moving on to bottle parties: 'perhaps we were more closeted', he wrote, 'but in our closets we asserted ourselves more defiantly in drag and outrageous campery. [...] It was nothing for one hundred people to crowd into one small apartment in Edinburgh or Glasgow, word having got round the cafes and pubs like wildfire'.[69]

During World War II, drag shows at Manchester's Union Pub on Canal Street were popular, with American troops stationed at nearby Burtonwood. The imprisonment of the publican for 'outraging public decency' in 1965 only served to consolidate the pubs reputation further. The Long Bar under the Odeon Cinema and opposite a notorious cottage on Bridgwater Street took off in the early 1960s. It was soon followed by Rouge (later Queens) and the Rockingham. Manchester's queer hub at this point was between Albert Square and Deansgate, and not Canal

Street, which later became Britain's first 'gay village'.[70] Roy found
Manchester 'much gayer than London', and if discretion was informing
the scene further south, here he saw 'drag walking along the street. In
London you would get arrested. But lots of them were doing it. I'm not
talking about the odd one here and there'.[71]

Outside the cities, private car ownership was also important in helping
to sustain rural networks like those exposed in Somerset, Yorkshire
and Surrey in the 1950s (and discussed later). Men seem to have been
prepared to travel considerable distances for queer parties and events.
For wealthier men, the circuit extended further, taking in European cities
like Paris and Berlin, as well as the south of France around Nice and parts
of Greece and Southern Italy. As people travelled more, so there was
more contact between local scenes; men would be given addresses of
bars, hotels and individuals in the places they were visiting. The A & B
club had the nearest thing to a listings: a book where members would
note down bars and cruising areas in London and other cities in Britain
and abroad.

Signs, language and labels

Newspapers and magazines like the *Link* (from 1915) carried
advertisements from 'artistic', 'broad-minded' or 'unconventional'
men 'seeking similar'.[72] One man was prosecuted after he placed an
advertisement in his local paper for a 'young man, aged about 18, to
travel with and assist gentleman'.[73] Wilde or Dorian Gray were often
evoked.[74] These advertisements indicate the importance of coded
language in a period when there was no universally accepted term for
homosexuality or the homosexual, and when being too explicit in letters
or conversation could be incriminating. Trevor Thomas remembers his
opening gambits from the interwar years: 'are you fond of music? Do you
like music? Oh yes, I like music very much!' Men might be 'so', 'poofs'
or 'queens'; the *Empire News* described the men in Brighton as 'Nancy
types';[75] 'masculine' working-class men might be 'tbh' ('to be had') or
'trade'. Guardsmen rent boys, meanwhile, knew their customers as
'twanks'.[76] 'Queer' gained ground as a loose term for sexual strangeness
from around World War I, whilst Noel Coward used 'gay' with evident
relish at its new double meaning in 'Green Carnation', a number from his
musical *Bitter Sweet* (1929). These various terms were not synonymous.

Trade, for example, could be a 'normal' working-class man who also had girlfriends; queens, whilst also generally working class, were effeminate and had sex more exclusively (and supposedly passively) with other men.

Polari, a combination of 'pig' Latin, word inversions and Romany, had developed as a distinctive queer patois in the nineteenth century, and by the 1920s, it was common in theatrical circles and around the docks, fostering a sense of connection between queens, prostitutes, immigrants and other 'outcasts'. It allowed for some defiant and outlandish conversation in public. A visit to the 'charpering carsey' after getting caught 'charvering' with an 'omi polani' with 'bona ecaf, strong lallies, and a huge cartzo' would signal a visit to the police station after getting caught having sex with a queer man (significantly in terms of understandings of homosexual identity a 'man(omi)-woman (polani)') with a cute face, strong legs and a big cock. Polari gained a national audience in the 1960s, with Julian and Sandy in radio's *Round the Horne*, and some terms such as 'dosh' and 'naff' became more common slang. Before the war, though, it was much more exclusive. John, a working-class chorus boy in the 1930s, observed that: 'there's no more mystery about it [now] but then it used to be great fun. It was common amongst only a certain class in the gay world. It was usually people like myself who were in the chorus, the common end of the structure, who used it'.[77] As a purely spoken language, polari had real flexibility, and different cliques would adapt and expand the vocabulary. The polari used by merchant seamen apparently confused West End queens.

Clothes performed a similar function. As we saw earlier, queens often used make-up, women's clothes, bright colours and flamboyant jewellery. In addition, camel coats, Liberty silk ties, bright shirts, a brooch or 'pinkie' ring, the button hole, silk scarves or suede shoes were all signs. Grant remembers that in the 1950s Brighton, queens all wore 'terribly flared trousers and terribly Hawaiian shirts with all sorts of tulle at the neck'. These often came from Filk'n's, a clothing store next to the town's Theatre Royal run by Phil and Ken (aka Rose Filk'n and Esme Filk'n). 'It was very daring to wear their sort of clothes, you didn't find it anywhere else [...] People used to come down specially for a weekend to Brighton and to go round to Aunt Rose's shop', recalled one customer.[78] Noel Coward meanwhile used high-fashion and unconventional dress to signal his 'theatricality' to a wider public and his sexual difference to his own circle of friends. The trademark smoking jacket, for example, was a motif he shared with his friend, Radclyffe Hall.[79]

On the one hand, these sartorial signals could foster a feeling of belonging and helped men make contact with each other. On the other, they might give you away or be used in evidence against you. Dudley Cave was wolf-whistled in Heaton park, Manchester, for his dapper green trousers and Harris tweed jacket and he became embarrassed to wear blue or green because he had read 'in Havelock Ellis or somewhere' that these were homosexual men's favourite colors.[80] Police used blotting paper to gather evidence of rouge and lipstick from the men they arrested, and dresses and effeminate clothing were mentioned in court cases, as we have seen. In 1962, it was the suede shoes and brightly coloured shirts of the clientele of the Kandy Lounge in Gerard Street, London, which were cited in evidence against the proprietor.[81]

Queer classes

Class made a difference in terms of where you went, who you met, how you saw yourself and the support you received from peers, friends and family. Working-class men were more likely to be arrested throughout the period. Those charged after the raids on the Caravan Club and Billie's Club in 1934 and 1936 respectively were mainly in labouring or service jobs, for example. Middle-class men went to these venues too, but without the make-up the queens often used, they were less visibly queer and so less likely to be arrested or barred. Their class status may also have meant that police were more likely to turn a blind eye.

The same was true of Oxford and Cambridge Universities in the 1920s and 1930s where men were insulated by relatively open and fashionable homosexual fraternities in the 1920s and 1930s. Goronwy Rees (later a member of the Wolfenden Committee) reported that during this period homosexuality became, 'among undergraduates and dons with pretensions to culture and a taste for the arts, at once a fashion, a doctrine and a way of life'. '[It] exercised an influence far beyond the boundaries of the university'.[82] At Cambridge, the Apostles Society became known for its queer membership. At Oxford, undergraduates divided into two camps, dubbed the 'hearties' and the 'aesthetes' in a clear homage to Wilde, Walter Pater and other artistic 'radicals' of the Victorian *fin de siecle*.[83] Some were now political radicals too, and by the 1930s, there was an association between homosexuality and left-wing politics at the universities: Guy Burgess, Anthony Blunt and Donald MacClean, later notorious as spies, were Cambridge communists; the future labour MP Tom Driberg, and the poets W. H. Auden and Stephen Spender were all Oxford left-wingers.

Beyond the universities, wealthier men had access to homes in London and the country which facilitated a private social circuit, largely insulated from the law (though not impervious to it – as Lord Montagu, Peter Wildeblood and Michael Pitt-Rivers found to their cost in the 1954). Those in the Bloomsbury group and the circle around Ivor Novello and Noel Coward could enjoy weekends at country homes in Kent and Sussex. Their bohemian and artistic occupations in addition allow for a degree of openness that was unimaginable in most middle- and upper middle-class professions. Lawyers, accountants, doctors and teachers had to go to elaborate lengths to cover their queer tracks in the workplace and with their families – including of course the so-called marriages of convenience. This left many men especially vulnerable to blackmail, a trade which thrived throughout the period.

Working-class men needed to be cautious at work too. In most working-class jobs, men had to exercise extreme caution. Grant recalls that at work in the 1950s 'you didn't lisp and you didn't have broken wrists. They could fire [...] you with a week's notice'.[84] Some occupations were more tolerant, however, and the theatres, merchant navy, bars, restaurants and hotels often had a disproportionate number of queer men on their staff. Nursing was similar, though Gwladys Edwards suggests that this was partly due to ignorance: as a trainee nurse in Birmingham she had no understanding of what one of her male peers had done wrong in a public toilet to warrant his arrest and removal from the hospital.[85]

If the police too a harder line with working-class men, it does also seems that they often enjoyed more support from their families and immediate communities in the interwar period than many middle- and upper middle-class homosexuals. Matt Houlbrook cites John's recollections of the East End in the 1950s: 'homosexuality [...] had always been absolutely accepted [...] we used to go to one of the pubs where the mums and dads used to go [...] they used to refer to the boys by their camp name, 'Hello Lola love, how are you dear? You going to give us a song?' '[86] Jack Robinson was welcomed warmly by his boyfriend's mother, and whenever he docked in Liverpool he found a double bed made up.[87] James felt that the real disgrace was pregnancy: 'therefore I think a lot of working class people [...] didn't mind if you put two boys in a bed together and two girls in a bed together. Then no-one could get pregnant'.[88] The Marquis of Granby, the Ken and the Round House in London's docks drew a mixed crowd including local dockers, married couples, queens and sometimes visitors from the West End. The Marquis hosted regular drag shows, which were also a feature of working-class pubs across east and south-east London. Don Trueman remembers the co-existence of different pub goers at the Royal Court pub in Liverpool: 'the gay guys used the little back room, the snug, we were in the public bar, we'd blow them kisses from time to time. They'd walk through the public bar to the gents and we'd say nice arse or something and they'd say 'Ooh, thank you' but they wouldn't follow it up if you weren't serious'.[89] Trueman recollects a separatism, but also indicates that there was sometimes an easy social and also sexual cross-over between the two groups.

The queens in the East End and Liverpool were, as we have seen already, a working-class 'type', and the way in which queer men behaved and understood was very much informed by class position and background. Many of the middle-class men who talked in the 1980s about their relationships and sex lives in the first half of the century recall being keen to read and find out more about their 'condition'. Henry Havelock Ellis's *Sexual Inversion*, the work and reputation of Edward Carpenter, Freud's theories of sexuality (first published in English in 1905) and the British Society for the Study of Sex Psychology (founded in 1913) are all mentioned in their testimony. For many men discovering a rationale for their desires and behaviour was important, partly because it gave a sense of legitimacy. George Ives saw such writing and discussion as crucial to his campaign for reform and was excited by the growing interest in the subject. 'What was there written about inversion 30 years ago?', he wrote in 1917: 'some privately printed essays by John Addington Symonds; that is all I can think of in English. Now there are some half dozen writers'.[90] As H. G. Cocks indicated, some of the sexologists these men were reading interpreted homosexuality in terms of gender misalignment – having a female 'soul' in a male body or being an 'intermediate type'. Effeminacy in men was, however, widely derided, and it was difficult to imagine it going hand in hand with middle-class respectability.[91] Many thus insisted on their own masculinity and conformity and in this way marked a difference from the working-class queens in the Marquis of Granby, The Running Horse or the Royal Court.

Other working-class men maintained both their 'normality' (as opposed to the middle-class 'homosexuals') and their masculinity (as opposed to the queens), despite the sex they were having with men.[92] John Beardsmore would go out with mates trying to pick up girls and when they failed would end up in bed together. They would also tell each other when they picked up other men. 'When [...] you met somebody who took you home for five bob or so many pints of beer you would say 'I went with a brown hatter last night' '.[93] Whilst Beardsmore clearly recognized a type – the middle-class 'brown hatter' – he did not categorize his peers in the same way; they were 'normal' men who had sex with men sometimes.

Many guardsmen who supplemented their income through prostitution were similarly open about their activities and seem to have felt little conflict over the sex they were having and their role as masculine defenders of the nation.[94] Their activities were nevertheless a continued cause for concern and scandal. *Reynolds News* observed the disproportionate number of 'young guardsmen implicated in perversion, and other offences no less heinous' – though David, himself a former guardsman, suggested that the 'reputation of the guards was exaggerated a bit'.[95] After a case in 1956 in which five members of the Cold Stream Guards were prosecuted, the defence argued that they had been seduced 'by civilian Herberts' with free entertainment and had then found themselves in the 'unscrupulous clutches of a perverted man'.[96] Homosexuality was again conjured as a privileged, immoral and corrupting civilian vice. There was often an assumption that it was the higher-class man who had the distinctive sexual identity, whilst the working-class partner was sexually pliant or just in need of the money.

Some upper middle-class and upper-class men testify to the erotics for them of the class divide. The working-class 'rough' and soldiers and sailors are described as figures of fantasy by Edward Carpenter, the MP Tom Driberg, J. R. Ackerley and the journalist Michael Davidson. Such men were often available as casual rent as John Beardsmore explained, but it was not necessarily just about sex. In the 1910s and 1920s, there was sometimes also a political dimension: relationships with lower-class men could be conceived as an act of cross-class comradeship and part of a process of social change. This was how Carpenter thought about his partnership with George Merrill, and Ives took a similar line in describing his relationships. It is a key theme in E. M. Forster's *Maurice* (1914) too.[97] At one remove from Edwardian romantic socialism, Tom Driberg's later account of his sexual adventuring is couched more in the language of social observation than social transformation. When he writes about the sex, he had with a tramp he picked up on London's Embankment he notes the man's 'pitiably thin, weak liquid load [...] (poverty again), not sufficient to form on the sheet the [...] stain which chamber maids call a 'map of Ireland' '.⁹⁸

Lovers

Casual encounters like that described by Driberg have often been used to characterize queer lives. This is partly because court cases and consequently newspaper reports most often related to opportunistic sex undertaken in public spaces. Being in a relationship – or wanting to be part of one – nevertheless often defined the way men lived day-to-day. In his autobiographies, J. R. Ackerley movingly describes how his yearning for an 'ideal friend' structured his life and the choices he makes. Men in relationships were necessarily discreet in their partnerships, but we get a glimpse of them through the diaries and letters of well-known figures and also in newspaper exposes and reports of tragedies and prosecutions. Noel Coward had two long-term lovers, Jack Wilson and then Graeme Payne; the composer Benjamin Britten had a forty-year relationship with the tenor Peter Pears; and Joe Orton was with Kenneth Haliwell throughout the 1960s. Whilst Orton details his relationship in his diary, it was exposed much more dramatically in 1967 when he was killed by Haliwell, who then committed suicide. Earlier relationships are also revealed through the press. In 1923, in Jersey, Louis Delanoe murdered his 'chum' Fred Langois and then committed suicide after Langois decided to move out of the home they had been sharing.⁹⁹ Four years earlier, an *Empire News* expose described a 'mincing' man living in Brighton with his older cross-dressing 'valet' who the reporter mistook for a housekeeper.¹⁰⁰ In 1937, two men committed suicide together in Finchley in North London and left a note asking to be buried together. Their landlord testified to the coroner that he had heard them play 'When the Poppies Bloom Again' on the gramophone the night they gassed themselves.¹⁰¹ A year later, two soldiers imprisoned for 'committing certain acts' were revealed to have set up home in Clacton, Essex, after serving in India together. Apparently more benignly two men who shared a home for sixty years in a small village in Northamptonshire died within hours of each other in 1939; they were described by the *Daily Mirror* as 'the perfect friends'.¹⁰² The press was able to celebrate the latter's apparently 'innocent' friendship without innuendo, whilst it damned the Clacton couple whose 'secret life' shamed the nation.

Oral histories often give a less sensational angle on the various ways in which men organized their relationships and domestic lives. Frank Oliver recalls the problems of showing 'any kind of affection' to his lover Andrew in public. In a subsequent relationship – which lasted for twenty-five years – he describes his mother's snobbery at his partner's class, which seems to have been more of an issue for her than his gender. Frank also describes a personal need for a degree of independence; after fifteen years, the two men decided to live in separate flats in the same block in Streatham, South London.[103] Sam, the dancer from Cambridge, had a long-term affair with a married sailor and developed a good relationship with his wife, becoming 'uncle Sam' to their children. Gerald, a professional soldier, describes a seven-year partnership with Phil and the equitable way in which they organized their domestic life. 'We done the housework between us. We shared everything fifty-fifty. If I saw the stove wanted cleaning I'd clean the stove. If he saw the chest of drawers wanted polishing he'd polish the chest of drawers [...] Whoever came home first made the meal'. The couple did not tell their friends and family. They felt they had probably guessed but also that this was a private matter. Phil said: 'As long as we love each other what's it to do with other people'.[104]

Other men describe relationships changing into enduring but nonsexual friendships. Peter notes: 'It's not a sexual relationship we have, it's something above that, it's something more golden, we've been together a long time'.[105] Harry said of his relationship with Bob: 'although we're sort of not a pair any more in the usual sense, we're still together'.[106] George Ives, the early campaigner for homosexual law reform we met earlier, did not have a long-term partner during his life, but he did create his own 'family' at his home in London's Primrose Hill. In 1917, he gave an inventory using the pet names of his housemates: 'Kit [James Goddard] has been with me some 35 years. His wife over 20. Wappy [Charles Gee], Pug [Harold Bloodworth] 9 or 10 [...] and the 2 Kit girls [Goddard's daughters] all their lives'. 'That', he concluded, 'is my little circle in the world'.[107] The Goddards lived with Ives until their deaths in the 1930s; their daughters until the 1940s. Bloodworth remained until Ives died in 1950.

These relationships indicate deep commitment and love; they also reveal a variety of domestic and living arrangements. The dynamics of Ives' household, Gerard and Phil's partnership, Frank and Jimmy's arrangements after fifteen years living together, Peter's loving but nonsexual partnership and Sam's relationship with his lover's family, each balance the intimate with the pragmatics of circumstance, the operation of the law and other outside pressures and expectations. For married couples, there was a template and a series of conventions which they were expected to live by – not least relating to monogamy and cohabitation. Such relationships had a visible place in society and were expected to be productive in terms of children. The expectations were undoubtedly restrictive and suffocating for many, and for homosexual men, there might have been a certain liberation in forging relationships which did not have to follow a particular pattern. They could make up their own rules. What comes through much of the testimony, however, is the problem of sustaining relationships which needed to be secret and which had no social recognition or support. This was especially the case for those men who did not have their own homes. J. Jeffrey, a valet who lived with his employers in London in the late 1920s, had nowhere private to take his boyfriend: for two years they met each week in Hyde Park.[108]

Reaction: the press, the law and the 'experts'

Interwar

Men conducted and understood their sexual and emotional relationships with other men in a variety of ways and had differing degrees of contact with the overlapping public and private subcultures. Not surprisingly, though, this sense of complexity is rarely evident in newspaper coverage, which tended to focus on the classic themes of effeminacy and the threat to 'youth' and nation. The *Morning Post* observed the declining standards of theatre after the World War I, for example, and the trend in the West End to 'exploit' effeminacy among men as 'a box office draw'. It noted with approval Sir Oswald Stoll's 1929 decision to 'veto all jokes dealing with effeminacy in men' in his theatres.[109] Commenting on Mordant Sharpe's play *The Green Bay Tree* in 1933, the theatre critic Temple Thurston complained of the 'influence of sex perversion' in the theatre and the impossibility 'in casting a play these days, to find the healthy manliness of youth'.[110] The association of theatre and homosexuality was long-standing, and theatres had become a common venue for men to meet and socialize with each other and also to work in an atmosphere of relative tolerance. Homosexual men were not of course intrinsically more 'cultured' or 'tasteful' than other men, but as Richard Dyer argues, 'culture' was a means of identifying as queer: it was something beyond the ordinary and the everyday.[111] What Thurston and the other newspaper commentators were in part voicing was a paranoid concern about the parading of such an alternative value system and set of possibilities in a public and cultured arena.

This effeminacy and decline in standards was evident well beyond the West End. During the depression of the early 1930s the Bishop of Chelmsford proclaimed that 'a great service would be done [...] if we could break all stained glass windows depicting Jesus as a pale, weak, effeminate and unmanly figure'.[112] Immediately before the World War II, the *Referee* launched a crusade against 'the moral evil for which effeminacy is a cloak'. 'Here in Britain', the paper stormed:

> we have today she-men in every walk of life – in literature, on the stage, in schools, in politics, even in the army. It is not the prerogative of the leisured. Oh no. [...] While we strive to build up the nation's health with laws and leagues [...] this vile canker is sweeping through the nation's manhood. It is an evil without shame. Indeed it is blatant, it proclaims itself a new fashion, a super civilization. This is its real peril.[113]

In 1938, *Reynolds* reported the drastic measures advocated by a Dorset doctor to combat this 'canker': special gas chambers should be attached to courts for the immediate execution of 'sex perverts' post-prosecution.[114]

Such opinion was by no means universal, however. If Thurston railed in the 1930s against theatrical effeminacy in the *Green Bay Tree*, another critic, Ivor Brown in the *Weekend Review*, saw Sharpe's play as a breakthrough. 'First the pansy joker became the stock-in-trade of every touring company; then it invaded the fashionable West End comedy; now it has been supplanted by the recognition that a male effeminate or unwomanly women is not, of necessity, a scream'. Sharpe's play, he felt, indicated 'a public opinion that is coming to its senses'.[115] Brown reinforced the connection between effeminacy and homosexuality but also doubted that either was a national problem or disgrace.

Earlier in 1921, the *Evening News* welcomed the 'cult of candour' after the Great War and related it to the advent of psychoanalysis.[116] 'Psychoanalysis', the *Sunday Times* reported in 1928, 'has made us deal more gently with abnormality, since it has made us uncertain as to what the norm really is – whether it is, indeed, more than a conventional mask covering our strangeness'.[117] Family background and psychological explanations for sexual behaviour were more frequently cited in court cases in the 1920s and 1930s.[118] *Reynolds News* covered the experiment of a magistrate in Bradford who attempted to treat rather than punish homosexual offenders.[119] A Marylebone magistrate heard of the supposed glandular causes of homosexuality in a case of 1937 and bailed the defendant for 12 months on condition he sought treatment. 'A few years ago one would not have listened to what has been said on [the defendant's] behalf', he remarked.[120]

Whilst this shift in emphasis might indicate a growing sympathy for these men and an uneasiness about dealing with them in the criminal courts, the insistence on treatment was a judgment in itself – one that many homosexuals internalized by seeking 'help' independently. They were, they believed, not only criminal but sick. Treatment varied according to the theories of homosexuality espoused by the practitioner and included psychoanalysis (especially after World War II),[121] injections to correct a supposed hormone imbalance and aversion therapy, which attempted to induce a reaction of deep revulsion to men's bodies in the homosexual. Alan Turing, the man who helped to crack the enigma code during the World War II, opted for injections of oestrogen rather than a prison sentence after his relationship with another man in Manchester was exposed and prosecuted. The injections lowered Turing's libido but also led to the growth of breasts and to depression. He was found dead in 1953, and though the coroner recorded an open verdict, it was almost certainly suicide. Peter Price recalls his aversion therapy around the same time. He was engaged to be married in the Wirral in the north of England when his mother discovered his queer jaunts to London in a letter he had been sent. She persuaded him to seek treatment. In a psychiatric hospital, he was given Guinness and queer pornography, and then an injection of antabuse which reacted with the alcohol and prompted prolonged vomiting. He was given no sick bowl or access to a toilet and recalls lying terrified in a bed of vomit and excrement.[122] He later discharged himself when he learnt that the next stage of treatment involved electric shocks.

For some men, however, the sexological, psychological and psychoanalytic theories and consultations were helpful – not in reforming their desires but in helping them come to terms with them. As we have seen already, a number of men read Havelock Ellis' *Sexual*

Inversion – by now half a century old – and found it affirming;[123] in the final stages of the World War II, Dudley Cave recalls visiting a psychiatrist after his discharge from the army. 'I thought, 'No doubt they'll give me hormones and make me better'! [...] The doctor [...] said: 'Well my advice to you is to find somebody of like mind and settle down with him and stop bothering'. When he said this there was an elation'.[124]

The 1950s

In 1948, the Mass Observation Survey reported 'the isolationist manner in which homosexual groups appear to function'. A draft appendix described a 'homosexual group' on a trip to Brighton. The men had a 'distinctive outlook' and were not at all keen on the company of non-homosexuals except for neuters, borderline cases and possible converts'.[125] It also found that 60 percent of those sampled were antipathetic to homosexuality (it was 'absolutely detestable', said one respondent; 'I shouldn't think they're human', said another). The percentage figure may not seem especially high except when we consider that a further 30 percent did not understand what homosexuality was ('it never occurred to me', said one). Of those who were aware of homosexuality, the disdain was more or less absolute; for the remainder, the burgeoning debate, analysis and press coverage of the 1950s would soon educate them about this type of person. A number of sociological studies provided 'authoritative' accounts, including J. T. Rees's *They Stand Apart: A Critical Survey of Homosexuality* (1955) and Michael Schofield's more sympathetic works – *Society and the Homosexual* (1952), *A Minority: a report on the life of the male homosexual in Great Britain* (1960) (both published under the pseudonym Gordon Westwood) and *Sociological Aspects of Homosexuality* (1965), which he published under his own name. Homosexuals were characterized as isolationist and outside the social body in much of this work. Alternatively, they were what the *Practitioner* magazine of 1954 described as a 'cancer' 'eating into the very vitals of the nation'.[126] In either case, queers were undermining postwar social reconstruction, not least by turning their back on family life (a judgment which the experience of East End families in this period rather gives the lie to). The Archbishop of Canterbury gave a sermon in which he called on Britons to reject 'wartime morality' and return to living 'Christian lives'.[127] In the House of Lords, Earl Winterton observed that 'few things lower the moral fibre and injure the physique of the nation more than tolerated and widespread homosexualism'.[128] The dangers of homosexualism were apparently underscored in 1951 when British spies Guy Burgess and Donald MacLean defected to the USSR having betrayed American secrets. The *Sunday Pictorial* exposed 'the squalid truth' that they were 'sex perverts' and asserted that 'homosexuals – men who indulge in unnatural love for another – are known to be bad security risks. They are easily won over as traitors'.[129] The *Pictorial* – tellingly defining 'homosexual' for a readership it assumed might be uncertain of the term – returned here to the enduring notion of queer treachery.

In 1952, the same paper warned parents of the dangers of 'evil [homosexual] men' who 'infest London and the social centers about many provincial cities'.[130] A number of cases over the coming years seemed to confirm observation. A 'vicious clique' of twenty-eight tracked by police through a single address book appeared before a judge in Birmingham in August 1954. What a judge described as 'a festering sore in the county of Surrey' – fifteen men in Dorking – was exposed after a policeman followed up names and numbers left 'on a wall in a public place'.[131] At Chippenham in Wiltshire in 1956, 'a web of vice' involving nineteen men who had sometimes 'dressed as women' and 'indulged flagrantly in certain practices' at parties were brought to justice.[132] A judge told eleven men from Evesham that they had 'brought dishonour on the neighborhood'.[133]

There were also some high-profile prosecutions. The actor Sir John Gielgud was prosecuted for cottaging in Chelsea in 1953, and the author Rupert Crofft-Cooke and his companion Joseph Alexander were imprisoned in the same year on the disputed evidence of two sailors. Most sensational of all was the prosecution in 1954 of the aristocrat Edward Douglas Scot Montagu, his cousin Michael Pitt Rivers and the journalist Peter Wildeblood. The case revolved around events at Lord Montagu's country estate at Beaulieu, Hampshire. Lord Montagu and film director Kenneth Hume were tried and acquitted of 'committing an unnatural offence' with two boy scouts in a beach hut on the estate. The jury was, however, undecided on a further charge of indecent assault against the boys, and a re-trial was ordered. In the interim, Wildeblood, Pitt Rivers and Lord Montagu were charged with sodomy, attempted sodomy and gross indecency with RAF men Edward McNally and John Reynolds. Pitt Rivers and Wildeblood were further accused of having had sex with each other. The case rested on the selective use of McNally and Reynolds' evidence. Only three of the men they mentioned were ever charged, suggesting that the police were particularly keen to follow through a prosecution on the most high-profile figure. It is likely that they were pressured into identifying the men in return for immunity in their own cases. Montagu, Pitt Rivers and Wildeblood were found guilty and imprisoned – Montagu for 12 months, Pitt Rivers and Wildeblood for 18 months.

In murder and assault cases, meanwhile, defence counsels frequently highlighted the provocation and insult of a homosexual approach. A twenty-two-year-old Norwich sailor was acquitted after the Judge told the jury they should be in no doubt that the forty-four-year-old murdered man was a 'pervert'.[134] A month later, an actor who was hit over the head with some gas piping in a London hotel room was described as a 'loathsome specimen of humanity'.[135] The perpetrator was acquitted. Cases in Rotherham and Manchester in 1950 and 1951 respectively saw murder charges reduced to manslaughter because of 'extreme provocation'.[136] Roles were recast in these courtrooms and press reports: the victim had got his just desserts. Such cases also highlight the dangers that could go with queer sex. As Houlbrook points out, 'the lines between emotional friendship, casual fuck, and predatory assault were never clear' during this period.[137] Queer men were vulnerable to blackmail, theft and violence and yet, as we see here, were unlikely to get much sympathy.

Newspapers became less reticent and euphemistic in the 1950s, partly, it has been suggested, in response to competition from television. We thus get these more sensational depictions of the predatory homosexual and his insidious networks of vice, and also the idea of a valiant police force and judiciary doing their best to combat the threat. Arrests did indeed go up. Court cases involving sodomy, gross indecency and indecent assault had risen – from 719 in 1938 in England and Wales to 2,504 in 1955.[138] This figure for one year compares with the total of 8,921 cases for the whole of the nineteenth century (see Chapter 4).

Whilst this might be good news from the point of view of the moralist, to queer men it began to suggest a witch-hunt – and it is certainly true that the new head of the metropolitan police (Sir John Nott-Bower), the Home Secretary (Sir David Maxwell Fyfe) and the Director of Public Prosecutions (Sir Theobald Mathew) had little sympathy for the homosexual. A witch-hunt, however, implies that these high-level figures were orchestrating a coordinating crackdown along the lines of Joe McCarthy's contemporaneous campaigns in the USA. Historians Matt Houlbrook and Patrick Higgins have shown convincingly that this was not the case in Britain. The impetus for action instead appears to have come from lower down the police ranks and was uneven and inconsistent. Whilst some provincial police forces pursued mass arrests, for example, this was not an approach favoured by the metropolitan police in London who focused on suspect bars and toilets. Moreover, the increase in arrests and prosecutions in the capital in the 1950s was down to the increased vigour of two or three specific police districts rather than being part of a coordinated clampdown.[139]

Witch-hunt or no witch-hunt, the level of prosecutions and the articles about 'evil men' and 'sex perverts' made the first half of the 1950s a period of real anxiety for many men. Cases like that of Wildeblood are mentioned almost universally by men interviewed about the 1950s and as a sensational reminder of the risks they were taking and the caution they needed to exercise. Barry bought the *News of the World* to keep abreast of court cases. 'I was aware of the legal danger, very much so'.[140] He marks time passing with these major scandals: 'that was the period of the Montagu scandal and Gielgud', he would note.[141] Bernard Dobson recalls discussing these cases 'a great deal' with friends, and John Alcock remembers being 'very frightened'. 'I thought that every policeman coming up to me was going to arrest me [...] the temperature at the time was quite unpleasant. We thought we were all going to be arrested and there was going to be a big swoop. The newspapers were full of it. I got so frightened that I burnt all my love letters from Hughie'.[142] James remembers having to be similarly cautious with photographs: 'the police could take your family album, your photograph album and ask: 'who is this? Who is that? What is going on here?' It was too risky'.[143] 'I never kept the names and addresses of my Brighton friends written down', Dennis observed, 'it was in my head but I never wrote it down on anything and I would certainly never dream of keeping a diary because I know loads and loads and loads of queans who were arrested and then they'd go through their rooms and they'd find a diary and they'd go through the names in that and it could snowball'.[144]

The prosecutions were personally devastating. Some committed suicide; others lost their jobs and found personal relationships in tatters. Confidences were betrayed as police put pressure on men to reveal the names of their friends. One of Hugh David's interviewees recalled of a 1950s sting:

> I lived in the West country in a very conservative seaside town. [...] and one particular member of our gay community was caught cottaging by the police. They threatened him with ten years in prison if he didn't tell them the names of all the gay men who lived in the area. So he went round in a police car to everywhere we worked or lived and a dozen of us ended up at the quarter sessions of the Exeter Assizes. [...] When it came to sentencing it was rather frightening for myself and another young chap. They were sending people down – to prison – for four to six years. We were just shaking in out shoes wondering what was going to happen. Fortunately we were put on probation.[145]

The Church of England focused on such misery and anxiety in their investigation into 'the problem of homosexuality'. The resulting report of 1954 advocated the legalization of sex between consenting men and an equal age of consent. As it stood the law led to blackmail and suicide, it argued.[146] This was a conclusion underscored by the contemporaneous case of Gilbert Nixon, a former Territorial Lieutenant Colonel, who killed himself with cyanide in his cell minutes after being sent down for a year at Somerset Assizes court for homosexual offences.[147]

There was dismay in some quarters at cases like Nixon's and also at the invasions of privacy and heavy sentencing in others.[148] The *Hampstead and Highgate Express* refused to cover cases of homosexual sex in the 1950s 'because of the misery that was caused'.[149] Theatre goers brought the West End performance of W. C. Hunter's *A Day By the Sea* to a halt with a standing ovation for Gielgud when he made his first entrance after his prosecution; his career continued to go from strength to strength. Wildeblood recalls the derision of some but also the support he received during his trial. He and Croft-Cooke gave vivid accounts of their treatment in *Against the Law* (1955) and *A Verdict on You All* (both 1955) and clearly envisaged an interested and possibly sympathetic readership. Fred Dyson, a Yorkshire miner convicted of cottaging at this time, kept his job and was supported by his colleagues. One told him: 'if thou can admit to being a poof all thou life, thou art a better man than us'.[150] Public opinion was not slavishly following the line about 'evil men' pedalled by the *Sunday Pictorial* and other papers.

Wolfenden and reform

There had never been so much discussion, coverage and analysis – both critical and supportive – and it was in this context that the *Sunday Times* called for an enquiry:

> the law [...] is not in accord with a large mass of public opinion [...] The case for a reform of the law as to acts committed in private between two adults is very strong [...] the case for an authoritative inquiry into it is overwhelming.[151]

In fact, a proposal for a Royal Commission to look at homosexuality and prostitution had already been made to Cabinet by Home Secretary Sir David Maxwell Fyfe. Prime Minister Winston Churchill and other ministers were opposed, partly because they felt any legal reform arising from such a commission would lose Tory votes. As a compromise, Fyffe agreed to down-grade the level of the investigation from Royal Commission to Departmental Committee, and in September the committee met for the first time under the chairmanship of John Wolfenden, Vice Chancellor of Reading University. The fifteen-strong body was made up of twelve men and three women, including lawyers, doctors, high court judges, MPs and the chairwoman of the Scottish Association of Girl Guide Clubs. It met sixty-two times over three years to review the law and heard evidence from 200 organizations and individuals, including the armed forces and the police.[152] Much of this evidence revolved around the familiar ideas about corruption, contagion, treachery and misery. It heard evidence from only three professed homosexuals – all educated and middle class. The committee nevertheless assumed that they were adequately representative of Britain's diverse queer population. Whilst eye consultant Patrick Trevor Roper and Cambridge University fellow Carl Winter gave relatively straightforward testimony about homosexual 'types' and communities, Peter Wildeblood projected a self-consciously respectable image and berated the promiscuous camp queen in his evidence, as in his book.

The committee reported in 1957 and produced a report with recommendations based on the premise that it should be the job of the law to preserve public order and protect the weak from exploitation. It should not, it argued, seek to regulate individual morality. On this basis, it suggested the tightening of provisions against street prostitutes and those who used them but advocated the relaxation of the laws on homosexual offences. It recommended that consensual homosexual sex between adults over 21 should be decriminalized; that buggery should be reclassified from a felony to a misdemeanor (reducing the potential length of sentences); and that offences which were more than 12 months old should not be prosecuted, except in the case of indecent assault. It also called for further research into the causes and treatment of homosexuality and suggested that oestrogen treatment be made available to all prisoners who wanted access to it.

The press response to the Wolfenden report was mixed. Whilst the *Mail* feared legalization would 'certainly encourage an increase in perversion' and the *Express* wanted 'family life' to continue to be protected from 'these evils', the *Times, Mirror, Guardian* and *Telegraph* were broadly sympathetic.[153] Even an interim report of the Public Morality Council suggested that the 'invert' should not be prosecuted so long as his sexual activities were not anti-social (though a letter of 1959 indicates sharp division within the council on the issue).[154]

The reform agenda was pressed in new films and writing which often focused on the ways in which the law led to misery and isolation. Two films on Wilde appeared in 1960, and a year later Dirk Bogarte starred in *Victim*, a tragic tale of blackmail and suicide. Rodney Garland's *A Heart in Exile* (1952) and Mary Renault's *The Charioteer* (1953) explored similar themes. There was an attempt in these novels and films to portray a respectable and discreet homosexual who was at one remove from a debauched and destructive underworld fraught with petty jealousies. Dirk Bogarde's character in *Victim* needs an intermediary to liaise with the denizens of the Salisbury in London's St Martin's Lane, whilst in the *Charioteer* Laurie is out of place at a queer party which is marred by an attempted suicide.

By the late-1950s, the desire to have sex with another man was more universally seen to be the result of an ingrained condition. Before and during the World War II, there had been different levels of knowledge and understandings such that male–male sex was not automatically linked to homosexual identities either by the men involved or by the society more broadly. Guardsmen prostitutes and rough trade had had sex with men and still considered themselves 'normal'. Now more polarized ideas about sexual identity had taken hold, and 'homosexual' was a commonly applied term for all men who had sex with other men. Who you desired and had sex with defined who you were. Identity politics in relation to homosexuality had been in play since at least the 1890s, but by the late 1950s, it seemed it was virtually the only way to think about love and sex between men and hence also the only way to structure a campaign for their legal rights.

The Homosexual Law Reform Society (HLRS) emerged in 1958 when it became clear that the conservative governments of Anthony Eden and Harold MacMillan had no intention of acting on Wolfenden's recommendations on homosexuality, despite the fact that his proposals on prostitution were being written into the Street Offences bill, which became law in 1959. HLRS was initiated by the English Literature lecturer A. E. Dyson and the Rev. Andrew Hallidie Smith who sent a letter to the *Times* calling for reform. It was signed by thirty-three religious leaders, politicians, philosophers, writers and artists. Soon after a committee was formed to orchestrate a campaign and at the organization's first public rally in Caxton Hall, London, in 1960, 1,000 people heard calls for the immediate implementation of Wolfenden's recommendations.

The HLRS was narrowly focused on legal reform and addressed public and political opinion rather than the homosexual 'community'. It was not overtly homosexual in its membership and nor was it conceived as a support group. It strove to retain a respectable and even conservative edge as a means of persuading government and a wider audience of the benefits of change. 'The society', observes Jeffrey Weeks, 'was torn between its genuine desire to improve the lot of homosexuals, and its acute – perhaps over acute – assessment of what public opinion would take. Inevitably, it veered in the direction of caution'.[155] The society's newsletter (*Spectrum*), regular talks and the tireless campaigning of men like Anthony Grey (the society's secretary from 1962 to 1970) nevertheless opened up debate and prepared the ground for the partial legalization of homosexual acts in 1967.

The North-West Homosexual Reform Committee, founded in 1964 by labour councillor Allan Horsfall from a miner's cottage in Atherton, Lancashire, had a social as well as a reform agenda. In 1969, the group became the Committee (and from 1971 the Campaign) for Homosexual Equality and was largely composed of homosexual men seeking not only political reform but an alternative social network. Lord Arran and Leo Abse, the key sponsors of reform in parliament, were dismayed by Horsfall's initiative.[156] Such a network would undermine their argument, which centred on the rights of *individual* homosexual men and their integration into society.

Despite these moves and an apparent softening of public opinion – around 40 percent now favoured reform – the police continued to employ chain arrest techniques, secret surveillance and *agents provocateurs* throughout the 1960s. Raids took place on bars in London and Manchester in the early part of the decade, and there was perhaps something of a rearguard action: sentencing twenty-three men in Nottingham in 1961, the Judge observed that the case gave the lie to reformers' claims that 'this sort of thing is not contagious'.[157] Resistance to homosexual law reform could be observed elsewhere too. The MP H. Montgommery Hyde, who spoke out in favour of reform in the house of commons in 1959, was deselected by his local conservative party on the basis that he 'condoned unnatural vice'. Even some proponents of reform sent out decidedly mixed messages. Lord Brabazan of Tara, calling for reform in the House of Lords, said: 'these people are self-eliminating. They do not breed. They do very little harm if left to themselves. [...] Because we do not understand the mysteries of sex; because we do not understand the terrible handicap of the invert, it should not be in our traditions to beat our breast and say 'we are holier than thou' and prosecute'.[158] The Rev. Timothy Beaumont, future president of the Albany Trust (the charitable and counselling wing of the HLRS), reported that 'God has called homosexuals among others to chastity and to use their energies in other channels'.[159] Many reformers were ironically using the same language of illness, sin and despair as those opposing legal change.

The cultural climate was beginning to shift though. The swinging sixties did not constitute the wholesale social and cultural revolution that has sometimes been supposed, but there was nevertheless a change in attitudes which came with economic expansion and affluence, and a growing frustration with puritanical moral codes which ran counter to civil rights notions of individual liberty filtering through from the USA. Harold Wilson's labour government of 1964 embarked on a series of social reforms on abortion, divorce and the death penalty. TV, radio and the theatre became more irreverent, and Joe Orton's plays famously toyed with supposedly fixed moral codes and sexual categories, as well as satirizing police corruption and the workings of the psychiatric and medical professions.[160] In *Round the Horne*, Kenneth Williams and Hugh Paddick performed the palari-speaking duo Julian and Sandy. The show traded in stereotypes, but the couple were enduring, acerbic and self-confident. TV documentaries in 1965 and 1967 included homosexual men speaking on their own behalf. The photographer Cecil Beaton wrote in his diary in 1967: 'the [recent] tolerance towards the subject has made a nonsense of many of the prejudices from which I myself suffered acutely as a young man'.[161]

This change in climate – and government – put the Wolfenden recommendations back on the political agenda. Whilst 44 percent still opposed reform in 1966, 39 percent were in favour, making it less of a potential vote loser. The Director of Public Prosecutions ruled in 1964 that all cases be referred to him before prosecutions were pursued. A year later, there was an attempt to get a bill through parliament decriminalizing homosexual acts along the lines Wolfenden suggested. It foundered because of the election of 1966, but immediately thereafter Lord Arran reintroduced the bill to the Lords and Leo Abse guided it through the Commons, where it passed 244 votes to 100 on its first reading. The Sexual Offences Act became law on 27 July 1967, decriminalizing sex between two consenting adults over the age of twenty-one in private. The act did not apply to Scotland, Northern Ireland or the Channel Islands, and homosexual sex also remained illegal in the merchant navy and armed forces. The distinction between public and private was key: for the purposes of the law 'public' was anywhere where a third party was likely to be present; and it remained illegal for more than two men to have sex together. Lord Arran underscored the conservative import of the act when he asked homosexual men 'to show their thanks by comporting themselves quietly and with dignity'.[162] Anthony Grey, who had worked so hard for law reform, was 'nearly sick'.

For many, the legislation was a clear advance: 'when the law changed', recalls George, 'I had been living with Steve for quite some years and it was a great sense of relief, we were now not against the law. That made a great deal of difference'.[163] The response was generally fairly muted, however. It gets a cursory mention in Joe Orton's diaries, and Kenneth Williams felt it would make no difference. The photographer Cecil Beaton was incredulous: 'this should be a time of great celebration'. It was, he felt, 'one of the most important milestones in English law'.[164]

The lack of euphoria is perhaps partly explained by the fact that the 1967 Sexual Offences Act did little for those like Orton who did not experience sex and love with another men only in terms of coupledom and domesticity.[165] These 'other' men remained beyond the law because of where they were picking up sexual partners, where they were having sex and how they were conducting themselves in public. When Fred

Dyson heard the news he kissed his friend and declared 'you can all look, it's legal now'; ironically he was laying himself open to arrest.[166]

The previous half century had seen the expansion of a visible queer scene, and then, postwar, its partial recession. The 'homosexual problem' had become a key area of discussion in the 1950s, and many queers felt more embattled and fearful than before, especially after experiencing the liberalism of the war years. Campaigns for law reform took a conservative route in their lobbying and campaigning work and touted an image of the homosexual which revolved around middle-class respectability, discretion and conformity.[167] Though the result was welcome, it was simply not substantial enough. Many men refused to 'comport themselves quietly' after 1967, and, as we will in the next chapter, they demanded both rights and respect for their sexual and subcultural difference. In the 1970s, there was anything but a smooth transition of the homosexual into 'normal' society.

Chapter 6

From Gay Reform to Gaydar, 1967–2006

Matt Cook

In September 1971, the Christian Festival of Light planned a rally to re-awaken Britain's sense of morality and to protest at moral pollution and obscenity on television. The pop star Cliff Richard and campaigner Mary Whitehouse were among the luminaries. Whilst the organizers had anticipated opposition, no one in the festival's London offices suspected that one of their straight-laced volunteers was in fact an infiltrator from the Gay Liberation Front (the GLF). With her help, 'brothers' and 'sisters' in the Front sent out misleading parking information and forged tickets for the rally in London's Westminster Hall. 'Operation Rupert' had swung into action, and small groups of conservatively dressed lesbians and gay men took their seats on the festival floor. Each group had planned its own special demonstration, cued into action by the end of the previous one. White mice scurried across the floor, a group of nuns performed the can-can and a banner was unfurled from the balcony proclaiming 'Cliff for Queen'. Michael James, dressed in 'a lovely coffee lace dress', eye shadow and wig, declared he had been saved to shouts of Hallelujah from the crowd.[1] When a woman told 'Bishop' Tony Salvis that this was a very sinful world, he replied: 'don't worry sister, keep right on sinning'.[2] GLFers set out to engage delegates in conversation on the issues, and Nettie Pollard felt that it worked: 'we were real people prepared to talk about it. […] I genuinely think it did have an effect and they did think twice'.[3,4] Some were not so receptive, however: the woman who released the mice was beaten with a handbag whilst being told repeatedly that Jesus loved her.[5]

Operation Rupert was part of a fresh visibility and radicalism on the part of some gay men who were unhappy with the conformist imperative of the 1967 act and the implicit dismissal of what had become a distinctive way of life for many. This chapter charts this assertive gay pride and the reservations many others had about it. It looks at the intersection of homosexuality and politics, at the impact of AIDS, at the changing scene and at the ways in which all this brought about further shifts in understandings of sexual identity and community. The conventional story of progressive liberation, this chapter suggests, is a problematic one, and the acceptance of sexual difference in British society continued to be highly contingent.

Gay liberation

The Festival of Light was not GLF's first 'zap'; that had taken place on Highbury Fields, north London, in November 1970 following a cottaging arrest. It was, though, one of the most theatrical demos and gave the GLF a platform from which to present some of its demands. It was also indicative of a new defiant mood amongst some gay men. Gay liberation politics in the States, especially following the Stonewall riots in New York in July 1969, inspired student activists Aubrey Walker and Bob Mellors to hold a meeting at the London School of Economic in October 1970. The Front went on to meet on a weekly basis, developing a philosophy evincing pride and touting sexual and subcultural difference as positive and life enhancing. Like Edward Carpenter and George Ives before them, GLFers turned to inner liberation as a means of challenging misogyny and sexism and achieving wider social change. They criticized gay male narcissism, lesbian butch/femme role playing, the ingrained racism and sexism of polari and the presumption that monogamy was necessarily the best basis for sexual and emotional relationships. The GLF manifesto listed a number of immediate demands covering equality under the law, the end to workplace discrimination, the reform of sex education in schools and the right for gay people to 'be free to hold hands and kiss in public'. From the outset, there was controversy about what was being sought: on the one hand there was the rights agenda and the demand for equality, on the other was a vision of transformed interpersonal relations and a revolutionized society. This tension about what liberation could be braced debate in gay and lesbian politics for the next thirty years.

Subgroups formed to pursue specific issues and activities. The Media Workshop coordinated the production of *Come Together*, the GLF paper; the Action Group orchestrated Gay Days in London Parks and various other events; the Anti Psychiatry Group crucially took on homophobic rhetoric in psychiatry and the idea that homosexuality was a mental illness (homosexuality was removed from the register of psychiatric illnesses in the UK in 1973); the Christmas Party Group organized parties for children in Notting Hill.

The very existence of the GLF and its chaotic general and group meetings were personally revelatory. Many of those involved remember the electrifying effect of gathering with so many others who were ready to speak openly and radically about sex and sexuality. John Fraser went from 'being nervous and shy and diffident and worried about my sexuality to embracing it totally' as a result of GLF gatherings.[6] Previous chapters have shown that men had been defiant in the past, but now there was a greater sense of collective support behind angry individuals.

A number of communes started through the GLF in which men and women experimented with shared money, wardrobes, food, drugs and beds. At the commune in Notting Hill, twelve mattresses were pushed together for sleeping and sex; money was pooled in a teapot. 'I loved the commune', remembers regular visitor Andrew Lumsden:

it was like stepping off the planet [...] You went into a no daylight zone where there were places to sleep strewn all over the floor [...] endless sounds always on, you were always offered dope or acid. The welcome was lovely. It was unstructured to a degree that was terrifying if you had led any kind of structured life and I think there were people who came and went very quickly, in about ten minutes.[7]

The Notting Hill Group was characterized by its radical drag – a deliberate attempt to sabotage ideas of conventional masculinity without attempting to 'pass' as female. Alaric Sumner found the insistence some placed on such 'revolutionary codes of behaviour' stressful – but also remembers it prompting 'perfectly sensible conversations' with locals. This was perhaps not surprising, given that Notting Hill and nearby Earls Court had developed as relatively gay friendly neighbourhoods in the 1950s and were seen to be two of the more accommodating areas of the city. Bricks and abuse were meanwhile regularly directed at the Brixton commune, especially by local school children. The men responded by distributing a leaflet at the school announcing: 'we are gay men living in Athlone Road. We do, and dress, and have sex and are what we want to be, which is nice for us and doesn't affect you'. In typical style, it continued: 'we believe in talking, in friendship, in understanding each other and we'll talk anywhere. [...] But we won't talk to those who attack us. We will attack back and there are a large number of us. We are very strong because we love each other'.[8]

The GLF was behind the first Gay Pride of July 1972, which saw 1,000 people march from Trafalgar Square to Hyde Park for a picnic and party. The event was a success, but by this point the Front in London had already begun to falter. Many women had walked out in the previous year because men's issues tended to get most attention and action despite the avowed commitment to combating sexism. The male 'radfems', like those in Notting Hill commune, were also in conflict with 'straighter' GLF men who were focussing on a rights rather than lifestyle agenda. Fraser remembers 'ordinary people' attending the meetings becoming 'completely alienated by this in-fighting'. In addition, a special branch investigation and subsequent trial of GLFers over supposed links to the left-wing revolutionary group the Angry Brigade left many feeling embattled and paranoid about phone tapping and surveillance. Elizabeth Wilson recalls that 'it somehow spoilt the fun [of GLF] and everything became grimmer after that'.[9] Julian Howes remembers that at the Bethnal Rouge commune in East London, 'everybody's address book was kept in a communal plastic bag because there was this idea that we were going to be raided [...] We would leave the dope lying around the kitchen but not the address books, which were kept by the kitchen window [...] so that you could throw [them] away if you had to'.[10]

By the end of 1972, the London GLF had disbanded with considerable bitterness. The organization had been short lived and had achieved virtually none of its immediate aims on legal and social reform; another three decades of campaigning by other groups were needed before they even got close. But what the GLF established and set in process was hugely significant: Lesbian and Gay Pride, Lesbian and Gay Switchboard, the support service Icebreakers and the theatre groups Gay Sweatshop and the Brixton Fairies, all had their roots at least partly in the GLF. *Gay News* (1974) emerged from the ashes of the organization in a joint initiative by former GLFers and the Campaign for Homosexual Equality. Groups like the Gay Christian Movement (from 1976), Gay Teenage Group (founded in 1979), Gay Black Group (from 1981), the Long Yang Club (from 1983) and the disabled lesbian and gay organization REGARD (1989), all hark back to the subgroups of the GLF era. These provided a forum for sharing particular experiences of being gay and raised the profile of groups of men who could feel marginalized within the 'scene'. Physical disability, for example, was often seen to be incompatible with an active sexuality, especially in a subculture which fetishized bodily 'perfection'. REGARD was important in challenging such assumptions and in providing support for disabled gay men and lesbians.

The GLF also provided a model for other gay rights groups. The Gay Activists Alliance (GAA), for example, emerged in 1978 'to co-ordinate at a national level the fight against the increasing attacks being made on homosexuality and homosexuals'. The GAA was behind the picketing of W. H. Smith for refusing to stock *Gay News;* in London it monitored police harassment; in Manchester it campaigned against the homophobic police chief James Anderton; and in Scotland, which had been exempt from the 1967 legislation, it focused on legal change. It took part too in the anti-fascist league in the wake of National Front attacks on gay venues in the mid-1970s.[11]

Experiments in communal living also endured. Ian Townsen moved from Lancaster into a gay squat in Railton Road, Brixton, in 1974. He remembers the ways in which the squatters attempted to up-end the idea of a separatist and ghettoized gay community by taking part in local action against police racism, for example. The squats later became part of the Brixton Housing Co-op and were a focus of black gay and lesbian art and political organising.

More than the specific zaps, campaigns and experiments in communal living, the GLF and later the GAA demonstrated the scope to 'come out' to more than a small circle and to pursue a distinctive lifestyle unapologetically. Bernard Dobson observed: 'It was being able to be more open, and also the support – not just from one or two people but from lots of people. I felt a kind of strength I had never felt before'.[12] In South Wales, Fred went to GLF events after he was widowed at eighty. 'When I married I never thought I'd meet gay people, I was hoping and praying that one day I would be able to mix in with gay people. Oh yes, and it's been one of the happier times of my life since'.[13] The GLF, claims former activist Jeffrey Weeks, 'transformed the social and sexual and relationship possibilities for many men' – and it did this both for those directly involved and for those who watched from the sidelines.[14]

The GLF certainly made the biggest splash in the early 1970s, but by the time it folded the Campaign for Homosexual Equality (CHE) was larger and was set to be much longer lasting. As the last chapter noted, CHE was formed in 1969 out of the North-Western Committee for Homosexual Reform, which had been the more socially active wing of the national committee in the run up to legal change in 1967. It tellingly changed from 'Committee' to 'Campaign' in 1971 and was more tightly structured than the GLF: it held annual conferences, passed resolutions in the manner of Trade Unions and lobbied rather than zapped political parties, churches and other organizations. By 1972, it had developed sixty local groups across the country and had a membership of 2,800, rising ultimately to double that. It was broader based in terms of the political colours of its membership and was more 'respectable'. There were, unsurprisingly, tensions between the two organizations. After taunts from GLFers, Hugh Corbett, a CHE member, derided 'the vulgarity of frenetic faggots frolicking through the streets' in CHE magazine *Lunch*.[15] After the demise of the GLF, however, CHE became more feisty – at least in it rhetoric.[16]

CHE's 'respectability' perhaps allowed other bodies to feel they could do business with it. At the 1979 conference in Brighton, the Mayor made the opening address to delegates, amongst them representatives from various churches, the Family Welfare Association, NACRO (the organization for ex-offenders) and the National Council for Civil Liberties. The problem, however, was that CHE continued to focus on the law as it related to gay men, preventing it from becoming an embracing organization for gay men and lesbians. There was little action on the discrimination faced by lesbians or any real consideration of sexism, and this scant attention was reflected in the membership and attendance at conferences: in 1976 at Southampton fewer than 50 of the 700 delegates were women.[17] The political separatism of gay men from lesbians was something that began to shift only with the campaign against Clause 28 in the late 1980s, and many women continued to feel that gay men could be ignorant, sexist and misogynist in their conduct and politics. Moreover, despite the CHE's growing profile, it had no clear political successes in the 1970s. Its chief tangible achievements during this time were pastoral and social. It set up the counselling service Friend, which began taking calls in 1971 and gained a permanent and secure London base on the back of funding from Islington Council and the Home Office in 1975. The social groups were also hugely successful, especially in areas where there had previously been only limited opportunities for gay men to meet each other. In Sheffield and Rotherham, the local CHE was behind the city hall and assembly room discos, fighting hard for the right to use Rotherham council premises and skilfully enlisting the support of the local press, vicar and MP.[18] In Kent, Sam found the CHE group combating his feelings of loneliness. In an interview at the time, he said he 'enjoyed life much more [...] they're always ringing me up and you're never alone, as you were before'.[19] Trevor Thomas found speaking out at the Sheffield CHE conference life changing. 'I was out, and could not have been more obviously out [...] I've summed it up in the phrase that three days in Sheffield did more for me than three years on valium'.[20]

The Scottish Minorities Group was, like the GLF, inspired by American gay liberation politics, but its starting point in terms of its campaign was different: the 1967 reform did not apply north of the border, and gay men were consequently more comprehensively criminalized. Established in 1969, it had fewer members than organizations in England – beginning with five and growing to 200 by 1972. It nevertheless raised the profile of Scottish gay men and arguably helped to stem the migratory flow south. Ian Dunn, a key mover in SMG, came out on Scottish television in 1971, and three years later, the group opened a campaigning and social base in Edinburgh's Broughton Street. In the same year, the city hosted the First International Gay Rights Congress, drawing attention directly to the anachronistic legal status of men in Scotland.

Northern Irish men were in a similar position legally and a number of organizations of the early 1970s – the counselling Elmwood Association, the Gay Liberation Society, the Union for Sexual Freedom and the Irish Gay Rights Association – all campaigned for change in the face of Rev. Ian Paisley's vituperative 'Save Ulster from Sodomy' campaign. The 1967 Sexual Offences Act was extended to Northern Ireland in 1982 after a case that went before the European Courts. In Scotland, reform had taken place two years earlier.

It is too simplistic to put this new activism and radicalism down to the 1967 Sexual Offences Act and the opportunities a new legal climate supposedly opened up. The inequality enshrined in the act in terms of the unequal age of consent and provisions on privacy certainly fired many gay men to make further demands, but the fresh attitude and pride espoused by gay men also had its roots in the changing cultural and political landscape. The civil rights movement in the USA in the 1960s had put the onus on individual freedoms as well as the rights of particular groups. Women's Liberation on both sides of the Atlantic marshalled related issues of equality and sexual, cultural and social independence. The student protests at the London School of Economics in 1967 and student riots in Paris in 1968 suggested that groups outside the political mainstream did have the power and the ability to express their particular concerns. The summer of love and the so-called sexual revolution meanwhile mobilized debate around issues of sexual pleasure and monogamy.

After World War II, homosexuality had come to be seen as a social problem and personal tragedy, and not as integral to any discourse of rights or a broader left-wing political agenda. Though some of his Oxbridge generation had made such links, the MP Tom Driberg saw his ' 'deviant' sex, his Catholicism, and his left-wing politics' as 'mutually irreconcilable'.[21] Stephen similarly saw his homosexuality as 'quite separate' from his politics and pacifism in the war years.[22] A long-standing thread of radical thinking had been that homosexuality was associated with a dissipated artistic and higher class elite, and Alan Horsfall suggests that this is partly why the Labour party was reticent about taking on gay rights: they feared alienating the working-class vote. Indeed in the 1970s, it was prominent Tories – amongst them Margaret Thatcher, Keith Joseph and Enoch Powell – who supported a relaxation of the law on homosexuality on the basis of their libertarian politics. By the later 1970s, this was beginning to shift, however. The GLF philosophy was informed by Marxism and was aligned with anti-racist, anti-apartheid, feminist and union organizations and campaigns. The GLF marched with the Trades Union Council (TUC) against Ted Heath in 1971, for example. This kind of cross-over support continued in the 1980s and 1990s. Most famously, a gay support group for the striking miners raised considerable funds for a community in the Dullais Valley in South Wales. After the 'Pits and Perverts' fund raiser (named in response to a *Sun* newspaper dig at the supposedly unlikely alliance), they brought the community a mini bus emblazoned with a pink triangle and the slogan 'Lesbians and Gays Support the Miners'. In return, miners and their families led the Gay Pride march in 1985, the biggest yet with over 15,000 participants. In the same year, the TUC passed resolutions on gay and lesbian rights in the workplace.

The new rights agenda and this overt politicization in the 1970s and 1980s confronted gay men with a different way of thinking about sex, lifestyle and their position within society – and many did not welcome it. Drinkers at the Coleherne pelted passing pride goers with bottles in 1972, and there were attempts to bar GLFers from some gay pubs.[23] The radicals seemed to make demands on all gay men, and many felt they were unrepresentative. Kevin Birch saw them as having fewer responsibilities than others; they appeared independent of restrictions. 'They were students, people new to the city, and those who had dropped out'.[24] Despite the open-door policy operated by the GLF, many felt unable to embrace a radical and visible politics for fear of family, work or community reaction, or because other responsibilities gave them too little time to dedicate to these activities. Some retained their conservative politics and were resentful of the presumption of a connection between gays and the left-wing. Others simply disliked the disruption to the status quo and the challenge to an established scene. John Fraser recalls friends who felt 'extremely threatened by this boat rocking'.[25] Even the new terminology raised heckles. Gregory, well into his 1970s by the time the GLF emerged, had long disliked what he saw as the self-advertisement of men like Quentin Crisp and disliked the label 'gay' for similar reasons. Norman also objected 'to them taking the word gay'.[26] Peter simply felt that the queer world 'had lost a bit of its charm': 'now you're gay or you're straight, you're one or the other. It's lost a certain amount of it's colour for the fact that it's no longer slightly underground'.[27]

Many black gay men saw the gay scene and gay politics as very white affairs. Philip Baker, for example, felt patronized and found 1970s gay life implicitly and explicitly racist.[28] Topher Campbell experienced the same in the 1980s and 1990s. In London, he recalls being grudgingly admitted to pubs and clubs; elsewhere in the country he 'was point blank refused entry or faced crude stereotyping'.[29] Growing up in Huddersfield in the 1980s, Ajamu felt the absence of black gay role models intensely. He related neither to prevailing gay stereotypes nor to the way black men were portrayed – 'as muggers, sexual preditors, immigrants (negative) and sports stars (positive)'. 'My saving grace', he writes, 'was black American porn which I purchased at the only sex shop. […] The problem with the porn at that time was that it fitted the hyper sexualized black male stereotype. So whilst on the one hand the pictures affirmed many of my own desires, I also found them deeply offensive'.[30]

If 'gay' was developing as a less middle-class identity than 'homo-sexual', it was implicitly as white, and many black and Asian men felt doubly excluded. The black newspaper *The Voice* was unsympathetic and highly critical of footballer Justin Fashinou when he came out in the *Sun* newspaper in 1990. The gay press meanwhile tended at least initially to sideline or ignore the growing black and Asian queer subculture that started with Lift in London in 1983 and grew to include Off da Hook, the Vox, Bootylicious and Club Kali in the 1990s and early 2000s. This felt duel marginalization and the distinctive experience that went with being black and gay made organizations like the Long Yang Club, for South East Asians, and the Gay Black Group crucial. 'When [the latter] first started', remembers founder member Zahid Dar, 'it was amazing the way people said 'yeh! I felt like that'.

> [They would] talk[] about their family and how they felt about being gay, the pressure to get married. Explaining to their parents, if they had come out to them, what 'gay' meant because such a term doesn't exist in Pakistani or Hindi [...] we all understood and that made us feel really good. I'd talked to gay groups before about being black and gay, with white people just nodding their heads and saying 'yes, yes'.[31]

Disco

The CHE, GLF and other groups changed the ways in which men socialized and related to each other, and this shift was occurring in parallel with huge changes in the commercial scene. Though UK gay clubs followed club trends in the states, they also gained impetus from an increasingly confident youth scene at home. There was a link between gay and punk venues, for example, and London's premier punk clubs – Louise's in Poland Street and Chaguerama in Covent Garden were both gay initially. At Northern Soul clubs like Wigan Casino and the Twisted Well in Manchester, it was fashion and dancing not sexual orientation that were paramount – a combination that appealed to many gay men, including Soft Cell's Mark Almond who was a regular. Bang!, the first large American-style club night, was launched by Jerry Collins in 1976. Inspired by Studio One in Los Angeles, it proved hugely popular and drew in celebrities like Rod Stewart, Rock Hudson and David Bowie. Heaven at Charing Cross (the first every nighter), Subway in Leicester Square (complete with two backrooms) and Copocobana in Earls Court (popular with a leather and clone crowd) followed. In Manchester, there was Heroes, in Newcastle Rockshots, in Liverpool the Flamingo and in Nottingham Take Two. 'Disco' was now determinedly at the heart of the gay scene and was an important symbol of liberation: 'only a few years earlier', notes Alkarim Jivani, 'gay men and lesbians had had to do with bars and dank basements'.[32]

Fashion changed too. The late 1960s were what Richard Dyer calls 'a turning point in sartorial history, the moment of men's rediscovery of the pleasures of unabashed dress and display'.[33] Colour came back and got ample outings in the new clubs and discos. Meanwhile, the leather, denim and chequered shirts worn by 'clones' at Copocobana overtly countered stereotypes of the effeminacy. Whilst uniformed and working-class men had long been figures of fantasy, in the 1970s men who were neither in the forces nor working class were adopting these styles to go clubbing and to take up a particular sexual pose. Partly rooted in British working-class culture and the long-standing fetishization of muscular youth (in Baron von Gloeden's famous Taormina photographs, for example),[34] the new style was also related to American physique magazines and pornography coming into Britain, and to growing transatlantic tourism – especially after Freddie Laker pioneered cheap flights with Skytrain in 1977.[35] Derek Ogg remembers men in Edinburgh's appropriately named Fire Island club 'wearing hard construction helmets and cut off jeans and work boots with rolled down socks and skimpy t-shirts'.[36]

These shifts in the scene opened the way in the 1980s and 1990s for clubs and bars catering for particular fetishes, like SM and uniform. *Spartacus* (launched in 1969 as the first UK magazine explicitly 'for homosexuals, about homosexuals, by homosexuals'),[37] *Jeremy* (from 1970), *Spartacus International Gay Guide* (annually from 1972) and *Gay News* (from 1974) provided information, reviews and listings, and with legions of advertising space helped to make it profitable for business people 'to service the new, expanded 'out' subculture'.[38]

A 1984 survey of gay London teenagers found that 25 percent had first had contact with 'other homosexuals' in a pub or club; 18 percent had done so through the London Gay Teenage Group and 13 percent through the London Lesbian and Gay Switchboard.[39] Both the commercial and the voluntary sector were clearly significant in providing an opening for these young men, and it is perhaps all too easy to dismiss bars and clubs as being 'only' about 'fun'. Peter Burton argues that 'it has been the commercial wing [of the gay subculture] that has brought homosexuality so far out of the closet'.[40] Certainly, it was part of the new visibility of gay life, and, as with the flamboyant protests of the GLF, it countered the 1950s image of the sad, tortured and lonely homosexual and suggested new terms for sexual engagement. The GLF had explicitly debunked monogamy and the heterosexual couple as the ideal model, and the commercialized gay scene provided new opportunities to pick up partners for casual sex and for sex on premises. Gay pornography and literature brought a new openness about sex which had hitherto been potentially dangerous and/or acutely embarrassing to discuss. There was a growing sense that sexual activities, roles and relationships could be more flexible and that it might be possible to make up new rules. Oral history evidence suggests that until the 1960s, sexual practices were often relatively limited and that there was a clearer definition of sexual roles, often relating to the gender identities discussed in the previous chapter. Buck remembers that 'in those days one did know who was Arthur and who was Martha but today, you really don't know'. Peter agreed: 'Is he butch or bitch?' they used to say. You were either feminine or masculine. If you were bitch, you buried your head in the pillow and if you were butch you were on top'.[41] There was 'a sort of orthodoxy within people's own minds' James observes: 'Variations of interest like S and M or leather were kept very hush hush'.[42] Chris, recalling his time on cruise ships, noted that sex toys, 'tit work' and fisting 'weren't even thought of' in gay sex in the immediate postwar period.[43]

The use of recreational drugs was also growing, adding to the sense for many that there was less risk and more pleasure to be had than in previous decades, at least for those young self-confident urbanites with some money to spare. Even for those who did not go clubbing or engage in the new politics, there was a greater sense of self-possession and possibility, and a shift in terms of what it meant to be gay – a term which now had as wide a currency as homosexual and also a defiant twist.

A new generation of writers and artists explored contemporary gay life and history and brought with them a diversity of images and ideas about gayness. Derek Jarman's *Sebastiane* (1976) harked back to the martyred saint and the homoeroticism that surrounded his legacy, whilst his *Jubilee* (1977) explored the links between the gay and punk countercultures. Ron Peck's *Nighthawks* (1978) used West End clubs (including Heaven) in a film about contemporary gay life, and Gay Sweatshop explored Edward Carpenter's legacy in *The Dear Love of Comrades* (1979). Later, in *Who Was That Man?* (1988), Neil Bartlett evoked queer life in London in the 1890s as a way of orientating himself in the city a century later. Jeffrey Weeks' *Coming Out* (1977) was a landmark history of homosexual politics in the nineteenth and twentieth centuries, and around the same time the French philosopher Michel Foucault's famously questioned the idea that a homosexual type of person had existed throughout history in his *History of Sexuality, volume I* (1976 in French and 1979 in English). He argued that this type was invented by the sexologists in the later nineteenth century, giving rise to the homosexual/heterosexual binary that we take to be self-evident now.

Though Foucault's thesis has been rightly criticized for being too gestural and sweeping, it has underpinned much subsequent work in the history of homosexuality which has shown – rather as this book does – that ideas and understandings of male–male sex and intimacy change over time.

High-profile musicians in the 1970s like David Bowie, Mick Jagger, Marc Bolan, Freddie Mercury and Elton John modelled a camp glamour and talked about their bisexuality; Bowie 'came out' in *Melody Maker* in 1972, only to retract in *Time* magazine in 1983 as the horror of the AIDS crisis was becoming apparent. Tom Robinson's 'Glad to Be Gay' was written for Gay Pride in 1976 and became a gay standard. If most were more equivocal than Robinson over their sexuality, 1970s rock certainly brought androgynous styling and ideas of sexual fluidity to a mass audience, opening out new possibilities. Tony Sayonas, a Liverpool teenager, recalls seeing Bowie putting his arm round another man on television: 'my heart nearly came through my chest. I thought, this is unbelievable and something snapped in me. [...] If I ever did get to meet him, which I doubt, I'd just say 'thanks very much' '.44

Reaction

Whilst the renewed visibility of gay lives and the burgeoning network of pubs, clubs and groups were hugely significant to gay men and helped to challenge antagonism towards homosexuality, British culture remained broadly hostile and grudging in its liberalism. An opinion poll for *Gay News* in 1975 found that most supported the 1967 legislation, but few thought further legal change was justified; 45 percent believed there should be curbs on gay men working in teaching and medicine, and the conception of gay men being a danger to children endured. Stereotypes were stubborn and gained regular outings on television and radio, though one of the most famous – the effeminate Mr Humphries in the department store sitcom *Are You Being Served* (1972–1983) can also be seen as an independent and self-confident, reporting riotous week-ends with 'the boys', for example.45 Many men struggled with rejection and isolation, and whilst some parents worked hard to 'come to terms' with having gay sons, many still viewed their 'choice' as tragic and/or abhorrent. The pressure to conform was intense, and the struggle many men experienced in squaring their sexual identity with the expectations of their friends, relatives, community, church or work colleagues became apparent in 'coming out' tales. Coming out became – literally – a defining moment, the point at which a sexual identity was openly claimed. Most did it gradually – telling some but not all family members, or friends but not work colleagues – but whatever the extent of revelation the very idea of being in or out of the closet reveals how central sexuality had become in terms of thinking about identity.

The new gay organizations and businesses could also have felt embattled. *Gay News* editor Denis Lemon was arrested for obstruction after taking photos of police harassment around the Colherne in Earls Court in 1978, and the newspaper was repeatedly subject to obscenity raids and prosecutions. It won a case centring on a front-page image of two men kissing in 1974 but three years later lost an action brought by veteran purity campaigner Mary Whitehouse. She accused the paper of 'blasphemous libel' for publishing James Kirkup's poem 'The Love that Dare Not Speak its Name', in which a Roman centurion has sex with Jesus of Nazareth. As editor Denis Lemon was fined £500 and given a nine-month suspended prison sentence in what was the first blasphemy case in Britain for over half a century. As Terry Sanderson argues, though, it was a Pyrrhic victory for Whitehouse: international condemnation greeted the verdict, pirate copies of the poem were distributed to a far greater audience than would otherwise have seen it and the circulation of *Gay News* itself increased significantly for the remainder of the year.[46]

The support *Gay News* received may have been heartening, but the jury had nevertheless come out in favour of Whitehouse, and some felt that such a verdict lent tacit support to other attacks on gay men. A week after the *Gay News* blasphemy case thirty-two-year-old Peter Benyon was murdered leaving the Rainbow Rooms in North London, and in 1978, Roy Phillips was killed outside a Liverpool gay bar. A CHE report covering the period 1977 to 1980 detailed dozens of violent homophobic attacks across the country, from Belfast to Windsor. In 1979, five members of Gay Sweatshop were attacked by nine men with metal bars as they left the Birmingham Repertory Theatre. One member of the company was left unconscious.[47] Men wearing gay badges, or known to be members of CHE and other gay organizations, were also vulnerable. Being visible could sometimes bring unwanted attention. When CHE held its conference in Brighton in 1979, leaflets were distributed, highlighting the risk posed by 'these perverts' 'concentrating in the town'. 'All able bodied men', the leaflet thundered, 'should be ready to drive these creatures back to the sewers where they belong'. The leaflet went on to detail conference plans and to list gay bars in the town where 'queers' might be found.[48] Five years later, a survey of gay teenagers in London found that 25 percent had experienced homophobic verbal abuse at school, whilst 16 percent had been beaten up.[49] Until the mid-1980s, there was no agenda in government, education or business for protecting, championing or – at school – nurturing gay men or teenagers. 'It might have helped', said one twenty-year-old, 'if we were told simply that not everyone's sexuality was the same'.[50]

Things began to change in this respect in the mid-1980s. Especially significant were certain local councils. The Greater London Council, under Ken Livingstone, did important early work in linking grants to equal opportunities policies and in providing support for gay and lesbian initiatives, including the London Lesbian and Gay centre in Cowcross Street (opened 1985) and the London Lesbian and Gay Switchboard housing service, which helped gay men and lesbians find safe accommodation. The council's Charter for Lesbian and Gay Rights published in the same year included 142 social policy recommendations and echoed many of the GLF's early demands. In 1986, the London Borough of Haringey sent letters to head teachers asking them to provide positive images of lesbians and gay men to students. Nottingham council funded support work aimed at elderly lesbian and gay men in 1987, and Manchester City Council put significant resources behind the lesbian and gay community, especially in the wake of police action against gay bars in the city. Under police chief James Anderton, officers had raided Napoleon's bar in Manchester's Bloom Street in 1984 and succeeded in closing it down for the night despite a Stonewall-style sit-down protest by twenty drag queens. The police action undoubtedly stiffened the resolve of the newly elected labour council which appointed two equal opportunities officers with specific responsibility for gay and lesbian issues in January 1985 with a Gay Men's Sub-committee to follow.

Just as left-wing local councils were taking up lesbian and gay issues as an integral part of public policy, political and religious groups were also seeking an angle on what was now a much more visible constituency. The Conservative party stressed the importance of personal liberty in their pamphlet on homosexuality of 1983 (*Homosexuality in Britain: A Conservative Perspective*), whilst the Socialist Workers Party's *Out, Proud and Fighting* (1988) saw 'the origins of gay oppression in the way that capitalism is organised'.[51] The Church of England explored the scope for 'the homosexual way' to be a 'Christian option' in 1980, and the Catholic Church in Britain published *Homosexuality: A Positive Catholic Perspective* five years later. As we have already seen, the TUC incorporated the rights of lesbian and gay workers into its policy framework in 1985.

These moves were a response partly to the increasing level of monitoring, complaint and campaigning on the part of gay and lesbian groups and a by now established gay press. The reports from CHE on homophobic violence in 1980 and the project on gay teenagers of 1984 were symptomatic of a new wave of research undertaken by gay pressure and support groups and some local councils. *Gay News, Capital Gay, Scots Gay* (from 1982), *Gay Times* (from 1984) and the *Pink Paper* (from 1987) in particular covered discrimination in depth and monitored media coverage of gay men closely. CHE's Gay Monitoring and Archive Project (1978) and its successor the Hall Carpenter Memorial Archive (1982) collated newspaper articles as well as other material relating to lesbian and gay life. In 1985, its research report *Are We Being Served?* highlighted silence, stereotype and hostility on television and the radio. Homophobia was increasingly challenged, and gay men and lesbians were also speaking more frequently on their own behalf in documentaries and gaining more sympathetic representation in other TV programmes. LWT was well ahead of the game with its adaptation of Quentin Crisp's *Naked Civil Servant* starring John Hurt in 1975. Ten years later, Channel 4 introduced Gordon onto its flagship soap *Brookside* and the BBC followed suit in *Eastenders* in 1986 when Colin and his boyfriend Barry moved on to Albert Square. Their first kiss led *Sun* to re-dub the show 'Eastbenders'.[52] In 1989, Channel 4 broke new ground with its lesbian and gay weekly magazine programme *Out on Tuesday*. This period also saw some high budget and widely distributed gay-themed movies: most notably Stephen Frears *My Beautiful Launderette* (1986) and Orton biopic *Prick up Your Ears* (1987) and Ismael Merchant and James Ivory's adaptation of E.M. Forster's *Maurice* (1987). Isaac Julian's *Looking for Langston* (1989) and *Young Soul Rebels* (1991) had less money behind them but importantly explored black gay experience. Also in the early 1980s, Boy George in Culture Club, Holly Johnson of Frankie Goes to Hollywood, Marc Almond in Soft Cell and Jimmy Summerville in Bronski Beat and then the Communards each joined camp with sex with love with politics and were uncompromising in asserting their right to difference in terms of style and sexual and gender ambiguity. In an echo of the Brixton commune's note to the local school kids who attacked them, Holly Johnson wrote in the cover of *Welcome to the Pleasuredome* 'I enjoy certain things, no one else has to enjoy them [...] Then again no one has the right to tell me it's immoral or selfish or wrong to do what I do'.[53] Reaching a mass audience, these artists were hugely significant in providing role models for a new generation of gay men. John recalls the significance of this music in terms of his own sexuality and style, opening up possibilities that would otherwise have seemed remote for him growing up in rural England.[54]

Modern Books in Camden High Street (the forerunner to the Zipper Store) opened in 1972, and seven years later, Gay's The Word in Marchmont Street was launched, serving not only as a book shop but also as something of a community centre. The gay publishers Millivres and Gay Men's Press (GMP) were launched in 1974 and 1979 respectively. The former specialized initially in the magazine market, whilst GMP published work by contemporary authors as well as 'classics' by Andre Gide and Edward Carpenter. Gay writing was now much more readily available and covered wide-ranging issues. In an attempt to counter what was seen as the overwhelming heterosexuality of sex education in schools, for example, Sheba released Joani Blank's *The Playbook for Kids about Sex* (1982) which incorporated discussion of homosexuality; a year later, GMP published a translation of the Dutch children's book *Jenny Lives with Martin and Eric* (1983). More academics began work on (homo)sexuality, especially in university humanities departments. Amongst the first was Sussex University's 'Sexual Dissidence and Cultural Change' MA programme, which was launched in 1991. The Tory MP Terry Dicks called for the university to 'be shut down and disinfected'.[55]

HIV and AIDS

By the 1980s, this activity, writing, art and activism was taking place with a sense of desperate urgency. In 1981, the US Center of Disease Control in the USA reported that five young gay men had died from a rare form of pneumonia in Los Angeles. The news came as St Mary's Hospital in London found immune cell abnormalities in blood samples from 100 gay men. A year later, on 4 July 1982, thirty-seven-year-old Terry Higgins became the first known person in Britain to die of an AIDS-related disease at St Thomas' Hospital in London. Reaction was muted. Despite the warning signs from the States, it was five months before the case was reported in *Capital Gay*. Higgins' friends were dismayed at the way he had been treated and concerned about what the death might portend. By the end of the year, they had set up the Terrence (initially Terry) Higgins Trust, which went on to lead the response to HIV and AIDS in Britain. At this stage though, there was little indication of the potential scale of the crisis. There was also a good deal of ignorance and denial. Tim Clark remembers that 'the risk did not seem great [...] Anyone infected kept it hidden [...] You turned yourself into an untouchable. There was little solidarity at this stage'.[56] *Scotsgay*, the Scottish gay monthly, was keen to distinguish the epidemic in the States – which had by this time claimed 1,000 lives – from what was happening in Britain and more specifically Scotland: 'There is unlikely to be the kind of epidemic we have seen in the USA. Social circumstances are so different here that the virus is unlikely to move through the gay scene with the same speed and ferocity as in the tightly incestuous gay communities of California and New York'.[57] The magazine was quick to point out that of the first two cases in Scotland, one was not a Scot and the other had recently visited New York. 'Working together and acting quickly in response to new developments, we can limit the damage' the magazine proclaimed. The problem was identifying what 'acting quickly' might involve; before AIDS was coined in 1982, it had been dubbed Gay cancer, or GRID (Gay-related immune deficiency), and there was a strong sense that the condition was associated with sexual identity rather than sexual practice, a myth that endured. Early Terrence Higgins Trust literature highlighted the dangers of anal sex, but recommended abstaining rather than using condoms. It advised sex with fewer men and sex with men in good health; it also suggested avoiding sex with men who had been sexually active in north America. The singer Holly Johnson, who later talked publicly about his own HIV+ diagnosis, initially reassured himself in these terms, telling himself: 'we've never been to America, we've never slept with Americans'.[58]

The London Lesbian and Gay Switchboard and the Health Education Authority held the first conference on AIDS on 21 May 1983.[59] The conference took place just as the media was beginning to take notice. *Horizon* broadcast 'The Killer in the Village' which speculated on the potential scale of the epidemic and the Middlesex Hospital in London counted five times as many news items in the six months between April and September of 1983 as in the entire previous fifteen months.[60] The THT (Terrence Higgins Trust) had swung into action on a number of fronts, most famously with its army of volunteer 'buddies' providing emotional and practical support for people living with AIDS (from 1982). Following the isolation of the virus (in 1983 in France and 1984 in the USA) and development of a test (in 1985), THT was able to issue more specific guidance on infection routes and risky sexual practice. By the late 1980s, Body Positive (in London, but soon a network of independent groups across the country), CRUSAID, Scottish AIDS Monitor in Edinburgh, Brighton's Open Door, Manchester's George House Trust and many other local groups were providing voluntary support to those effected by the virus. In 1988, on the back of intensive fund raising, the Mildmay Hospice and London Lighthouse opened their doors to provide specialist respite care. These centres, together with the newly formed Immune Development Trust, pioneered the use of complimentary and touch-based therapies, which, Nick Bridgmont has argued, were symbolically crucial in a climate when people with AIDS were being branded untouchable.[61] Princess Diana was lauded by many for breaking the taboo around casual contact in her visits to hospitals.

The level of charitable and support work owed much to an existing tradition of community mobilization. Simon Watney recalls that 'many of us involved in the early days of the epidemic had known one another as young gay men on the gay scene [and from] a political culture that had revolved around the London Lesbian and Gay Switchboard, and many other organizations and groups'.[62] The structure and impetus of these earlier groups arguably helped to prevent the British crisis reaching French, Spanish and Italian proportions, though injecting drug use did account for many more cases in these countries.[63]

The government was slower to act than the gay 'community' – a term which was finally felt by many to have some sort of resonance and meaning. It was not until 1985 that an AIDS unit was set up in the Department of Health and Social Security and £2.5 million earmarked for an advertising campaign. A year later, a cross-Department committee was established to coordinate government efforts, and a cabinet minister, Social Services Secretary Norman Fowler, stood before the press in Downing Street to exhort the public to use condoms. The National AIDS Trust was launched, and Health Authorities were required to report all their AIDS-related work.

The response was criticized by the voluntary sector on a number of levels. Some felt it had acted only when it became clear that it was not only homosexuals and drug users who might be affected.[64] The government moreover steadfastly refused to fund targeted safer sex campaigns, despite the trajectory of the epidemic in Britain. More specifically, in the first government-sponsored campaign – 'Don't Die of Ignorance' – London Lesbian and Gay Switchboard's number was published without proper consultation or additional funding; the phone lines collapsed under the inevitable influx of calls from a terrified public and also men and women who became aware of switchboard's number for the first time and wanted to discuss coming out. 'A large number of provincial housewives came out that year', recalls Lisa Power, a switchboard volunteer at the time.[65]

The government effort had become more concerted by 1989. Grants were announced to the London Lighthouse, Body Positive and the Mildmay Mission Hospital, and AIDS funding for local authorities was ring fenced, though North West Thames region – covering the worst affected region in the country – illegally diverted £8.5 million in funding to other projects.[66] There was continuing resistance to targeted care, and a survey of 1992 found that 66 percent of government agencies with a HIV remit had done no specific work with gay men; only 3.5 percent said they had engaged in substantial amounts of work. 'Gay men in the AIDS field faced a terrible compromise', writes Simon Garfield, 'either to put gay men's needs second and gain funding or to face the possibility of having statutory funding removed'.[67]

Medical professionals were meanwhile struggling to cope with the wide range of symptoms patients were presenting. With a compromised immune system, individuals were susceptible to rare infections and cancers, several of which doctors had not been used to dealing with before. Amongst them were KS, a kind of skin cancer, PCP, a form of pneumonia and CMV which led to blindness. The drug AZT had initially looked like a promising treatment, but its efficacy when used in isolation was doubted. At the Vancouver AIDS conference in 1996, however, it was announced that when used in combination with other drugs AZT was effective in slowing the replication of the HIV virus. Despite some unpleasant side effects including nausea and lypodistrophy (the redistribution of body fat), the availability of the so-called combination therapy in Britain allowed many men to regain their health. By the early 2000s, around 200 gay men with HIV were dying each year, about the same mortality rate as 1986. By contrast, approximately 1,000 gay or bisexual men were dying each year in the first half of the 1990s. By the end of 2004, over 16,000 people with HIV had died in the UK; almost 10,000 of this number were men who are believed to have contracted the virus from sex with another man. London was still the centre of the UK epidemic: 56 percent of gay men in Britain with the virus lived in the capital, although the relative number of new diagnoses elsewhere in Britain was increasing year on year. Approximately 58,000 people in UK were living with HIV; gay or bisexual men accounted for just under half of this number were men who had sex with men.[68]

Bare statistics say little about the devastating progress of the virus. People with AIDS had to deal regularly with diarrhoea, night sweats and severe weight loss. Tim described his lover Ricardo lying on the sofa 'week after week with fevers'. 'He'd have to change his nightclothes three times a night because he'd been soaked in sweat. He'd shake and shake for periods of about 40 minutes, then he'd get hot and then incredibly cold'.[69] Derek Jarman wrote matter-of-factly in September 1993 of the treatments he was receiving:

> I've been at Barts [St Bartholemew's Hospital, London] for nearly two weeks. My kidneys and bone marrow are monitored under the deluge of Gancyclovir and Foscarnet. I have an injection each day to bolster my neutrophils, the infection has not cleared up yet but is on its way. Two weeks ago I had an eye operation, very sore and painful, and I have another on Thursday. I am almost blind and have certainly read my last book and newspaper.[70]

Jarman spoke highly of his care at Barts in the early 1990s and by this point specialized AIDS wards often had a unique atmosphere with patients proactive in their own treatment. Earlier – and especially before the isolation of the virus in 1985 – fear had gripped many hospital workers. Ian Weller, a doctor at the Middlesex Hospital, remembers that 'one night I was sitting in a patient's room, and this hand came round the door with food on it and just dumped it. I laughed with the patient, who said 'it happens all the time'. Within five minutes a bunch of flowers flew across the room – whoosh! That time I didn't even see the hand'.[71]

There was by the later 1980s growing evidence of discrimination by employers, and insurance and mortgage companies, and some organizations – including THT – were advising men not to take the new HIV test. Knowledge, in this case, was not felt to be empowering because there was precious little that could be done with it; it could indeed make matters considerably worse. The stigma of AIDS was potent, especially for those who had not come out to family, friends or work mates. Isolation was common, and the demonization of gay men as carriers of the 'plague' re-inscribed the old connection of homosexuality and pathology in many minds, giving new ammunition to moralists who touted AIDS as a punishment from God and the 'natural' fruit of sexual immorality. Manchester police chief James Anderton famously envisaged gays 'swirling around in a cess pit of their own creation'.[72] Brian Hitchen of the *Daily Star* asked 'how long are we going to support spurious AIDS charities for those who brought this awful curse upon themselves'. Sir John Junor, the *Mail on Sunday* columnist agreed: 'It is said that by shaking hands with patients in an AIDS ward, Princess Diana showed that the disease need not make them into social outcasts. But since each had only his homosexual promiscuity to blame for the disease, isn't that exactly what they should be?'[73] The Terrence Higgins Trust, according to the chair of the Conservative Family Campaign, was a 'homosexual front which provides gay pornography to teenagers under the guise of health education'. In its Charter of Responsibility for AIDS Sufferers, published in 1991, the organization demanded HIV-infected citizens disclose their status to employers, be banned from certain occupations – including food preparation – and accept incursions on their personal freedoms.[74] Calls for the quarantining of gay men and drug users were made. This kind of attitude underlay much reporting on HIV and AIDS in the 1980s and early 1990s, and coverage of high-profile deaths – of Rock Hudson in 1985, the actor Ian Charleston in 1989, Kenny Everett and Freddie Mercury in 1991 and Derek Jarman in 1994 – often came with implicit and explicit messages of blame and shame. *The Daily Mail* reported that film heart-throb Hudson had 'died a living skeleton – and so ashamed'.[75] Jarman was pilloried in some obituaries. Many gay men felt doubly embattled. Recounting his experiences of being gay and coping with AIDS-related illnesses, Ken from Brighton spoke of the electric shock therapy he had been subject to on account of his sexuality, the multiple physical attacks he had endured, the rejection he had felt from his family when he revealed his HIV status and the callous chorus of a group of men who had followed him home one night: 'singing to the tune of Rod Stewart's *Sailing* they had chorused: 'You are dying, you are dying, you are dying, but we don't care' '. Rupert in London recounted stall-holders shouting out 'AIDS!' as he walked by.[76] 'There was a period of about 6 months when it was touch and go', observed Michael James, 'the hatred that was coming out was totally naked from the *Sun* and the *Daily Mail* and all those papers. The gloves were off […] I really believed that they were going to round up all the gays and put them in concentration camps'.[77]

Many gay men were defiant and angry in the face of such stigmatization, discrimination and ignorance. Following Larry Kramer's example in New York, ACT UP – AIDS Coalition to Unleash Power – was launched in London in an attempt to re-radicalize AIDS and gay politics. Activists floated helium-filled condoms carrying safer sex information over the walls of Pentonville prison in London to highlight the lack of prison provision and the catastrophe of HIV and AIDS amongst prison inmates. By 1991, ACT UP had groups across the country – in Edinburgh, Manchester, Leeds and Norwich – though the London chapter collapsed after the treasurer was prosecuted for embezzling funds. GMFA (Gay Men Fighting AIDS) started work in the same year with direct interventions on safer sex in cruising areas, pubs and clubs; THT, they alleged, was dancing to the tune of a government bent on resisting targeted funding and safer sex campaigns.

By 1993, Ken in Brighton had embroidered the names of 130 men he had known and who had died onto a banner. He had become in his own words 'a professional funeral goer': 'there were three in one day once'.[78] He described feelings of guilt at surviving these mostly younger men. Jarman listed sixteen friends who had died by the same year;[79] and when Rupert's dinner party guest asked how many of the thirteen people around the table were positive 'all except the person who had asked put up their hand'.[80] Tim talks of the agony and isolation of grief after his lover Ricardo's death. 'I am only 27, I could have another 50 years ahead of me, and yet the person who I wanted to share that time with isn't going to be here. That's something I find very difficult to understand [...] I was 22 when I met him, and he shaped the person I am today. He was the motivation for everything I did'.[81]

Such a stigmatized illness and death left families struggling too. Martin Hazel describes visiting a family in 1985 who had been ostracized by their church after their son's death and had been unable to find an undertaker to deal with the funeral because he had died of an AIDS-related illness. Others found it too difficult to reveal the cause of death to extended family and family friends. Simon Watney eloquently describes the funeral of his friend Bruno in 1986 and the trauma of his parents who felt 'condemned to silence, to euphemism [...] in this the most devastating moment of their lives as parents'. For Watney himself, there was a painful tension in crossing into this other world of a family funeral which did not reflect the life of the man he had known. 'The irony of the difference between the suffocating life of the suburbs where we found ourselves, and our knowledge of the world in which Bruno had actually lived, as a magnificently affirmative and life-enhancing gay man, was all but unbearable'.[82]

This was not a unique experience, and many felt this collision of two worlds and two world views. In many cases, there was a reciprocity and a generosity of spirit, as family, friends and voluntary and professional medical and support workers formed tightly knit networks around the men they cared for. But other family members could not come to terms with the friends and lovers of their brothers and sons, and nonfamily members found themselves shut out of medical decisions and funeral arrangements. As there was no legal recognition of same-sex couples, surviving lovers had no rights in the law when it came to illness, death and inheritance. The issue fired arguments for partnership rights, for living wills on the part of the person with AIDS and also for pre-emptive funeral arrangements. Undertakers were often left with very specific instructions about what should happen. Ken went to one funeral where 'we all let go of coloured balloons. You could see the balloons drifting off to heaven'.[83] I attended one where glasses of champagne and joints pre-rolled were handed out to each mourner. Others requested particular music, readings and acts of remembrance, often beyond and in defiance of established funereal rituals. David Ruffell felt that for him it was a way of 'taking control' in circumstances in which he had felt powerless.[84]

In the context of this profound grief and anger, many gay artists and writers began to focus in their work on HIV and AIDS and on issues of untimely illness and death. 'What are artists affected by HIV to do if not to include it in their working practice' declared the writer Adam Mars Jones in response to criticism of the trend.[85] There was a felt imperative to bear witness and to memorialize at a time of widespread ignorance or indifference at the scale of loss. Commemorative quilts were sewn, and writers such as Oscar Moore, Paul Monette and Derek Jarman charted their lives with AIDS in, respectively, newspaper columns, memoirs and diaries. 'I had to write of sad times as a witness', wrote Jarman. 'Please read the cares of the world that I have locked in these pages; and after, put this book aside and love'.[86]

There was an insistence in much of this work on safeguarding what many saw as a distinctive subculture and lifestyle, and this became an important part of the 'battle' with the disease and with the homophobic backlash. There was a refusal amongst many to conform to a series of social norms which they felt had done them few favours. 'AIDS', wrote

John Shiers in 1987, 'inevitably means major changes in the organisation of our sexual lives [...] it does not, however, have to imply monogamy, celibacy or a return to 'traditional' moral values'.[87]

Hepatitis had been the biggest health problem for gay men prior to HIV and AIDS, and there had been a major outbreak in London in the mid- to late-1970s. But from the 1920s and especially after the war, diseases such as syphilis, gonorrhoea and NSU (nonspecific urithritis) when contracted were relatively easily treated. Robert observed that amongst his colleagues in the merchant navy, these illnesses were regarded as an occupational hazard. None of Stanley and Baker's interviewees used condoms for anal sex in the 1970s.[88] This changed once HIV emerged and transmission routes became clearer, however. THT and other organizations began to focus on the kinds of sex men were having and the relative risks involved. Leaflets and pamphlets from HIV and AIDS organizations in the UK remained largely sex positive, focussing on levels of risk and endorsing a proactive approach on the part of gay men in negotiating the kinds of sex they were prepared to engage in. At one level, this often involved men telling partners their limits before sex; at another it took men into a fuller exploration of sensuality, desire, fantasy and fetish. The Joy of Gay Sex, first published in 1977, was updated and reissued by Gay Men's Press in 1993 and Peter Tatchell's Safer Sexy appeared a year later. This was not an era, both books argued, in which it was necessary to be abstemious. Some men of course made decisions to have less or no sex and changed their sexual behaviour significantly. Philip Baker said he began to 'look at things like one nighters in a different light' post-AIDS, whilst Eduardo Pereira observed that 'sometimes it's simply not worth it'.[89] David became celibate after losing close friends in the early years of the epidemic.[90] Overall, though, surveys of sexual behaviour by Project Sigma found that men were not having less sex because of HIV and AIDS, and neither were they having less partners. In their analysis of the sexual lives of 1,083 men between 1987 and 1995, there was no evidence of an increase in monogamy, with a majority of men in couples (who accounted for 58 percent of those surveyed) having open relationships (26 percent monogamous; 32 percent open). They also found an increase in anal sex and in rimming (oral anal sex).[91] Whereas a 1985 gay sexual lifestyles survey dismissed rimming as a rarity,[92] the Project Sigma study found it to be common by the mid-1990s, partly, they supposed, because it was labelled a 'low-HIV risk activity'. The project concluded 'more men are having sex now than they were at the start of the study: this may be a sign that they are more comfortable with sex and less afraid of the risks of sex'.[93]

Levels of condom use varied, and Project Sigma found many men being strategic: using them with casual partners but not with their boyfriends, for example. Older gay men used them less than younger, and HIV-positive men were using them 'to a degree well in excess of negatives and those not tested'. The prevalence of condom use also shifted with time and levels of concern about the epidemic. It increased sharply in 1986–1987, tailed off to 1993 and then rose again, possibly as death rates began to peak.[94] A survey of men in Scotland found that the decision not to use a condom at this stage appeared to be based on love, trust and a partner's sexual reputation, rather than on prevailing health and education advice or specific knowledge about the HIV status of the partner.[95]

The 1980s backlash

Press coverage of gay men and AIDS in the 1980s was unsympathetic, sensational and overtly homophobic. The 'gay plague' had struck, and this, together with the (in fact very modest) expenditure of local councils on lesbian and gay groups mentioned earlier, were seized upon by the tabloids and some conservative politicians who were keen to highlight the country's moral slide. 'The current fashion for the flouting and propagating of homosexuality and lesbianism is both anti-family and anti-life' observed the MP Dr Rhodes Boyson in the Daily Express.[96] In a period of recession and unemployment, gay and lesbian threats to the family and morality were convenient diversions and were strategically deployed to justify the dissolution of Greater London Council and other city-wide authorities in 1986. The move stripped bodies like the London Lesbian and Gay Centre, Hall Carpenter oral history project and Lesbian and Gay Switchboard of some of their funding and impeded the development of city-wide strategies for HIV prevention and support. The government played the family and morality ticket strongly in its 1987 election campaign, and after Prime Minister Margaret Thatcher's third successive election victory, she used her conference speech of that year to 'question those who claim an inalienable right to be gay'. The government followed up this rhetoric with legislative action, inserting the infamous Clause 28 into the 1988 Local Government Act. The clause ruled that:

> A local authority shall not (a) intentionally promote homosexuality or publish material with the intention of promoting homosexuality; (b) promote the teaching in any maintained school of the acceptability of homosexuality as a pretended family relationship.

The legislation was virtually unworkable and no prosecution was brought, but the measure nevertheless inculcated considerable uncertainty amongst local authorities about what was permissible in terms of, for example, safer sex information. Libraries were also confused about the books that could be stocked and how far sex and social education could go.

Though at one level, Clause 28 can be read as an attempt to cling onto supposed moral certainties in a changing culture, at another it seemed to reflect a broader hardening of attitudes towards homosexuality. In 1983, 62 percent of people disapproved of gay relationships – already an increase on the figures for the late 1970s. By 1985, the figure was 69 percent, and in 1987 it had reached 74 percent. In the same year – and providing ammunition to the government on Clause 28–93 percent said gay men should be forbidden from adopting children; 86 percent said the same of lesbians.[97] It is of course important to remember that such figures always belie complex patterns of support in which most of us live and which might allow a father to pour scorn on 'rights' of 'queers' but offer something very different to his gay son.

The climate was nevertheless pernicious for gay men. Gay bashing continued unabated. David left London after two separate and vicious attacks outside the National Theatre and near the Vauxhall Tavern gay bar in London in the late 1980s.[98] Peter Burton felt disorientated after being beaten up in Brighton, partly because it had felt like such a focused attack on his identity.[99] In 1990, *Time Out* and the *Independent* reported four homophobic murders near gay venues or cruising grounds in London between June and August; there were also three serious assaults. *Gay Times* counted fifty-five murders of gay men in Britain between 1986 and 1989; twenty-eight of them in London.[100] Colin Ireland – dubbed 'the gay slayer' – killed five gay men in 1993, and a year later eleven men died in an arson attack on a gay cinema in Clerkenwell. The clear-up rate for these murders stood at 55 percent against 92 percent for all murders. Scotland Yard refused to monitor attacks on gay men until 1994 insisting no purpose would be served.

There was a seeming indifference to these crimes, and in addition, the police had stepped up action against gay men. Although consensual sex in private between men over twenty-one had been decriminalized in 1967, men who contravened the age prescription or who had sex in cottages or parks were still infringing the law. Indeed in 1991, the law on soliciting and procuring was extended under Clause 25 of the Criminal Justice Act. The year 1989 saw 2,022 prosecutions for indecency between men in England and Wales, a 50 percent increase on the previous year and the highest figure since 1955. When we add convictions for sodomy, soliciting and procuring, the total is 3,065, the highest ever number of arrests and prosecutions for consensual sexual activity between men since records began.[101] Public order and breach of the peace charges could also be used, and on these counts a couple kissing goodbye in a London street and a man dressed in women's clothes in Aberdeen were fined £40 and £50 respectively in 1988 and 1989.[102] Assault charges were used to convict sixteen men involved in consensual sadomasochistic sex in private in the Operation Spanner case of 1990. The men were imprisoned for terms of up to four and a half years. Subsequent appeals failed.

Police raids also continued. In 1986, the police entered the Vauxhall Tavern in London and arrested twelve men for being drunk inside the premises. A year earlier, a raid on Gay's The Word bookshop led to charges in which works by Wilde, Tennessee Williams, Jean Genet, Allan Ginsburg and Jean Paul Sartre were cited. After a massive campaign, the charges were eventually dropped. Mary Whitehouse was still hitting the headlines with her morality campaigns. She brought an unsuccessful private prosecution against the director Michael Bogdanov for 'procuring an act of gross indecency' between the two actors who mimed gay rape in Howard Brenton's *Romans in Britain* at the National Theatre in 1980. Four years later, she attacked Channel 4 for screening two of Jarman's films. The police and campaigners like Whitehouse were pushing to circumscribe and marginalize gay social and cultural life. The *Times* observed that 'this country seems to be in a galloping frenzy of hate, where homosexuals are concerned, that will soon, if not checked, lead to something like a pogrom'.[103]

When Clause 28 was introduced, it was the final straw and it became the focus for lesbian and gay anger at this broader backlash. The clause specifically delegitimized lesbian and gay households and those bringing up children, and the debate which ensued importantly placed the relationship between homosexuality and the nurturing and education of children high on the political, social and cultural agenda. That lesbians and gay men were themselves family members and that many were also parents seemed something of a revelation to many. Was it gay men and lesbians who destroyed families or those who disowned them? The campaign against the clause was astonishing in its scale and vigour. Ten thousand people marched in London in one of the two marches organized in the city in 1988; there were 15,000 at the Manchester event in the same year. A special train was chartered to take London protestors to the latter, and Lisa Power remembers selling pink champagne on the platform, whist British Rail announced the imminent departure of the 'Pink Express'.[104] The campaign deployed GLF-style stunts. Two women famously abseiled into the House of Lords and then chained themselves to news reader Sue Lawley's chair as she attempted to deliver a live bulletin. Outrage! – formed in 1990 by Peter Tatchell, Simon Watney and others following the homophobic murder of the actor Michael Boothe – staged a series of highly visible direct action events, including a kiss-in at the statue of Eros in Piccadilly Circus. The site was key to the queer history of the capital as previous chapters have shown, and the statue at its centre – the protestors insisted – was a symbol of the power of queer love as well as straight. Tatchell threatened an outing campaign, especially in relation to hypocritical Church of England clergy. Under Outrage! pressure the Bishop of London David Hope admitted in 1995 that his sexuality was 'a grey area'. More colourfully, the Sisters of Perpetual Indulgence held a sparklingly camp ceremony on the Kent coast in 1991 to create Derek Jarman 'Saint Derek of Dungeness of the Order of Celluloid Knights'. He was to be a queer positive rival to the 234 new saints created by Pope John Paul II.

Outrage!, the Sisters of Perpetual Indulgence and others now self-consciously used 'queer' rather than 'gay' to describe themselves and their defiant politics. By the late 1980s, the radical edge that initially surrounded 'gay' had softened, and it had become a standard descriptive term. Using 'queer' was a way of regaining this radical impetus. It was also part of an academic debate about the conventional divisions between 'gay' and 'straight'. If gay defied medical and legal definition, queer defied the idea that the desire for the same sex placed the individual in a rigid identity category. Theoretically at least 'queer' served as an umbrella for all sexual dissidents who saw themselves outside a traditional set of norms and values. Queer certainly expressed a powerful sense of dissidence and disenchantment; whether it served genuinely as a more inclusive term extending to men and women, those who had sex with members of the same sex as well as those who had sex with the opposite sex, is still a matter of debate. Many also felt uncomfortable using a term that was still regularly evoked in attacks on gay men. The literary critic Alan Sinfield observed that 'if you are struggling to be gay in rural Britain, the last thing you want is someone more fortunate telling you don't measure up because you can't think of yourself as 'queer'.[105]

Also at the forefront of the gay 'fight back' was Stonewall, formed in specific response to Clause 28 by twenty gay men and lesbians, among them actor Michael Cashman (Colin from *Eastenders*) and Ian McKellen, who had sensationally come out during a radio debate. The founders were acutely aware that none of the existing organizations were talking directly to government on Clause 28, the age of consent, immigration, adoption and parenting, housing rights and partnership recognition. They thus sought to establish a tightly organized and professionally run body to lobby on these and other key issues. A Chief Executive was appointed and specialists in law and government recruited.

Stonewall's supposed 'fraternisation with the enemy' made it the target of some fierce criticism from other gay and lesbian groups and individuals – especially when Ian McKellen accepted a knighthood in 1989 in the midst of the Clause 28 furore. The tensions were a muted echo of those between the GLF and CHE. For some, the legal rights and equality agenda pursued by Stonewall steered gay politics too far towards assimilation and respectability. Outrage! Saw themselves as more visibly defiant in their celebration and expression of sexual and cultural difference, and in their reconnection to GLF ideas about the transformation of social and sexual relations more broadly.

Though much heartfelt anger was generated in the disagreements between Outrage! and Stonewall, there was in truth as much to connect as to divide them. Stonewall did not oppose direct action by group but rather saw lobbying as a necessary additional tactic. The groups in fact sometimes worked together – on police homophobia in the early 1990s, for example. Peter Tatchell of Outrage! and Stonewall Chief Executive Angela Mason were also personally linked by their earlier activism in the GLF, and Mason kept the initial list of GLF demands pinned on the wall of her office.[106]

The reinvigoration of gay and queer politics in the late 1980s and early 1990s drew in many who had never been involved before, leading

Capital Gay to observe in 1990 that the lesbian and gay movement had 'come of age':

> Well-known figures, who have previously been quiet about their sexuality have come out fighting, we have had protest letters and taken to the streets in the biggest ever lesbian and gay demonstrations, the media coverage has been massive and the visibility of our community has rarely, if ever, been greater.[107]

Gay Times echoed the sentiments in 1992 after the mammoth Europride event in London that year: there was, it claimed 'a sense of being an unstoppable movement, part of a tribe that had scattered but is now reunited'.[108] The numbers of Pride marchers grew year on year. In 1985, 15,000 people took part, but Clause 28 brought 40,000 people out in 1988. *Capital Gay* proclaimed '200,000' in its mast head for 1995, and two years later, there were estimates of 300,000 people.[109] Provincial Pride events also emerged. Belfast Pride was launched in 1990, Brighton and Manchester hosted annual festivals from 1992 and Pride Scotia in Edinburgh began in 1995. As a direct response to the failure of the appeal against the Operation Spanner verdicts, SM Pride was launched in 1992; its importance underlined by police raids on The Mineshaft in Manchester (1994) and the Whiplash (1994), Saidie Maisie (1996) and Gummi in London (1996).

The scale and publicity attracted by pride events was part of a growing visibility of gay life; more men were taking part, and it was not only the politically active who were coming out to families and work colleagues. Well into his 1970s, Barry came out at a dinner party: 'I found myself sitting next to a woman of about 40, and she turned to me and she said, your wife isn't here, and I replied, I heard myself say and I couldn't believe it, I turned and I said, no, I'm homosexual. It rather stunned her. [...] Then we talked about something quite different, quite amicably may I say'.[110] Barry's own sense of disbelief at his statement is suggestive of a change in the social and cultural climate which had even taken him by surprise.

The commercial scene was also exuding confidence. By the early 1990s, Manchester's gay village around the city's Canal Street was well established with fifteen venues within 150 yards of each other. The local council had moved to pedestrianize and improve lighting along the canal in support of these developments. Something similar was happening in London's Soho, with long-established pubs like Comptons on Old

Compton Street joined by a series of new European-style bars like the Village from 1992. With street-level plate glass windows rather than shutters and doorbells for entry, these new bars signalled a determination to be out and visible. London was becoming a popular gay holiday destination, making for an increasingly cosmopolitan – though in Soho a very male-dominated – scene. Gay pubs and clubs were also becoming popular with straight men and women and were by many seen to be at the cutting edge of music and drug culture. Twenty percent of clubbers in gay clubs in London, Manchester and Brighton were straight by the late 1990s. Tim Nicholson observed: 'I gravitate[d] towards gay men and gay clubs simply because they were more civilised; I would much rather deal with an unwanted grope than an unwanted fist in my face'.[111] In the bigger cities, the scene was now multilayered with a range of clubs and pubs catering to different fashions, music tastes and fetishes. The Bell had been the indie gay venue in London for the 1980s and early 1990s, and from 1995 Duckie brought comedy, performance and indie music together in a winning formula. Together with Popstarz and Wig Out, these clubs provided an alternative to the Soho scene. Though the annual pride march retained some of its radical edge, the festival was now an overtly commercial enterprise, with entry charges from 1998 and big name sponsorship. British gay men were meanwhile flocking in ever increasing numbers to other European cities and to specifically gay resorts in Sitges, Gran Canaria, Ibiza and Greece. Gone were the vacations in Brighton: 'that stopped at the end of the sixties', remembers Grant, 'they started going abroad. Holland, Morocco, Spain'.[112]

Gay men were also gaining a higher profile in the arts and media. Depictions still often revolved around stereotype, but they were becoming more sophisticated and diverse. Following the success of Channel 4's *Out on Tuesday* (1989), Greater London Radio launched *Gay and Lesbian London* in 1993, and Radio 5 won awards for *Out This Week*. Much camper were BBC2's *Gaytime TV* (from 1996) and the game show *Blankety Blank* hosted from 1999 by veteran drag queen Lilly Savage. In the same year, *Queer as Folk* and *Gimme Gimme Gimme* in 1999 moved away from the earnest positive imaging of the soaps; earlier *Shopping and Fucking* (1996) had done something similar at London's Royal Court Theatre and later on the West End stage. By now, the internet had also radically changed gay life, especially with the launch of Gaydar in 1999. Cruising for sex could now be a very domestic affair with men checking out profiles of hundreds of men living locally, each listing their sexual likes and dislikes. Anecdotal evidence suggests that famous cruising grounds like Hampstead Heath in London and Carlton Hill in Edinburgh were visited by fewer and fewer men. Gaydar and other internet sex and dating sites again shifted the ways in which men negotiated sex, found out intimate details about prospective partners and assessed trustworthiness and levels of commitment.

There was by the late 1990s the beginning of a cultural shift and a recession in the frantic homophobia of the late 1980s. The initial panic around HIV and AIDS had receded to some degree, especially with combination therapy after 1996. The crisis was not over; funding was certainly inadequate and health education arguably needed to be targeted more carefully, but gay men were beginning to feel less embattled. The age of consent for gay men had been lowered to eighteen (1993), and following a joint campaign by Outrage!, Stonewall and GALOP (the Gay London Policing Group – founded in 1984), the number of convictions for consenting sex between men fell by 75 percent in 1994. The police also made strides in recruiting gay officers and monitoring homophobic crime more systematically.[113] The police were beginning to be seen by gay men as a body which might protect as well as prosecute.

Tony Blair's new labour government of 1997 included the first openly gay cabinet minister – the Culture Secretary Chris Smith, who had come out publicly in 1985. Within months of the election, foreign partners of British lesbian and gay men were given immigration rights on the same terms as straight couples (though the rules became tougher overall). Attempts to equalize the age of consent for gay men at sixteen were repeatedly stalled by the House of Lords in a campaign orchestrated by Baroness Young. By now, though, there was an inevitability about the measure, not least because of Britain's membership of the European Union. It finally passed into law in 2001. A year earlier, the hated Clause 28 was repealed, and the European court forced the government's hand in allowing gays in the military.

Each of these changes came on the back of intense lobbying by Stonewall in particular, and there were fierce debates in parliament and the media, as well as some anti-gay publicity stunts. Attempts were made, for example, to bring the first prosecution under Clause 28 in a civil action against Glasgow city council. The Christian Institute accused the council of flouting Clause 28 in its support for Gay Pride event Glasgay and reproduction of 'pornographic' safer sex advice on its website. Kent County Council introduced its own local version of Clause 28 in response to the moves for repeal at the national level. As with the age of consent debacle, the debate for the retention of the clause was fired with homophobic inventive, but the difference now was that such opinion was often ridiculed. In 2005, the Civil Partnerships bill became law, giving men and women who registered their relationships almost identical legal protection as married heterosexual couples.

By this time, many men were no longer seeing their sexuality as incompatible with fatherhood, and in the later 1990s, there were a significant number of gay men who were actively involved in bringing up children, sometimes with male partners, sometimes with lesbian co-parents. At the first conference on lesbian and gay parenting in November 1998, it was observed that Britain was by far the most liberal place in terms of gay parenting in Europe: 'despite the periodic tirades in the media and the lack of legal recognition of lesbian and gay relationships, public attitudes are more tolerant than at any time in the past'.[114] Bars to adoption and fostering on the grounds of sexuality were coming down, especially after a landmark court ruling in 1997 which stated that the law allowed for adoption applications of a single person regardless of their sexuality. The Adoption and Children's Act of 2002 followed, allowing joint adoption by gay couples. This came after Dame Elizabeth Butler-Sloss, the highest ranking family law judge, publicly gave her support to gay parents.

For many, these changes signalled a battle almost won. Others were more sceptical, seeing an identity and sexual lifestyle that had been radical and subversive becoming commodified and sanitized.[115] The rights agenda had apparently won out over the socially transformative hopes of some GLFers. Peter Tatchell hit out in 1999 at the 'amoral hedonism and historical amnesia' that he saw dominating gay culture. He claimed that the single-issue campaigns betrayed the transformative politics of the 1970s, and there was a widespread indifference to homophobia and sexual repression both at home and abroad.[116] Gay life had been depoliticized for all but a relatively few activists. If bars and clubs were visible and open compared to the discreet venues in the 1950s, some argued that gay culture was being contained and restricted through its integration into a consumerist ethic and mainstream culture. It became in some ways more difficult to protest about marginalization and homophobia because gays were apparently now comfortably accommodated on television, in the major cities, and under the law. Such accommodation did not, however, mean that people were not still

positioned within what Jeffrey Weeks calls 'a hierarchy of acceptability'.[117] By carefully arranging where you studied, lived, worked and
socialized in the later 1990s and early 2000s, it was possible largely
to avoid feeling personally isolated or ridiculed because of the sex
and relationships you were having. There nevertheless remained an
entrenched cultural resistance to the kinds of lives many gay men were
living, and many were still battling with anti-gay abuse and violence.
Gay teenagers continued to suffer at school where anti-gay bullying had
not abated. The 2005 play Bashment at London's Stratford East Theatre
dealt with the prevalence of homophobia in rap and amongst some Afro-
Caribbean men. In London, Outrage! protested against rap lyrics at
successive Mobo music award ceremonies. The nail bomb at the Admiral
Duncan gay pub in London's Old Compton Street in 1999 (part of a
multitarget racist and homophobic hate campaign) and the murder of
Jody Dobrovski on Clapham Common in 2005 showed the hatred many
continued to harbour towards gay men.

At the start of the twenty-first century, there was thus a sense of
schizophrenia. Homophobic invective no longer spilled with quite such
frequency from the mouths of politicians and the press; 'inclusion' and
'diversity' became watchwords for government and employers. Much
public opinion had shifted dramatically from the 1980s and early
1990s. And yet, this was not a panacea. Homophobia endured and was
entrenched, and some felt that homosexuality was being accepted on
decidedly straight terms.

Many men had lived through a series of changes in ideas about
identity and behaviour which had forced them to reappraise their sense
of themselves, their relationships and their communities. Such changes
also marked out differences between the generations. Richard Dyer,
for example, was acutely aware of shifts in the idea of coming out. For
him, before the advent of GLF, it meant 'learning and adopting camp
behaviour and taste'. For a younger colleague, it involved 'coming
straight into an already altered gay world'.[118] Many who had lost
friends and lovers in the 1980s found the generation coming out in the
1990s to be apathetic. Older gay men and some who lived outside the
major cities could feel alienated by the self-conscious sophistication
of urban queers and an 'excessively youth orientated subculture'.[119]
Even for the in-crowd, however, the expectations of gay life and culture
provoked real anxiety. 'I have not met a single gay men in the past ten
years', writes sociologist Tim Edwards, 'who does not suffer from major

hang ups concerning his appearance, from weight and musculature to grey hair, no hair or hair in the wrong places, to style, dress, demeanour and confidence, let alone cock size and sexual performance'. Edwards in part blames the 'relentless imagery' of young, toned, largely white men who populate the gay press and gay websites, but he also finds it disturbing that we have failed to resist such imagery or to 'come up with other options' given 'thirty years of political mobilising'.[120] Twentieth-century Britain saw countless men crippled by self-loathing on account of their 'perverse' desires and inability to fit in to 'normal society'. The twenty-first century irony is that the self-loathing some experience might now be borne out of an inability to fit into a queer scene and queer culture.

In his 1991 documentary *Strip Jack Naked*, Ron Peck observed that in making a gay film and in particular his own *Nighthawks* (1978), 'no single character could stand for everyone, it was too big and diverse a world'. Peck treads a fine line between attempting to capture a community and simultaneously acknowledging how problematic the notion is: how do you connect such a hugely diverse group of men with very different conceptions of sex and sexual possibility, friendships and relationships, radicalism and language. There is a shared history of men who love and have sex and relationships with other men; it is a history which this book has tried to configure. But experiencing different moments of crisis and transition, living in different parts of the country, and coming from different religious, ethnic or cultural backgrounds means ultimately that every gay, queer or homosexual man has a different access to and relationship with that past.

List of Illustrations

1. Tomb effigy of Richard Lionheart. Erich Lessing/AKG – Images.

2. The Wilton Diptych. National Gallery Collection/By Kind Permission Of The Trustees Of The National Gallery, London/Corbis UK Ltd.

3. Lot and the inhabitants of Sodom. British Library.

4. Torture and execution of Hugh Despenser at Hereford. AKG – Images.

5. Benjamites flee into wilderness; Bulgars and Albigensians engaged in illicit kissing and embracing. Topham Picturepoint/TopFoto.

6. Impalement of crowned male. Gothic ivory comb. Musei Civici d'Arte Antica di Bologna.

7. Tomb slab of Sir William Neville and Sir John Clanvowe. Alan Bray/University of Chicago Press.

8. Abraham's wife given over to pharaoh; heretics and princes of the world kissing and embracing. Bodleian Library, University of Oxford.

9. Daniel Mytens: King James I. HIP/TopFoto.

10. William Larkin (attrib): The First Duke of Buckingham. AKG – Images.

11. Lord Castlehaven. Folger Shakespeare Library.

12. R. B. Parkes, Edward Kynaston. Victoria & Albert Museum.

13. John Hayls: Samuel Pepys. Topham Picturepoint/TopFoto.

14. Jacob Huysmans (attrib.): John Wilmot, The Earl of Rochester. Visual Arts Library (London)/Alamy.

15. The Woman-Hater's Lamentation. Guildhall Library.

16. The Complete Beau. Frontispiece to *An Essay in Defence of the Female Sex*. British Library.

17. Jonathan Wild in the Condemned Hold. British Library.

18. Kingsbury (attrib): A Milliner's Shop. Lewis Walpole Library, Yale University/Greenwood World Publishing.

19. This is not the Thing, or Molly Exhalted. British Library.

20. Trial at the Old Bailey Court. British Library.

21. The Arse-Bishop Josling a Soldier. British Library.

22. Confirmation or the Bishop and the Soldier. HIP/The British Library/TopFoto.

23. Anne Hurle for Forgery and Methuselah Spalding [for an unnatural offence] on their way to Execution at Newgate. British Library.

24. Disgraceful Proceedings in Manchester: Men Dressed as Women. British Library.

25. Men in Women's Clothes: the Dressing Room. British Library.

26. Young Men Charged With Appearing in Women's Clothes. British Library.

27. Men in Women's Clothes. British Library.

28. The War Memorial to the 24th Infantry Division in Battersea Park, London. TopFoto.

29. The Dumbells Concert Party. PA-005741/Canada. Dept. of National Defence/National Archives of Canada.

30. Tea at Lyons Corner House. British Library.

31. Chorus boys back stage at London's Adelphi Theatre. Hulton-Deutsch Collection/Corbis UK Ltd.

32. 'O Sir, spare a copper'. Courtesy of Paul Raymond Publications Ltd.

33. *Victim*, starring Dirk Bogarde. Park Circus Ltd.

34. Cover of *The Heart in Exile*. Penguin Books Ltd.

35. Cover of *Physique Pictorial*. Athletic Model Guild LLC.

36. The first Gay Pride march. Library of the London School of Economics & Political Science, Hall-Carpenter Archives.

37. Bang Disco. Robert Workman Photographer Ltd.

38. Gay Liberation Front badges. Library of the London School of Economics & Political Science, Hall-Carpenter Archives.

39. South London Gay Centre. Ian Townsen.

40. Culture Club backstage. Corbis UK Ltd.

41. Lesbians and gays support the miners. Pam Isherwood/Photofusion Picture Library.

42. AIDS memorial panel. Mark Power/Magnum Photos.

43. Mardis Gras parade. Scott Nunn.

44. *Pink Paper*, December 2005. Pink Paper.

Further Reading

Chapter 1: Male–Male Love and Sex in the Middle Ages, 1000–1500

Boswell, John. 1980. *Christianity, Social Tolerance, and Homosexuality: Gay People in Western Europe from the Beginning of the Christian Era to the Fourteenth Century.* University of Chicago Press.

Bray, Alan. 2003. *The Friend.* University of Chicago Press.

Burger, Glenn, and Steven F. Kruger, editors. 2001. *Queering the Middle Ages.* University of Minnesota Press.

Burgwinkle, William E. 2004. *Sodomy, Masculinity, and Law in Medieval Literature: France and England, 1050–1230.* Cambridge University Press.

Chaplais, Pierre. 1994. *Piers Gaveston: Edward II's Adoptive Brother.* Clarendon.

Dinshaw, Carolyn. 1999. *Getting Medieval: Sexualities and Communities, Pre- and Postmodern.* Duke University Press.

Foucault, Michel. 1978. *The History of Sexuality*, vol. 1: *An Introduction.* Translated by Robert Hurley, Penguin.

Frantzen, Allen J. 1998. *Before the Closet: Same-Sex Love from "Beowulf" to "Angels in America".* University of Chicago Press.

Hergemoller, Bernd-Ulrich. 2001. *Sodom and Gomorrah: On the Everyday Reality and Persecution of Homosexuals in the Middle Ages.* Free Association Books.

Jaeger, C. Stephen. 1999. *Ennobling Love: In Search of a Lost Sensibility.* University of Pennsylvania Press.

Jordan, Mark D. 1997. *The Invention of Sodomy in Christian Theology.* University of Chicago Press.

Keiser, Elizabeth B. 1997. *Courtly Desire and Medieval Homophobia: The Legitimation of Sexual Pleasure in Cleanness and its Contexts.* Yale University Press.

Lochrie, Karma. 1999. *Covert Operations: The Medieval Uses of Secrecy.* University of Pennsylvania Press.

McGuire, Brian. 1994. *Brother and Lover: Aelred of Rievaulx.* Crossroad.

Payer, Pierre J. 1984. *Sex and the Penitentials: The Development of a Sexual Code 550–1150.* University of Toronto Press.

Quinn, Patricia A. 1989. *Better Than the Sons of Kings: Boys and Monks in the Early Middle Ages.* Peter Lang.

Zeikowitz, Richard E. 2003. *Homoeroticism and Chivalry: Discourses of Male Same-Sex Desire in the Fourteenth Century.* Palgrave Macmillan.

Chapter 2: Renaissance Sodomy, 1500–1700

Bergeron, David M. 1999. *King James and Letters of Homoerotic Desire.* University of Iowa Press.

Betteridge, Tom, editor. 2002. *Sodomy in Early Modern Europe.* Manchester University Press.

Bray, Alan. 1982/1995. *Homosexuality in Renaissance England.* Gay Men's Press, Columbia University Press.

Bredbeck, Gregory W. 1991. *Sodomy and Interpretation: Marlowe to Milton.* Cornell University Press.

Carvajal, Federico Garza. 2003. *Butterflies Will Burn: Prosecuting Sodomites in Earl Modern Spain and Mexico.* University of Texas Press.

DiGangi, Mario. 1997. *The Homoeroticism of Early Modern Drama.* Cambridge University Press.

Franceschina, John. 1997. *Homosexualities in the English Theatre from Lyly to Wilde.* Greenwood Press.

Gerard, Kent, and Gert Hekma, editors. 1989. *The Pursuit of Sodomy: Male Homosexuality in Renaissance and Enlightenment Europe.* The Haworth Press.

Goldberg, Jonathan. 1992. *Sodometries: Renaissance Texts, Modern Sexualities*. Stanford University Press.

Hammond, Paul. 2002. *Figuring Sex between Men from Shakespeare to Rochester*. Clarendon Press.

Herrup, Cynthia B. 1999. *A House in Gross Disorder: Sex, Law, and the 2nd Earl of Castlehaven*. Oxford University Press.

Merrick, Jeffrey, and Bryant T. Ragan, Jr., editors. 2001. *Homosexuality in Early Modern France: A Documentary Collection*. Oxford University Press.

Orgel, Stephen. 1996. *Impersonations: The Performance of Gender in Shakespeare's England*. Cambridge University Press.

Rocke, Michael. 1996. *Forbidden Friendships: Homosexuality and Male Culture in Renaissance Florence*. Oxford University Press.

Ruggiero, Guido. 1985. *The Boundaries of Eros: Sex Crime and Sexuality in Renaissance Florence*. Oxford University Press.

Sigal, Peter, editor. 2003. *Infamous Desire: Male Homosexuality in Colonial America*. University of Chicago Press.

Smith, Bruce R. 1991. *Homosexual Desire in Shakespeare's England: A Cultural Poetics*. University of Chicago Press.

Young, Michael B. 2000. *King James and the History of Homosexuality*. New York University Press.

Zimmerman, Susan, editor. 1992. *Erotic Politics: Desire on the Renaissance Stage*. Routledge.

Chapter 3: Modern Sodomy: The Origins of Homosexuality, 1700–1800

Altman, Dennis, and others. 1989. *Homosexuality, Which Homosexuality*. GMP Publishers.

Duberman, Martin B., Martha Vicinus, and George Chauncey, Jr., editors. 1989. *Hidden from History: Reclaiming the Gay and Lesbian Past*. New American Library.

Fout, John C., editor. 1992. *Forbidden History: The State, Society and the Regulation of Sexuality in Modern Europe*. University of Chicago Press.

Goldsmith, Netta Murray. 1998. *The Worst of Crimes: Homosexuality and the Law in Eighteenth-Century London*. Ashgate.

Haggerty, George E. 1999. *Men in Love: Masculinity and Sexuality in the Eighteenth Century*. Columbia University Press.

Harvey, A.D. 1994. *Sex in Georgian England*. Duckworth.

Herdt, Gilbert, editor. 1994. *Third Sex, Third Gender: Beyond Sexual Dimorphism in Culture and History*. Zone Books.

Higgs, David, editor. 1999. *Queer Sites: Gay Urban Histories since 1600*. Routledge.

Hitchcock, Tim. 1997. *English Sexualities, 1700–1800*. St Martin's Press.

Kimmel, Michael S., editor. 1990. *Love Letters between Certain Late Noblemen and the Famous Mr. Wilson*. The Haworth Press.

Maccubin, Robert Purks, editor. 1987. *'Tis Nature's Fault: Unauthorized Sexuality during the Enlightenment*. Cambridge University Press.

McFarlane, Cameron. 1997. *The Sodomite in Fiction and Satire, 1660–1750*. Columbia University Press.

Merrick, Jeffrey, and Bryant T. Ragan, Jr., editors. 1996. *Homosexuality in Modern France*. Oxford University Press.

Merrick, Jeffrey, and Michael Sibalis, editors. 2001. *Homosexuality in French History and Culture*. The Haworth Press.

Norton, Rictor. 1992. *Mother Clap's Molly House: The Gay Subculture in England 1700–1830*. GMP.

O'Donnell, Katherine, and Michael O'Rourke, editors. 2003. *Love, Sex, Intimacy and Friendship between Men, 1550–1800*. PalgraveMcmillan.

Rousseau, G. S. 1991. *Perilous Enlightenment*. Manchester University Press.
Straub, Kristina. 1992. *Sexual Suspects: Eighteenth-Century Players and Sexual Ideology*. Princeton University Press.
Trumbach, Randolph. 1977. "London's Sodomites: Homosexual Behavior and Western Culture in the 18th Century." *Journal of Social History*, 11: 1–33.
Trumbach, Randolph. 1998. *Sex and the Gender Revolution*, vol. 1: *Heterosexuality and the Third Gender in Enlightenment London*, vol. 2: *The Origins of Modern Homosexuality*. University of Chicago Press, 2008.

Chapter 4: Secrets, Crimes and Diseases, 1800–1914

Bartlett, Neil. 1988. *Who Was That Man: A Present for Mr Oscar Wilde*. Serpent's Tail.
Brady, Sean. 2005. *Masculinity and Male Homosexuality in Britain, 1861–1913*. Palgrave.
Cook, Matt. 2003. *London and the Culture of Homosexuality, 1885–1914*. Cambridge University Press.
Cocks, H. G. 2003. *Nameless Offences: Homosexual Desire in the Nineteenth Century*. IB Taurus.
Cocks, H. G., and Matt Houlbrook. 2005. *The Modern History of Sexuality*. Palgrave.
Cohen, editor 1993. *Talk on the Wilde Side: Towards a Genealogy of a Discourse on Male Sexualities*. Routledge.
Croft-Cooke, Rupert. 1967. *Feasting With Panthers: A New Consideration of Some Late Victorian Writers*. WH Allen.
Crompton, Louis. 1984. *Byron and Greek Love: Homophobia in Nineteenth Century England*. Faber and Faber.
Dowling, Linda. 1994. *Hellenism and Homosexuality in Victorian Oxford*. Cornell University Press.
Foldy, Michael. 1997. *The Trial of Oscar Wilde: Deviance, Morality and Late-Victorian Society*. Yale University Press.
Hyde, H. Montgomery. 1973. *The Trials of Oscar Wilde*. Dover.
———. 1976. *The Cleveland Street Scandal*. WH Allen.
Kaplan, Morris. 2005. *Sodom on the Thames: Sex, Love and Scandal in Wilde Times*. Cornell.
Nye, Robert, editor. 1999. *Sexuality*. Oxford University Press.
Sedgwick, Eve. 1985. *Between Men: English Literature and Male Homosocial Desire*. Columbia University Press.
———. 1990. *The Epistemology of the Closet*. University of California Press.
Sinfield, Alan. 1994. *The Wilde Century: Effeminacy, Oscar Wilde, and the Queer Moment*. Cassell.
White, Chris, editor. 1999. *Nineteenth Century Writings on Homosexuality: A Sourcebook*. Routledge.

Chapter 5: Queer Conflicts: Love, Sex and War, 1914–1967

Baker, Paul, and Jo Stanley. 2003. *Hello Sailor! The Hidden History of Gay Life at Sea*. Longman.
Bech, Henning. 1997. *When Men Meet Men: Homosexuality and Modernity*. Translated by Teresa Mesquit, and Tim Davies, Polity Press.
Bullough, Vern. 1994. *Science in the Bedroom: A History of Sex Research*. Basic Books.
Castle, Terry. 1996. *Noel Coward and Radclyffe Hall: Kindred Spirits*. Columbia University Press.
Cole, Sean. 2000. *Don We Now Our Gay Apparel: Gay Men's Dress in the Twentieth Century*. Berg.
Cooper, Emmanuel. 1994. *The Sexual Perspective: Homosexuality and Art in the Last Hundred Years in the West*. Routledge.
Crisp, Quentin. 1968/1978. *The Naked Civil Servant*. Fontana/Collins.

David, Hugh. 1997. *On Queer Street: A Social History of British Homosexuality, 1895–1995*. Harper Collins.

Dennis, Peter, editor. 1992. *Daring Hearts: Lesbian and Gay Lives in 50s and 60s Brighton*. QueenSpark.

Dollimore, Jonathan. 1991. *Sexual Dissidence: Augustine to Wilde, Freud to Foucault*. Clarendon.

Dyer, Richard. 2002. *The Culture of Queers*. Routledge.

Hall Carpenter Archives. 1989. *Walking After Midnight: Gay Men's Life Stories*. Routledge.

Higgins, Partick. 1996. *Heterosexual Dictatorship: Male Homosexuality in Post-War Britain*. Fourth Estate.

Hoare, Philip. 1997. *Wilde's Last Stand: Decadence, Conspiracy and the First World War*. Duckworth.

Houlbrook, Matt. 2005. *Queer London: Perils and Pleasures of the Sexual Metropolis, 1918–1957*. Chicago University Press.

Hyde, H. Montgommery. 1970. *The Other Love: An Historical and Contemporary Survey of Homosexuality in Britain*. Heineman.

Jivani, Alkarim. 1997. *It's Not Unusual: A History of Lesbian and Gay Britain in the Twentieth Century*. Michael O'Mara.

Porter, Kevin, and Jeffrey Weeks. 1991. *Between the Acts: Lives of Homosexual Men, 1885–1967*. Routledge.

Sinfield, Alan. 1999. *Out on Stage: Lesbian and Gay Theatre in the Twentieth Century*. Yale.

Weeks, Jeffrey. 1977. *Coming Out: Homosexual Politics in Britain, from the Nineteenth Century to the Present*. Quartet.

Whittle, Stephen, editor. 1994. *The Margins of the City: Gay Men's Urban Lives*. Arena.

Chapter 6: From Gay Reform to Gaydar, 1967–2006

Cant, Bob, and Susan Hemmings, editors. 1988. *Radical Records*. Routledge, 156.

Coxon, A. M. 1996. *Between the Sheets: Sexual Diaries and Gay Men's Sex in the Era of AIDS*. Cassell.

Edwards, Tim. 2006. *Cultures of Masculinity*. Routledge.

Gardiner, James. 1996. *Who's a Pretty Boy Then: One Hundred and Fifty Years of Gay Life in Pictures*. Serpent's Tale.

Garfield, Simon. 1994. *The End of Innocence: Britain in the Time of AIDS*. Faber.

Hadleigh, Boze. 1999. *Sing Out!: Gays and Lesbians in the Music World*. Robson.

Hall Carpenter Archives. 1989. *Walking After Midnight: Gay Men's Life Stories*. Routledge.

Jarman, Derek. 1992. *At Your Own Risk: A Saint's Testimony*. Hutchinson.

Mayes, Stephen, and Lyndall Stein. 1993. *Positive Lives: Responses to HIV – A Photodocumentary*. Cassell.

Power, Lisa. 1995. *No Bath But Plenty of Bubbles*. Cassell.

Spencer, Colin. 1995. *Homosexuality: A History*. Fourth Estate.

Watney, Simon. 1987. *Policing Desire: Pornography, AIDS and the Media*. Comedia.

Weeks, Jeffrey, Brian Heaphy, and Catherine Donovan. 2001. *Same Sex Intimacies: Families of Choice and Other Life Experiments*. Routledge.

Whittle, Stephen, editor. 1994. *The Margins of the City: Gay Men's Urban Lives*. Arena.

Notes

Chapter 1: Male–Male Love and Sex in the Middle Ages, 1000–1500

1. Roger of Hovedon (Benedict of Peterborough), *Gesta regis Henrici Secundi Benedicti abbatis*, 2 vols., edited by William Stubbs, Rolls Series 49 (London: Longman, 1867), 2: 7, quoted in C. Stephen Jaeger, *Ennobling Love: In Search of a Lost Sensibility* (Philadelphia: University of Pennsylvania Press, 1999), 11.

2. Hovedon, *Gesta regis*, 2: 126, quoted in Jaeger, *Ennobling Love*, 12.

3. John H. Harvey, *The Plantagenets, 1154–1485* (London: Batsford, 1948), 33–34; Noel I. Garde (pseud. Edgar Leoni), *Jonathan to Gide: The Homosexual in History* (New York: Vantage, 1964), 191–195; James A. Brundage, *Richard Lion Heart* (New York: Scribner, 1974), 88, 202, 257; Michael Goodich, *The Unmentionable Vice: Homosexuality in the Later Medieval Period* (Santa Barbara, CA: ABC-Clio, 1979), 11; John Boswell, *Christianity, Social Tolerance, and Homosexuality: Gay People in Western Europe from the Beginning of the Christian Era to the Fourteenth Century* (Chicago: University of Chicago Press, 1980) (hereafter Boswell, *CSTH*), 48, 231–232; *Encyclopaedia Britannica*, 15th ed., 30 vols. (1980), 15: 827; William A. Percy, "Richard I, the Lionhearted," in *Encyclopedia of Homosexuality*, 2 vols., edited by Wayne R. Dynes (New York: Garland, 1990), 2: 1109–1110.

4. Jaeger, *Ennobling Love*, 11–13; M. J. Ailes, "The Medieval Male Couple and the Language of Homosociality," in *Masculinity in Medieval Europe*, edited by D. M. Hadley (London: Longman, 1999), 232–234.

5. Klaus van Eickels, "*Homagium* and *Amicitia*: Rituals of Peace and their Significance in the Anglo-French Negotiations of the Twelfth Century." *Francia* 24, no. 1 (1997): 133–140.

6. John Gillingham, "Richard I and Berengaria of Navarre." *Bulletin of the Institute of Historical Research* 53, no. 128 (1980): 157–173; John Gillingham, *Richard Lionheart*, 2nd ed. (London: Weidenfeld & Nicolson, 1989), 7, 107, 130, 161–162, 283, 298–299; John Gillingham, *Richard I* (New Haven: Yale University Press, 1999), ix, 84, 233, 263–266.

7. See David M. Halperin, *How to Do the History of Homosexuality* (Chicago: University of Chicago Press, 2002), 106–133, for a detailed account of four competing, 'pre-homosexual' categories of male sex and gender deviance of potential relevance to the Middle Ages: effeminacy, pederasty, friendship, inversion.

8. Alan Bray, *Homosexuality in Renaissance England* (New York: Columbia University Press, 1995), 24–26; Gregory W. Bredbeck, *Sodomy and Interpretation: Marlowe to Milton* (Ithaca, NY: Cornell University Press, 1991), 48–77.

9. Christopher Marlowe, *Edward II*, scene 1, in *The Complete Works of Christopher Marlowe*, 5 vols., edited by Roma Gill (Oxford: Clarendon, 1994), 3: 3–5.

10. On 23 May 1995, the Gay and Lesbian Alliance Against Defamation (GLAAD) organized a leafleting campaign in theatres in the US at which *Braveheart* premiered, claiming that the film included 'gratuitous anti-gay violence'.

11. Michael D. Sharp, "Remaking Medieval Heroism: Nationalism and Sexuality in *Braveheart*." *Florilegium* 15 (1998): 251–266.

12. On Edward's homosexuality, see Boswell, *CSTH*, 299; J. S. Hamilton, *Piers Gaveston, Earl of Cornwall 1307–1312: Politics and Patronage in the Reign of Edward II* (Detroit, MI: Wayne State University Press, 1988), 16–17, 109; J. S. Hamilton, "Edward II," in *Encyclopedia*, edited by Dynes, 1: 344–346; J. S. Hamilton, "Menage a Roi: Edward II and Piers Gaveston." *History Today* 49, no. 6 (1999): 26–31.

13. Pierre Chaplais, *Piers Gaveston: Edward II's Adoptive Brother* (Oxford: Clarendon, 1994), 6–7.

14. "Chronicle of the Civil Wars of Edward II," quoted in Chaplais, *Piers Gaveston*, 11.

15. *Vita Edwardi Secundi, Monachi cuisdam Malmesberiensis*, edited by Noël Denholm-Young (London: Nelson, 1957), 7, 17, 28.

16. Vita Edwardi Secundi, 15.

17. Chaplais, *Piers Gaveston*, 10–11.

18. Alan Bray, *The Friend* (Chicago: University of Chicago Press, 2003), 27–29; Alan Bray, "Edward II," in *Who's Who in Gay and Lesbian History: From Antiquity to World War II*, edited by Robert Aldrich and Garry Wotherspoon (London: Routledge, 2001), 141–142.

19. Elizabeth A. R. Brown, "Introduction" and "Ritual Brotherhood in Western Europe," in *Ritual Brotherhood in Ancient and Medieval Europe: A Symposium*, special issue of *Traditio* 52 (1997): 261–283, 357–381.

20. Adomnán, *Life of St Columba*, edited and translated by Alan Orr Anderson and Marjorie Ogilvie Anderson (Oxford: Clarendon, 1991), 64–67.

21. Michael Meckler, "Carnal Love and Priestly Ordination on Sixth-Century Tiree." *Innes Review* 51, no. 2 (2000): 95–108.

22. Florence of Worcester, *Chronicon ex Chronicis*, 2 vols., edited by Benjamin Thorpe (London: English Historical Society, 1848–1849), 1: 178–179; Henry of Huntingdon, *Historia Anglorum*, edited by Thomas Arnold (London: Longman, 1879), 185.

23. "The Knight's Tale," in *The Riverside Chaucer*, edited by Larry D. Benson (Boston: Houghton Mifflin, 1987), 41, ll. 1129–1139. See also "The Friar's Tale," 124, ll. 1399, 1405; "The Pardoner's Tale," 199, ll. 702–704; "The Shipman's Tale," 203, ll. 36, 40–42.

24. "Manuale ad usum Sarum," in *Manuale et processionale ad usum insignis ecclesiae eboracensis*, edited by W. G. Henderson, Surtees Society 63 (1875), Appendix 1: 19.

25. Gerald of Wales, *Topographia Hibernica*, in *Giraldi Cambrensis Opera*, 8 vols., edited by J. S. Brewer, James F. Dimock and G. F. Warner, Rolls Series 21 (London: Longman, 1861–1891), 5: 167, quoted in Bray, *The Friend*, 23.

26. Bray, *The Friend*, 22–25; Mark D. Jordan, "A Romance of the Gay Couple." *GLQ* 3 (1996): 301–310, 305, critiquing John Boswell, *The Marriage of Likeness: Same-Sex Unions in Pre-Modern Europe* (London: HarperCollins, 1994), 193; Brown, "Ritual Brotherhood," 366–399.

27. *Amys and Amylion*, edited by Françoise H. M. Le Saux (Exeter: University of Exeter Press, 1993), 32.

28. Sheila Delany, "A, A and B: Coding Same-Sex Union in *Amis and Amiloun*," in *Pulp Fictions of Medieval England: Essays in Popular Romance*, edited by Nicola McDonald (Manchester: Manchester University Press, 2004), 63–81; Richard E. Zeikowitz, *Homoeroticism and Chivalry: Discourses of Male Same-Sex Desire in the Fourteenth Century* (New York: Palgrave Macmillan, 2003), 37–38.

29. Delany, "A, A and B," 72–75.

30. 2 Kings 1:26; Brian McGuire, *Friendship and Community: The Monastic Experience, 350–1250* (Kalamazoo, MI: Cistercian Publications, 1988), 94–95.

31. Reginald Hyatte, *The Arts of Friendship: The Idealization of Friendship in Medieval and Early Renaissance Literature* (Leiden: Brill, 1994), 45–72; McGuire, *Friendship and Community*.

32. Boswell, *CSTH*, 221–222; Michael Morgan Holmes, "Aelred of Rievaulx," in *Who's Who in Gay and Lesbian History*, edited by Aldrich and Wotherspoon, 6–7; Ruth Mazo Karras, "Friendship and Love in the Lives of Two Twelfth-Century English Saints." *Journal of Medieval History*, 14, no. 4 (1988): 308–311; Brian McGuire, *Brother and Lover: Aelred of Rievaulx* (New York: Crossroad, 1994), 40–50.

33. McGuire, *Brother and Lover*, 64–66.

34. Jaeger, *Ennobling Love*, 110–116.

35. *The Letters of Saint Anselm of Canterbury*, translated by W. Fröhlich, 3 vols. (Kalamazoo, MI: Cistercian Publications, 1990–1994), 1: 305.

36. Jaeger, *Ennobling Love*, 43–50.

37. Boswell, *CSTH*, 190; Allen J. Frantzen, *Before the Closet: Same-Sex Love from "Beowulf" to "Angels in America"* (Chicago: University of Chicago Press, 1998), 198–199.

38. Jaeger, *Ennobling Love*, 130–131.

39. Jaeger, *Ennobling Love*, 135.

40. Walter Map, *De nugis curialium*, edited and translated by M. R. James (Oxford: Clarendon, 1983), 80–81, discussed in McGuire, *Brother and Lover*, 134; Jaeger, *Ennobling Love*, 132.

41. St Thomas Aquinas, *Summa Theologiæ*, edited and translated by Dominican Fathers, 61 vols. (London: Eyre & Spottiswoode, 1980–), 43: 244–245.

42. Mark D. Jordan, *The Invention of Sodomy in Christian Theology* (Chicago: University of Chicago Press, 1997).

43. Derrick Sherwin Bailey, *Homosexuality and the Western Christian Tradition* (London: Longmans, Green & Co., 1955), 1–28; Boswell, *CSTH*, 92–98.

44. Aelfric's *Anglo-Saxon Version of* Alcuini Interrogationes Sigewulfi in Genesis, edited by G. E. MacLean, in *Anglia* 7 (1884), 48.

45. London, British Library, MS Cotton Claudius B.IV, fol. 23v.

46. Vern L. Bullough and James Brundage, *Sexual Practices and the Medieval Church* (Buffalo, NY: Prometheus, 1982), 66–69; Carolyn Dinshaw, *Getting Medieval: Sexualities and Communities, Pre- and Postmodern* (Durham, NC: Duke University Press, 1999), 3–11.

47. *John Mirk's Instructions for Parish Priests*, edited by Gillis Kristensson (Lund: Gleerup, 1974), 80; *Book of Vices and Virtues*, edited by W. Nelson Francis, *Early English Text Society* o.s. 217 (London: Oxford University Press, 1942), 46.

48. "The Parson's Tale," in *Riverside Chaucer*, 318, 320.

49. *The Revelation of the Monk of Eynsham*, edited by Robert Easting, *Early English Text Society* o.s. 318 (Oxford: Oxford University Press, 2002), 79.

50. "Cleanness," in *Sir Gawain and the Green Knight, Pearl, Cleanness, Patience*, edited by J. J. Anderson (London: J. M. Dent, 1996), 81.

51. Anderson, *Cleanness*, 88–89.

52. Allen J. Frantzen, "The Disclosure of Sodomy in *Cleanness*." *PMLA* 111, no. 3 (1996): 451–464; Elizabeth B. Keiser, *Courtly Desire and Medieval Homophobia: The Legitimation of Sexual Pleasure in Cleanness and its Contexts* (New Haven, CT: Yale University Press, 1997).

53. Michael Hanrahan, "Speaking of Sodomy: Gower's Advice to Princes in the *Confessio Amantis*." *Exemplaria* 14, no. 2 (2002): 424–427.

54. Thomas Walsingham, *Chronicon Angliae*, edited by Edward Maunde Thompson, Rolls Series 64 (London: Longman, 1874), 375–376.

55. Karma Lochrie, *Covert Operations: The Medieval Uses of Secrecy* (Philadelphia: University of Pennsylvania Press, 1999), 178–226; Karma Lochrie, "Presumptive Sodomy and its Exclusions." *Textual Practice* 13, no. 2 (1999): 295–310.

56. Alan of Lille, *The Plaint of Nature*, translated by James J. Sheridan (Toronto: Pontifical Institute of Mediaeval Studies, 1980), 69; Peter Damian, *Book of Gomorrah* (Letter 31), in *The Letters of Peter Damian, 31–60*, translated by Otto J. Blum, *The Fathers of the Church: Mediaeval Continuation* 2 (Washington, DC: Catholic University of America Press, 1990), 31.

57. Walsingham, *Historia anglicana*, edited by Henry Thomas Riley, Rolls Series 28 (London, 1864; reprinted 1965), 2: 148.

58. Adam of Usk, *The Chronicle of Adam of Usk 1377–1421*, edited by Chris Given-Wilson (Oxford: Clarendon, 1997), 62–63.

59. Katherine J. Lewis, "Becoming a Virgin King: Richard II and Edward the Confessor," in *Gender and Holiness: Men, Women and Saints in Late Medieval*

Europe, edited by Samantha J. E. Riches and Sarah Salih (London: Routledge, 2002), 86–100.

60. William E. Burgwinkle, *Sodomy, Masculinity, and Law in Medieval Literature: France and England, 1050–1230* (Cambridge: Cambridge University Press, 2004), 46–52; C. Stephen Jaeger, *The Origins of Courtliness: Civilizing Trends and the Formation of Courtly Ideals* 939–1210 (Philadelphia: University of Pennsylvania Press, 1985), 176–189; Mathew S. Kuefler, "Male Friendship and the Suspicion of Sodomy in Twelfth-Century France," in *Gender and Difference in the Middle Ages*, edited by Sharon Farmer and Carol Brown Pasternack (Minneapolis: University of Minnesota Press, 2003), 162–163.

61. Orderic Vitalis, *Ecclesiastical History*, 6 vols., edited and translated by Marjorie Chibnall (Oxford: Clarendon, 1968–1980), 4: 188, quoted in Jaeger, *Origins of Courtliness*, 180.

62. Vitalis, *Ecclesiastical*, 5: 286–292. On Ganymede, see Boswell, *CSTH*, 250–265.

63. William of Malmesbury, *Gesta regum anglorum*, 2 vols., edited by William Stubbs, Rolls Series 90 (London: Eyre & Spottiswoode, 1887), 2: 369–370, quoted in Jaeger, *Origins of Courtliness*, 181.

64. Malmesbury, *Gesta regum*, 530–531.

65. Bailey, *Homosexuality*, 124; Frank Barlow, *William Rufus* (New Haven: Yale University Press, 2000), 101–109.

66. Edward A. Freeman, *The Reign of William Rufus and the Accession of Henry the First*, 2 vols. (Oxford: Clarendon, 1882), 1: 157–159.

67. Zeikowitz, *Homoeroticism and Chivalry*, 116–118.

68. *Flores Historiarum*, 3 vols., edited by H. R. Luard, Rolls Series 95 (London: Eyre & Spottiswoode, 1890), 3: 229; *Chronica Monasterii de Melsa*, edited by E. A. Bond, Rolls Series 43 (London: Longman, 1866–1888), 2: 355.

69. Jean Froissart, *Chroniques*, 15 vols., edited by Siméon Luce, Gaston Raynaud, Léon Mirot and Albert Mirot (Paris: Société de L'Histoire de France, 1869–1975), 1: 34.

70. *Chronicon Galfridi le Baker de Swynebroke*, edited by Edward Maunde Thompson (Oxford: Clarendon, 1889), 33–34; Ranulf Higden, *Polychronicon*, 9 vols., edited by C. Babington and J. R. Lumby (London, 1865–1886), 8: 325–327.

71. Michael Evans, *The Death of Kings: Royal Deaths in Medieval England* (London: Hambledon & London, 2003), 124–134.

72. Robert Mills, *Suspended Animation: Pain, Pleasure and Punishment in Medieval Culture* (London: Reaktion, 2005), 83–105.

73. Elaine Tuttle Hansen, *Chaucer and the Fictions of Gender* (Berkeley, CA: University of California Press, 1992), 229–233.

74. Evans, *Death of Kings*, 129.

75. Bray, *The Friend*, 275–276; Kuefler, "Male Friendship," 161–162; Zeikowitz, *Homoeroticism and Chivalry*, 128–129.

76. Gerald of Wales, Itinerarium Kambriæ et Descriptio Kambriæ, in Giraldi Cambrensis Opera, edited by Brewer, Dimock and Warner, 6: 215.

77. Robert Bartlett, *Gerald of Wales 1146–1223* (Oxford: Clarendon, 1982), 14, 20–25.

78. Rhonda Knight, "Procreative Sodomy: Textuality and the Construction of Ethnicities in Gerald of Wales's *Descriptio Kambriæ*." *Exemplaria* 14, no. 1 (2002): 47–77.

79. *Rotuli parliamentorum*, 6 vols. (London, 1767–1777), 2: 332.

80. Goodich, *Unmentionable Vice*, 7–10; Arno Karlen, "The Homosexual Heresy." *Chaucer Review* 6 (1971): 44–63.

81. Oxford, Bodleian Library, MS Bodley 270b, fols. 11v, 123v.

82. Malcolm Barber, *The Trial of the Templars* (Cambridge: Cambridge University Press, 1978), 69.

83. Barber, *Trial of the Templars*, 249.

84. Malcolm Barber, "The Trial of the Templars Revisited," in *The Military Orders*, vol. 2: *Welfare and Warfare*, edited by Helen Nicholson (Aldershot: Ashgate, 1998), 329–342.

85. Barber, *Trial of the Templars*, 191.

86. Barber, *Trial of the Templars*, 193–204.

87. Barber, *Trial of the Templars*, 221–223.

88. Anne Gilmour-Bryson, "Sodomy and the Knights Templar." *Journal of the History of Sexuality*, 7, no. 2 (1996): 151–183.

89. Thomas Walsingham, *Annales Ricardi Secundi*, edited by Henry Thomas Riley, Rolls Series 28 (London: Longmans, Green, Reader & Dyer, 1866), 182–183.

90. James A. Brundage, *Law, Sex, and Christian Society in Medieval Europe* (Chicago: University of Chicago Press, 1987), 593.

91. Dinshaw, *Getting Medieval*, 57–61.

92. Thomas Wright, *Political Poems and Songs Relating to English History*, 2 vols., Rolls Series 14 (London: Longman, Green, Longman & Roberts, 1859–1861), 2: 128.

93. Dinshaw, *Getting Medieval*, 64–68.

94. Dinshaw, *Getting Medieval*, 56.

95. Alan Stewart, *Close Readers: Humanism and Sodomy in Early Modern England* (Princeton, NJ: Princeton University Press, 1997), 38–44.

96. Bede, *Ecclesiastical History of the English People*, translated by Leo Sherley-Price (London: Penguin, 1990), 103–104 (bk 2, ch. 1).

97. John Bale, *The Actes of Englysh Votaryes* (London: Thomas Raynalde, 1548), quoted in Stewart, *Close Readers*, 42.

98. Roger of Hovedon, *Chronica*, 4 vols., edited by William Stubbs, Rolls Series 51 (London: Longmans, 1870), 3: 288–289.

99. Chaplais, *Piers Gaveston*, 9–10.

100. M. R. Godden, "The Trouble with Sodom: Literary Responses to Biblical Sexuality." *Bulletin of the John Rylands University Library of Manchester* 77 (1995): 99–101.

101. Boswell, *CSTH*, 215–216, 366.

102. Frantzen, *Before the Closet*, 237–239; David J. Bromell, "Anselm of Canterbury," in *Who's Who in Gay and Lesbian History*, edited by Aldrich and Wotherspoon, 24–25; R. W. Southern, *Saint Anselm: A Portrait in a Landscape* (Cambridge: Cambridge University Press, 1990), 148–153.

103. McGuire, *Brother and Lover*, 100–101.

104. Bromell, "Anselm of Canterbury," 25.

105. Judith M. Bennett, " 'Lesbian-like' and the Social History of Lesbianisms." *Journal of the History of Sexuality*, 9, no. 1 (2000): 1–24.

106. Bray, *The Friend*, 14–16; Siegfried Düll, Anthony Luttrell and Maurice Keen, "Faithful Unto Death: The Tomb Slab of Sir William Neville and Sir John Clanvowe, Constantinople 1391." *Antiquaries Journal*, 71 (1991): 174–190.

107. Düll, Luttrell and Keen, "Faithful Unto Death," 183–184.

108. Nigel Saul, *Richard II* (New Haven, CT: Yale University Press, 1997), 311, 457, note 100.

109. London, British Library, Harleian MS 2259, fol. 27v, quoted in Düll, Luttrell and Keen, "Faithful Unto Death," 184.

110. *Westminster Chronicle, 1381–1394*, edited and translated by L. C. Hector and Barbara F. Harvey (Oxford: Clarendon, 1982), 480–481.

111. Düll, Luttrell and Keen, "Faithful Unto Death," 178.

112. John M. Bowers, "Three Readings of *The Knight's Tale*: Sir John Clanvowe, Geoffrey Chaucer, and James I of Scotland." *Journal of Medieval and Early Modern Studies*, 34 (2004): 279–287.

113. Bowers, "Three Readings," 282.

114. Michel Foucault, *The History of Sexuality*, vol. 1: *An Introduction*, translated by Robert Hurley (London: Penguin, 1978), 43.

115. Pierre J. Payer, *Sex and the Penitentials: The Development of a Sexual Code 550–1150* (Toronto: University of Toronto Press, 1984), 12–13, 40–43, 135–139.

116. Payer, *Sex*, 138.

117. Poenitentiale Pseudo-Ecberti, or Old English Penitential, canon 2.6, quoted in Frantzen, *Before the Closet*, 178.

118. *Canons of Theodore*, canons 138–147, 183–185, quoted in Frantzen, *Before the Closet*, 179–180.

119. Payer, *Sex*, 135; Frantzen, *Before the Closet*, 124–129, 145, 171.

120. Frantzen, *Before the Closet*, 164–165.

121. Frantzen, *Before the Closet*, 151–154.

122. *Penitential* of 'Bede,' canon 3.24, quoted in Frantzen, *Before the Closet*, 177.

123. P. L. Heyworth, "Jocelin of Brakelond, Abbot Samson, and the Case of William the Sacrist," in *Middle English Studies Presented to Norman Davis in Honour of his Seventieth Birthday*, edited by Douglas Gray and E. G. Stanley (Oxford: Clarendon, 1983), 180–184, 193–194.

124. *Dean and Chapter of Durham*, Locellus 25, no. 115, quoted in R. L. Storey, *Thomas Langley and the Bishopric of Durham* (London: SPCK, 1961), 196.

125. *Records of Visitations Held by William Alnwick, Bishop of Lincoln 1436–1449*, part I, in *Visitations of Religious Houses in the Diocese of Lincoln*, 3 vols., edited by A. Hamilton Thompson (Horncastle: Morton & Sons, 1918–1929), 2: 188, 191, 197.

126. *Visitations Held by William Alnwick, Bishop of Lincoln 1436–1449*, part 2, in *Visitations of Religious Houses*, edited by Thompson, 3: 220–224.

127. Sarah Salih, "Sexual Identities: A Medieval Perspective," in *Sodomy in Early Modern Europe*, edited by Tom Betteridge (Manchester: Manchester University Press, 2002), 123–124.

128. See, for instance, London, British Library, Harley 1527, fol. 107r; Oxford, Bodleian Library, MS Bodley 270b, fols. 78r, 90r.

129. Frantzen, *Before the Closet*, 156–162.

130. Walter Horn and Ernest Born, *The Plan of St Gall*, 3 vols. (Berkeley, CA, University of California Press, 1979), 1: 252–253; Patricia A. Quinn, *Better Than the Sons of Kings: Boys and Monks in the Early Middle Ages* (New York: Peter Lang, 1989), 165.

131. *The Monastic Agreement of the Monks and Nuns of the English Nation*, translated by Thomas Symons (London: Thomas Nelson, 1953), 8.

132. Horn and Born, *Plan of St Gall*, 1: 252; Quinn, *Better Than the Sons of Kings*, 45–52, 66; V. A. Kolve, "Ganymede/*Son of Getron*: Medieval Monasticism and the Drama of Same-Sex Desire." *Speculum* 73 (1998): 1038–1041.

133. Michael Rocke, *Forbidden Friendships: Homosexuality and Male Culture in Renaissance Florence* (Oxford: Oxford University Press, 1996).

134. Quinn, *Better than the Sons of Kings*, 168–174.

135. *Medieval Latin Poems of Male Love and Friendship*, edited and translated by Thomas Stehling (Garland: New York, 1984), 71.

136. Quinn, *Better than the Sons of Kings*, 175–182.

137. Burgwinkle, *Sodomy*, 33–40; Ilene H. Forsyth, "The Ganymede Capital at Vézelay," *Gesta* 15 (1976): 241–246; Kolve, "Ganymede/*Son of Getron*"; Quinn, *Better Than the Sons of Kings*, 178–182.

138. Burgwinkle, *Sodomy*, 54.

139. Damian, Liber Gomorrhianus, in *Blum, Letters of Peter Damian*, 16.

140. Quinn, *Better than the Sons of Kings*, 183–189; Kuefler, "Male Friendship," 162, 169–170.

141. Frantzen, *Before the Closet*, 172–173, drawing on Bray, *Homosexuality*, 41–56.

142. Frantzen, *Before the Closet*, 142–144.

143. Bailey, *Homosexuality*, 145–146; Boswell, *CSTH*, 292–293; Goodich, *Unmentionable Vice*, 77.

144. Marc Boone, "State Power and Illicit Sexuality: The Persecution of Sodomy in Late Medieval Bruges." *Journal of Medieval History*, 22, no. 2 (1996): 135–153; Helmut Puff,

Sodomy in Reformation Germany and Switzerland 1400–1600 (Chicago: University of Chicago Press, 2003); Rocke, *Forbidden Friendships.*

145. Richard M. Wunderli, *London Church Courts and Society on the Eve of the Reformation* (Cambridge, MA: Medieval Academy of America, 1981), 83–84.

146. "General Prologue," in *Riverside Chaucer*, 34, l. 691.

147. *The Chronicle of Richard of Devizes of the Time of King Richard the First*, edited by John T. Appleby (London: Thomas Nelson, 1963), 65–66.

148. Wayne Dynes and Warren Johansson, "London's Medieval Sodomites." *The Cabirion* 10 (1984): 5–7, 34; *Encyclopedia of Homosexuality*, edited by Dynes, 2: 1259.

149. Anthony P. Bale, "Richard of Devizes and Fictions of Judaism." *Jewish Culture and History* 3, no. 2 (2000): 55–72.

150. David Lorenzo Boyd and Ruth Mazo Karras, "The Interrogation of a Male Transvestite Prostitute in Fourteenth-Century London." *GLQ* 1 (1995): 459–465.

Chapter 2: Renaissance Sodomy, 1500–1700

1. Michael Rocke, *Forbidden Friendships: Homosexuality and Male Culture in Renaissance Florence* (New York: Oxford University Press, 1996); Allen J. Frantzen, *Before the Closet: Same-Sex Love from Beowulf to Angels in America* (Chicago: University of Chicago Press, 1998), p. 190; *Sir Gawain and the Green Knight, Pearl, Cleanness, Patience*, edited by J. J. Anderson (London: Dent, 1996), p.86.

2. For Rome: Craig A. Williams, *Roman Homosexuality* (New York: Oxford University Press, 1999); Lynn E. Roller, "The Ideology of the Eunuch Priest," *Gender and Body in the Ancient Mediterranean*, edited by Maria Wyke (Oxford: Blackwell, 1998); Will Roscoe, "Priests of the Goddess: Gender Transgression in Ancient Religion," *History of Religions*, 35 (1996): 195–230; John Boswell, *Christianity, Social Tolerance, and Homosexuality* (Chicago: University of Chicago Press, 1980); For modern Islam: Levon H. Malikian, "Social Change and Sexual Behavior of Arab University Students." *Journal of Social Psychology* 73 (1967): 169–175; for Morocco and Turkey: *Sexuality and Eroticism among Males in Moslem Societies*, edited by Arno Schmitt and Jehoeda Sofer (New York: Haworth Press, 1992); S. S. Davis and D. A. Davis, *Adolescence in a Moroccan Town* (New Brunswick: Rutgers University Press, 1989) — the Moroccan transvestite dancer has been described to me by Vincent Crapanzano; for Oman, Unni Wikan, *Behind the Veil in Arabia* (Chicago: University of Chicago Press, 1982), G. Feuerstein and S. al-Marzooq, "The Omani *Xanith*." *Man*, 13 (1978): 665–667. For the Indian hijra: S. N. Ranade, "A Study of Eunuchs in Delhi" (Government of India, Delhi, 1983, unpublished), p.117 (I thank Serena Nanda for a copy of this work); Satish Kumar Sharma, *Hijras* (New Delhi: Gian, 1989); M. D. Vyas and Yogesh Shingala, *The Life Style of the Eunuchs* (New Delhi: Anmol, 1987); Serena Nanda, *Neither Man nor Woman: the Hijras of India* (Belmont, CA: Wadsworth, 1990); Kira Hall, "Hijra/Hijrin: Language and Gender Identity" (PhD thesis, University of California, Berkley, 1995); Zia Jaffrey, *The Invisibles* (New York: Vintage, 1996); Gayatri Reddy, *With Respect to Sex* (Chicago: University of Chicago Press, 2005); for passive adult men: Lawrence Cohen, "The Pleasures of Castration: the Postoperative Status of Hijras, Jankhas and Academics," *Sexual Nature, Sexual Culture*, edited by P. R. Abramson and S. D. Pinkerton (Chicago: University of Chicago Press, 1995); for men and boys: Shivananda Khan, "Under the Blanket: Bisexualties and AIDS in India," *Bisexualities and AIDS*, edited by Peter Aggelton (London: Taylor & Francis, 1996), "Through a Window Darkly: Men Who Sell Sex to Men in India and Bangladesh," *Men Who Sell Sex*, edited by Pete Aggleton (Philadelphia: Temple University Press, 1999), "Culture, Sexualities, and Identities: Men Who have Sex with Men in India." *Journal of Homosexuality* 40 (2001): 99–115; *Contexts: Race, Culture and Sexuality* (London: Naz Project, 1996), p.36 (60 percent of men have sex with men), *Khush* (London, 1996); Shakuntala Devi, *The World of Homosexuals* (New Delhi: Vikas, 1976, 1978), p.94; see also, Jeremy Seabrook, *Love in a Different Climate* (London: Verso, 1999), which claims an originality it does not have.

3. For modern discussion, see S. F. Daw, "Age of Boys' Puberty in Leipzig, 1727–49, as Indicated by Voice Breaking in J.S. Bach's Choir Members." *Human Biology*, 42 (1970): 87–89; David Wulstan, "Vocal Colour in English Sixteenth-Century Polyphony." *Journal of the Plainsong and Mediaeval Music Society*, 2 (1979): 19–60; Richard Rastall, "Female Roles in All-Male Casts." *Medieval English Theatre*, 7 (1985): 25–50.

4. Bruce R. Smith, *Homosexual Desire in Shakespeare's England* (Chicago: University of Chicago Press, 1991), 43–52.

5. David Knowles, *The Religious Orders in England* (Cambridge: Cambridge University Press, 1959, 1961), vol. 3; David N. Mager, "John Bale and Early Tudor Sodomy Discourse," *Queering the Renaissance*, edited by Johnathan Goldberg (Durham, NC: Duke University Press, 1994); Alan Stewart, *Close Readers* (Princeton: Princeton University Press, 1997), ch. 2; G. W. Bernard, *The King's Reformation: Henry VIII and the Remaking of the English Church* (New Haven: Yale University Press, 2005).

6. Knowles, *Religious Orders*, III, 291–303, 480–482; David Knowles and R. Neville Hadcock, *Medieval Religious Houses: England and Wales* (New York: St Martin's, 1971), 62, 120; Stewart, *Close Readers*, 47–48.

7. Robert Burton, *The Anatomy of Melancholy*, edited by Floyd Dell and Paul Jordan-Smith (New York: Tudor, reprint of 1927 ed.), 652, part 3, section 2; for the Latin original, see, *The Anatomy of Melancholy*, edited by T. C. Faulkner, N. K. Kiessling and R. L. Blair (Oxford: Clarendon Press, 1994), III, 50.

8. Michael B. Young, *King James and the History of Homosexuality* (New York: New York University Press, 2000), 10–17, 21–22; David M. Bergeron, *King James and Letters of Homoerotic Desire* (Iowa City: University of Iowa Press, 1999), 32–64.

9. Young, *King James*, 29, 150; Paul Hammond, *Figuring Sex between Men from Shakespeare to Rochester* (Oxford: Clarendon Press, 2002), 129.

10. Hammond, *Figuring*, 129; Young, *King James*, 29–31, 42–44, 74, 120; Bergeron, *King James*, 65–97.

11. Bergeron, *King James*, 175, 179, 189, 199–200; Young, *King James*, 31–34, 44–47, 60; Roger Lockyer, *Buckingham* (New York: Longman, 1981).

12. Young, *King James*, 49, 125, 76; *The Letters of John Chamberlain*, edited by N. E. McClure (Philadelphia: American Philosophical Society, 1939), 2 vols., I, 144, 442, 479, 553, 560, 570, 580.

13. Cynthia B. Herrup, *A House in Gross Disorder: Sex, Law and the 2nd Earl of Castlehaven* (New York: Oxford University Press, 1999), 38–48, 95–96, 113–114, 87.

14. G. R. Quaife, *Wanton Wenches and Wayward Wives* (New Brunswick: Rutgers University Press, 1979), 175–177.

15. David Rollison, "Property, Ideology and Popular Culture in a Gloucestershire Village, 1660–1740." *Past and Present*, 93 (1990): 70–97.

16. Michael Shapiro, *Gender in Play on the Shakespearean Stage* (Ann Arbor, MI: University of Michigan Press), Appendix B, 221–223.

17. Arthur F. Kinney, editor, *Markets of Bawdrie: The Dramatic Criticism of Stephen Gosson* (Salzburg: Institut für Englische Sprache und Literatur, 1974), 175, 177; John Rainoldes, *Th' Overthrow of Stage-Plays* (1599) (New York: Garland, 1974), 10–11, 32, 34–35, 18; William Prynne, *Histrio-Mastix* (1633) (New York: Johnson Reprint, 1972), 212.

18. Prynne, *Histrio-Mastix*, 390–391, 418–419; Clement Walker, *Relations and Observations* (London, 1661), 2 vols., II, 257; *The Diary of John Evelyn*, edited by E. S. De Beer (Oxford: Clarendon Press, reprint 2000), 6 vols., III, 96–97.

19. Miller Maclure, editor, *Marlowe: The Critical Heritage 1588–1896* (London: Routledge & Kegan Paul, 1979), 35, 37; Giovanni Dall'Orto, " 'Nature is a Mother Most Sweet': Homosexuality in Sixteenth- and Seventeenth-Century Italian Libertinism," *Queer Italia*, edited by Gary Castaro (New York: Palgrave Macmillan, 2004), 86–87, 100–101; *Documentos inéditos para la historia de España* (Madrid: 1936), I, 101–103 as translated in Lockyer, *Buckingham*, 43.

20. Fredson Bowers, editor, *The Complete Works of Christopher Marlowe* (Cambridge: Cambridge University Press, 1981, 2nd ed.), 2 vols., "Edward II": II, 16–17 (I.i.50–73); II, 22–23 (I.ii.46–67); II, 29 (I.iv.178–181); II, 45 (II.ii.224).

21. Smith, *Homosexual Desire*, 189–223; Jonathan Goldberg, *Sodometries: Rennaissance Texts, Modern Sexualities* (Stanford, CA: Stanford University Press, 1992), 114–137.

22. "Edward II": II, 35 (I.iv.391–397); Gregory W. Bredbeck, *Sodomy and Interpretation: Marlowe to Milton* (Ithaca, NY: Cornell University Press, 1991), 58–80; Young, *King James*, 57; *Works of Michael Drayton*, edited by J. William Hebel (Oxford: Blackwell, 1931), 5 vols., I, 194, ll.1268–1269; Young, *King James*, 58, 63.

23. C. H. Herford and Percy and Evelyn Simpson, editors, *Ben Jonson* (Oxford: Clarendon Press, 1925–1951), 11 vols: "The Alchemist," V, 353 (III.iv.75–82), "On Sir Voluptuous Beast," VIII, 34; "Epicoene," V, 164–165 (I.ii.1–30).

24. Herford and Simpson, *Jonson*: "Poetaster," IV, 209, 252–254 (I.ii.15–17, III.iv.205–209, 259–262, 273–276); "The Devil is an Ass," VI, 221 (III.iv.11), VI, 208 (II.viii.56–80).

25. Arnold Davenport, editor, *The Poems of John Marston* (Liverpool: Liverpool University Press, 1961), 78; J. Cocke, quoted in E. K. Chambers, *The Elizabethan Stage* (Oxford: Clarendon Press, 1974), 4 vols., IV, 256–257; Middleton, "Ingling Pyander," Satire V in *Mycro-Cynicon* (1599), *Works*, edited by A. H. Bullen, VIII, 130–134; *The Diary of Sir Simonds D'Ewes 1622–1624*, edited by Elizabeth Bourcier (Paris: Didier, 1974), 92–93; Rafael Carrasco, "Lazarillo on a Street Corner: What the Picaresque Novel Did Not Say about Fallen Boys," *Sex and Love in Golden Age Spain*, edited by Alain Saint-Saëns (New Orleans: University Press of the South, 1996), 57–69; Luiz Mott, "Pogode português: a subcultura gay em Portugal nos tempos inquisitoriais," *Ciência e Cultura*, 40 (1988): 120–139, 134.

26. Arnold Glover and A. R. Waller, editors, *The Works of Francis Beaumont and John Fletcher* (Cambridge: Cambridge University Press, 1906), 10 vols., "The Humorous Lieutenant," IV.ii–iv, 341–349, IV.vi, 352–353, V.v.362–363; Fredson Bowers, et al., editors, *The Dramatic Works in the Beaumont and Fletcher Canon* (Cambridge: Cambridge University Press, 1966–1996), 10 vols., "Love's Cure," III, 32 (II.i.174), "The Captain," I, 615 (IV.ii.126–129), I, 618–619 (IV.iii.58–74).

27. Bowers, editor, *Works*, "The Night Walker or Little Thief," VII, 551–556 (II.i.55–II.iii.81).

28. Bowers, editor, *Works*, VII, 563–565 (III.i.28–85), VII, 579–581 (IV.i.1–56), VII, 588–589 (IV.iv.1–46), VII, 571 (III.iii.78–80).

29. Bowers, editor, *Works*, "The Honest Man's Fortune," X, 76–77 (IV.i.96–146).

30. Bowers, editor, *Works*, X, 58–59 (III.i.115), X, 61–62 (III.i.197–206), X, 74–75 (IV.i.50–95).

31. Bowers, editor, *Works*, X, 72 (III.iii.195–227), X, 81–82 (IV.i.260–296), X, 105–106, 110–111 (V.iv.228–272); Rocke, *Forbidden Friendships*, 108–109, 170–172.

32. Glover and Waller, editors, *Works*, "The Maid's Tragedy," I, 2–3, 37, 41, 61, 73–74.

33. Tim Parrott, editor, *The Plays of George Chapman: The Comedies* (New York: Russell and Russell, 1961), 2 vols., "Sir Giles Goosecap," II, 619–620 (I.iv.26–29), II, 668 (V.ii.309–311); William Shakespeare, *The Sonnets*, edited by C. L. Barber (New York: Dell, 1960).

34. Robert Latham and William Matthews, editors, *The Diary of Samuel Pepys* (London: Bell and Sons, 1970–1983), 11 vols., I, 224, II, 7, IX, 435–436, IV, 209.

35. B. R. S. Fone, editor, *An Apology for the Life of Colley Cibber* (Ann Arbor, MI: University of Michigan Press, 1968), 71; H. Highfill, K. A. Burnim and E. A. Langhans, editors, *A Biographical Dictionary of Actors* ... (Carbondale, IL: Southern Illinois University Press, 1973–1993), 16 vols., IX, 83; J. W. Johnson, *A Profane Wit* (Rochester, NY: University of Rochester Press, 2004), 385n, 75; *Lorenzo Magalotti at the Court of*

Charles II, edited and translated by W. E. Knowles (Waterloo, Ont.: Wilfrid Laurier University Press, 1980), 48.

36. Highfill, et al., *Biographical Dictionary*, IX, 81, 83; Richard M. Wunderli, *London Church Courts on the Eve of the Reformation* (Cambridge, MA: Medieval Academy of America, 1981), 84; Benlow and Hawkyard, Appendix C, in *Gender in Play*, edited by Shapiro, 226; Bowers, editor, *Works of Beaumont and Fletcher*: "Love's Cure," III, 26 (I.iii.177–178), III, 33–34 (II.ii.23–25), III, 37 (II.ii.140–141), III, 69 (IV.iii.37–40), III, 74–76 (IV.iv.8–62).

37. *Pepys Diary*, edited by Latham and Matthews, IV, 209–210, IX, 21, 58–59, IV, 164, 301, V, 219, 220, 224–226, IX, 297, IX, 218, 220.

38. *Pepys Diary*, VII, 138, 315, 404, I, 174, I, 312, II, 15–17, IV, 28.

39. *Pepys Diary*, I, 250, IV, 177, II, 206–207, II, 239, III, 37–38, III, 116, III, 295, IV, 12, 109, 193–194, 202–205, 406, 426, 428, V, 256, 260.

40. *Pepys Diary*, IX, 337, IV, 92, 262, IV, 133, 213–214, VI, 61, 74, 88, III, 69, 70, 72, 74, I, 271, V, 18, I, 222, VI, 35.

41. *Pepys Diary*, I, 139, VI, 317, 321, VII, 70, 100, VII, 104, IV, 276, IX, 184, VII, 169, V, 185, III, 191, VII, 47, IV, 237, III, 6, VIII, 49, I, 286, IV, 216, 433, VII, 31, IX, 159, V, 23, 67, IV, 350, 245, VIII, 14.

42. Jeremy Treglown, editor, *The Letters of John Wilmot, Earl of Rochester* (Chicago: University of Chicago Press, 1980), 160, 230; *The Complete Poems of John Wilmot, Earl of Rochester*, edited by David M. Veith (New Haven: Yale University Press, 1968), 51, 117.

43. Harold Love, editor, *The Works of John Wilmot, Earl of Rochester* (New York: Oxford University Press, 1999), "Valentinian," 160–161 (II.ii.170–188), 63 (III.i.67–74), 167–168 (III.ii.61–65), 223–224 (V.v.1–14).

44. *Mundus Foensis: or the Fop Displayed* (London, 1691), 9, 12–13; *Poems on Affairs of State, Vol. 5: 1688–1697*, edited by William J. Cameron (New Haven: Yale University Press, 1971), 38, 365 (Essex), 38, 60, 122, 386 (Bentinck, also 41–42, 153–154, 221, 333, 440); 366 (Keel); *Vol. 6: 1697–1704*, edited by, F. H. Ellis, 18 (also 244, 370).

45. Charles Shadwell, *The Fair Quaker of Deal* (London, 1710, 1715 ed. cited), 22, 24, 26–27, 80–81; John Dennis, *The Critical Works*, edited by E. N. Hooker (Baltimore: The Johns Hopkins Press, 1939), 2 vols., I, 153–156.

46. *An Account of the Proceedings against Captain Rigby* (London, 1698), reprinted in *A Compleat Collection of Remarkable Tryals* (London, 1718), 2 vols., I, 236–242; A. G. Craig, "The Movement for the Reformation of Manners, 1688–1715" (PhD thesis, University of Edinburgh, 1980), 168–175.

47. *Tryals*, II, 239; Craig, *Movement*, 170, 52; *The Tryal and Condemnation of ... Earl of Castlehaven* (London, 1699) in *Sodomy Trials*, edited by Randolph Trumbach (New York: Garland, 1986); *The Sodomites Shame and Doom* (London, 1702), 1.

48. *Tryals*, II, 240.

49. Corporation of London Record Office: Sessions Papers, 16 June 1699.

50. Dennis Rubini, editors, *Letters from James Vernon to Duke of Shrewsbury, 1696–1708* (Wakefiled, Yorkshire: Academic Books, microform, 1988), III, 111–115, 119.

51. Craig, *Movement*, 170–171.

52. *The Sodomites Shame and Doom*, 2; Ned Ward, *The London Spy* (London, 1699, cited from 1706 ed.), 68, 212.

Chapter 3: Modern Sodomy: The Origins of Homosexuality, 1700–1800

1. Magnus Hirschfeld, *The Homosexuality of Men and Women*, translated by Michael A. Lombardi-Nash (Amherst, NY: Prometheus Books, 2000; originally published 1914), 529–561; Edward O. Laumann, John H. Gagnon, Robert T. Michael and Stuart Michaels, *The Social Organization of Sexuality: Sexual Practices in the United States* (Chicago: University of Chicago Press, 1994); Anne M. Johnson, Jane Wadsworth, Kaye Wellings, Julia Field, with Sally Bradshaw, *Sexual Attitudes and Lifestyles* (Oxford: Blackwell

Scientific, 1994); W. D. Mosher, A. Chandra and J. Jones, "Sexual Behavior and Selected Health Measures: Men and Women 15–44 Years of Age, United States, 2002" (Advance data from vital and health statistics; no. 362. Hyattsville, MD: National Center for Health Statistics, 2005).

2. Thomas Baker, *Tunbridge-Walks: or the Yeoman of Kent* (London, 1703); D. E. Baker, *Biographia Dramatica* (London, 1812; reprint, New York: AMS Press, 1966), 3 vols., I.i.15–16; *A Complete List of All the English Dramatic Poets*, attached to Thomas Whincop, *Scanderberg* (London, 1747), 166–167; *Dictionary of National Biography*.

3. *The Tryal ... of ... Sodomites ... 1707*; Corporation of London Record Office (CLRO hereafter): SR (October 1707), Newgate calendar, 15 October; Hertfordshire R.O.: D/EP/F32 (17 October 1707); John Dunton, *Athenianism* (London, 1710), 2 vols., II, 95–96; *The Women-Haters' Lamentation* (London, 1707).

4. *A Full and True Account of ... a ... Gang of Sodomites* (London, 1709); Edward Ward, *The Secret History of Clubs* (London, 1709) 284–301; *Oxford English Dictionary*, s.v. molly; Wayne Dynes, *Homolexis* (New York, 1985), *passim*; for faggot as early nineteenth-century West Country for prostitute: Polly Morris, "Sexual Reputation in Somerset, 1733–1850" (PhD thesis, University of Warwick, 1985); Dunton, *Atheneanism*, 95; *Women-Haters' Lamentation*.

5. Ward, *History of Clubs*, 284–298; David Rollison, "Property, Ideology and Popular Culture in a Gloucestershire Village 1660–1740," *Past and Present*, no. 93 (1981), 70–97.

6. Jonathan Wild, *An Answer to a Late Insolent Libel* (London, 1718), 30–32: reprinted in F. S. Lyons, *Jonathan Wild* (London, 1936), 278–281; *Select Trials at the Sessions House in the Old Bailey* (London, 1742), 4 vols. (New York: Garland, 1985, reprint in 2 vols.), edited by Randolph Trumbach, III, 74–75 (or *Trials at the Old Bailey*, hereafter SP (12–15 April 1727), 5–6); *St James's Evening Post* (15–18 April 1727); for Wild and Hitchen, see Gerald Howson, *Thief-Taker General* (New York: St Martin's Press, 1970).

7. For Partridge: SP (13–16 July 1726), 6; London Metropolitan Archive (LMA hereafter): MJ/SR/2458, Bond 82. The *Select Trials* do not print Partridge's name, giving only P_____. The cases brought to trial may be found conveniently in the *Select Trials*, II, 362–372, III, 36–40. The sessions rolls with material for 1726 are in LMA: MJ/SR/2458–2475 (2473 is too decayed to consult); CLRO: SR (April 1726 to January 1726/7).

8. *The London Journal* (7 May 1726), 2.

9. *Select Trials*, II, 366–367, 370–372: Orme and Wright; Stoneham "for boasting of his having committed sodomitical practices in the house of John Clapp": CLRO: SR (April 1726), R. 17, "in the house of Margaret Clap": CLRO: SR (May 1726), Bonds 5, 8; Clap's coffeehouse: CLRO: SR (December 1726): April Poultry Compter: #3, May Poultry Compter, #1; Margaret Clap's arrest, trial and pillorying: CLRO: SR (April 1726), R. 40, R. 19, R. 8, SR (July 1726) calendar of Wood Street Compter, 28 February, SR (December 1726), April, Wood Street Compter, *Select Trials*, III, 37–38, *London Journal* (23, 30 July 1726); Plump Nelly Roper: *London Journal* (17 December 1726), CLRO: SR (July 1726), bond #9, SR (December 1726), R. 21; Robert Whale and York Horner: *London Journal* (23 April, 9 July, 3 December 1726), LMA: MJ/SR/2458, bond 82, MJ/SR/2459, Newgate calendar, #57; Towleton and Mugg: LMA: MJ/SR/2459, Newgate calendar, #s 58, 59; Wright: *Select Trials*, II, 367.

10. Robert Holloway, *The Phoenix of Sodom* (London, 1813), in *Sodomy Trials*, edited by Randolph Trumbach (New York: Garland, 1986), 28; *Select Trials*, II, 362–363, 365, III, 37. Newton's age: LMA: MJ/SR/2462, indictment 53.

11. *Select Trials*, III, 36, II, 368.

12. A genuine narrative of all the street robberies committed since October last by James Dalton and his accomplices (London, 1728), 31–43; Holloway, *Phoenix of Sodom*, 29–30; *Select Trials*, III, 40; LMA: MJ/SR/2466: New Prison List, July 1726:_____(sic) Brown.

13. *Select Trials*, II, 362–372, III, 36–40.

14. Thomas Baker, *The Female Tatler* (London, 1709), cited in Howson, *Thief-Taker General*, 64; Fanny Burney, *Evelina* (1778; New York, 1958, Everyman edition), 23–24; Mary Hays, *Letters and Essays* (London, 1793), 84–85; idem., *Appeal to the Men of Great Britain in behalf of Women* (London, 1798), 200–202; Priscilla Wakefield, *Reflections on the Present Condition of the Female Sex* (London, 1798), 153, 164–165.

15. *London Journal*, 23 April 1726; LMA: MJ/SR/2459, Newgate calendar, #61; MJ/SR/2465, Recog. 41; CLRO: SR (May 1726), bond 7; SR (April 1726), R. 47; *Select Trials, passim*.

16. SP (1758) no. 2, part 3, 87–90.

17. CLRO: SR (October 1729), Recog. 78; R. Campbell, *The London Tradesman* (London, 1747), 327.

18. SP (1732), no. 6, 166–170.

19. *The London Chronicle*, 4–6 January 1757; and *London Chronicle*, 17–19 July 1764 and *London Evening Post*, 17–19 July 1764 for John Gill; *London Chronicle*, 11–13 September 1764.

20. On Somerset: Polly Morris, "Sodomy and Male Honor: The Case of Somerset, 1740–1850," *The Pursuit of Sodomy: Male Homosexuality in Renaissance and Enlightenment Europe*, edited by Kent Gerard and Gert Hekma (New York: Haworth, 1989), 383–406.

21. Jeffrey Merrick, "Sodomitical Inclinations in Early Eighteenth Century Paris," *Eighteenth Century Studies*, 30 (1997): 289–295; an unpublished paper by Bryant T. Ragan, Jr. which I am grateful to be able to cite; William A. Peniston, *Pederasts and Others: Urban Culture and Sexual Identity in Nineteenth-Century Paris* (New York: Harrington Park Press, 2004).

22. Hirschfeld, *Homosexuality of Men and Women*, 335; George Chauncey, *Gay New York* (New York: Basic Books, 1994), 140.

23. Antony Simpson, "Masculinity and Control in Eighteenth-Century London" (PhD thesis, New York University, 1984), 429, n. 8, 828–829; Trumbach, "Sodomitical Assaults, Gender Role, and Sexual Development in 18th Century London," *Pursuit of Sodomy*, edited by Gerard and Hekma, 427, n.13.

24. SP, no. 5, part 2 (1751): 186–188; see also Trumbach, "Sodomitical Assaults," 412–413.

25. SP, no. 5 (1730): 10–13.

26. SP, no. 6 (5–10 July 1749): 127–128; no. 5 (1735): 82; *Select Trials*, I, 158–160; SP, no. 3, part 2 (1760): 121–123; no. 7, part 2 (1732), 217. These cases are discussed in Trumbach, "Sodomitical Assaults"; Randolph Trumbach, *Sex and the Gender Revolution: Heterosexuality and the Third Gender in Enlightenment London* (Chicago: University of Chicago Press, 1998), 59–63.

27. SP, no. 7, part 3 (1755): 317–323.

28. A Faithful Narrative of the Proceedings in late affair ... John Swinton ... [and] a particular account of ... Robert Thistlethwayte ... and ... Mr W. French (London, 1739) reprinted in *Sodomy Trials*, edited by Trumbach.

29. Arthur N. Gilbert, "Buggery and the British Navy, 1700–1861." *Journal of Social History*, 10 (1976): 72–98.

30. Gilbert, "The *Africaine* courts-Martial: A Study of Buggery and the Royal Navy." *Journal of Homosexuality*, 1 (1974): 111–122. Jan Oosterhoff, "Sodomy at Sea and at the Cape of Good Hope during the Eighteenth Century," *Pursuit of Sodomy*, edited by Gerard and Hekma, 229–235, at 234.

31. Matt Houlbrook, *Queer London* (Chicago: University of Chicago Press, 2005); Chauncey, *Gay New York*; 30 percent of Mexican men: J. M. Carrier, "Mexican Male Bisexuality," *Two Lives to Live: Bisexuality in Men and Women*, edited by Fritz Klein and Timothy J. Wolf (New York: Harrington Park Press, 1985), 81; Joseph Carrier, *De Los Otros: Intimacy and Homosexuality among Mexican Men* (New York: Columbia University Press, 1995); Héctor Carrillo, *The Night Is Young: Sexuality in Mexico in Time*

of AIDS (Chicago: University of Chicago Press, 2002); for Costa Rica, three books by Jacobo Schifter, *Lila's House: Prostitution in Latin America* (New York: Harrington Park Press, 1998), *From Toads to Queens: Transvestism in Latin American Setting* (New York: Harrington Park Press, 1999), *Public Sex in a Latin Society* (New York: Harrington Park Press, 2000); for Peru: Carlos F. Cáceres, "Sexual Culture and Sexual Health Among Young People in Lima in the 1990s" (PhD thesis, University of California, Berkley, 1996), "Male Bisexuality in Peru and the Prevention of AIDS," *Bisexualities and AIDS*, edited by Peter Aggelton (London: Taylor and Francis, 1996), "Fletes in Parque Kennedy: Sexual Cultures Among Young Men Who Sell Sex to Other Men in Lima," *Men Who Sell Sex*, edited by Peter Aggleton (Philadelphia: Temple University Press, 1999).

32. CLRO: Guildhall Justice Room Book, Notebook 37 (9 August 1788), Notebook 29 (12 January 1785).

33. The Trial of John Lowther for an Assault on John Bushnell (London, 1761).

34. *London Chronicle* (LC hereafter), 5–7 July 1787; 22–25 December 1787.

35. LC, 4–6 November, 11–13 November, 7–9 December, 9–11 December 1790, 13–15 January, 1791, 4–6 August 1791; SP, 30–31 August, 1 September 1721.

36. LC, 1–4 December 1759.

37. SP, no. 5, part 2 (1778), 246–250.

38. SP (July 1797), 450–454, #464.

Chapter 4: Secrets, Crimes and Diseases, 1800–1914

1. Patrick Colquhoun, *A Treatise on the Police of the Metropolis …* , 7th ed. (London, 1806), 46.

2. Lord Alfred Douglas, "Two Loves," *Chameleon* (December 1894), quoted in Richard Ellman, *Oscar Wilde* (Harmondsworth, 1987), 421–425.

3. See on this, Jeffrey Weeks, *Coming Out: Homosexual Politics in Britain From the Nineteenth Century to the Present*, revised edition (London, 1990), 41–42.

4. *Times*, 28 November 1835.

5. See J. M. Beattie, *Crime and the Courts in England*, 1660–1800 (Oxford, 1986), 459.

6. See, for instance, indictment against Edward Harrison and James Neill, Central Criminal Court, 5 July 1841, National Archives, London (hereafter TNA), CRIM 4/175.

7. Anon. [Robert Holloway], *The Phoenix of Sodom*, or the Vere Street Coterie (London, 1813), 46.

8. *Parliamentary Papers*, judicial statistics, various volumes.

9. Anon. [Robert Holloway], *The Phoenix of Sodom, or the Vere Street Coterie* (London, 1813), quoted in Paul Hallam, *The Book of Sodom* (London, 1993), 119, 120.

10. Criminal Law Amendment Act 1885, s. 11, quoted in Jeffrey Weeks, *Coming Out*, 14.

11. Sir William Blackstone, *Commentaries on the Laws of England* (London, 1767), 215–216.

12. *Cowdroy's Manchester Gazette*, 23 August 1806; *Times*, 25 August 1806.

13. Lord Ellenborough to Earl Spencer 12 September 1806, British Library Add. Mss. 75899 (Althorp Papers), vol. dc.

14. Hesney Wedgwood to Lord Russell (not dated, November 1835), TNA HO 17/120 Xv13.

15. This remark was reported by John Addington Symonds. See John Addington Symonds to Edmund Gosse, 23 February 1891, in Herbert M. Schueller and Robert Peters, editors, *The Letters of John Addington Symonds*, 3 vols. (Detroit, 1969), III, 554–555.

16. William Bankes' trial was said to have attracted crowds of 2,000. *Times*, 8 June 1833.

17. Percy Fitzgerald, Chronicles of Bow Street Police Office (London, 1888), 214.

18. *Times*, 2 September 1825.

19. Daily Reports From the Various Police Offices, 1830, TNA HO 62/2 and 62/5.

20. See Iain McCalman, Radical Underworld: Prophets, Revolutionaries and Pornographers in London 1795–1840 (Cambridge, 1988), 207.

21. John Church, *The Foundling; or, the Child of Providence* (Printed for the Author, London, 1823), v, 123.

22. Anon., The Bishop!! Particulars of the Charge Against the Hon Percy Jocelyn, Bishop of Clogher, For and Abominable Offence with John Morelley, A Soldier ... (London, John Fairburn, 1822), 15, 19.

23. See H. G. Cocks, Nameless Offences: Homosexual Desire in Nineteenth Century England (London, 2003), 29.

24. Anon. [Robert Holloway] *The Phoenix of Sodom, or the Vere Street Coterie* (London, 1813), 45–46.

25. *Times*, 25 August 1825.

26. *Times*, 19 April 1820, 3.

27. "An Advocate of Police Reform," to the Home Office, 27 May 1827, TNA HO 44/18 ff. 426–427.

28. Anon., The Yokel's Preceptor, or, More Sprees in London (c.1840), quoted in Hallam, *The Book of Sodom*, 129.

29. *Times*, 11 April 1843.

30. *Times*, 30 July 1864.

31. See, for example, the activities of Samuel Cooper, *Times*, 16 February 1849.

32. *Times*, 20 April 1830; 26 April 1830.

33. Central London Free Church Council to the Home Office, 25 October 1912, TNA MEPO 2/5815.

34. For a later list of notorious urinals, see Matt Houlbrook, *Queer London: Perils and Pleasures in the Sexual Metropolis, 1918–1957* (Chicago, 2005), 53.

35. *Times*, 4 November 1842.

36. *Times*, 23 March 1871.

37. *Lancaster Gazette*, 20 August 1806, 3.

38. *Voluntary Examination of Thomas Rix, Late of Manchester ...*, 15 September 1806, Althorp Papers, British Library Additional Manuscript 75899, vol. dc. On this case, see H. G. Cocks, "Safeguarding Civility: Sodomy, Class, and the Limits of Moral Reform in Early 19th Century England," *Past and Present*, 190 (February 2006).

39. *Illustrated Police News*, 2 October 1880.

40. *Manchester Evening News*, 1 October 1880.

41. Proceedings of the Central Criminal Court, 13 April 1850, TNA CRIM 10/31. Original emphasis.

42. *Manchester Evening News*, 30 September 1880.

43. *Manchester Evening News*, 30 September 1880.

44. *Times*, 7 May 1870.

45. *Times*, 16 May 1870. This is the first recorded use of the word 'drag' to refer to wearing women's clothes, although it had obviously been used in that way for several years.

46. *Times*, 16 May 1870.

47. *Times*, 30 May 1870.

48. *Queen v Boulton and Others ...*, TNA DPP 4/6, 623.

49. Holloway, *Phoenix of Sodom*, quoted in Hallam, *Book of Sodom*, 116.

50. See Houlbrook, *Queer London*, ch. 7.

51. Charles Kingsley, *Life and Works*, Vol. 1, 260, quoted in James Eli Adams, *Dandies and Desert Saints: Styles of Victorian Masculinity* (Ithaca: Cornell University Press, 1995), 98.

52. David Hilliard, "Un-English and Unmanly: Anglo-Catholicism and Homosexuality." *Victorian Studies*, 25, 2 (1982) 181–210, 188.

53. Quoted in John Shelton Reed, *Glorious Battle: The Cultural Politics of Victorian Anglo-Catholicism* (Nashville: Vanderbilt University Press, 1996), 211.

54. The Confessional Unmasked: Showing the Depravity of the Romish Priesthood, the Iniquity of the Confessional and the Questions put to females in Confession (London: Protestant Electoral Union, 1871), 37.

55. This is how O'Brien described them in the House of Commons debate on 5 November 1884. *Times*, 6 November 1884, 6.

56. William O'Brien, *Evening Memories: Being a Continuation of Recollections by the Same Author* (Dublin, 1920), 22.

57. *Times*, 4 November 1884, 6.

58. *Times*, 4 November 1884, 6.

59. *Times*, 17 January 1890.

60. The term sexology was first used in 1860, but this referred to relations between the sexes rather than to specific types of sexual behaviour. See Chris Waters, "Sexology," in H. G. Cocks and Matt Houlbrook, editors, *Palgrave Advances in the Modern History of Sexuality* (London, 2005), 41–63.

61. Waters, "Sexology," 45.

62. Robert Nye, editor, *Sexuality* (Oxford, 2000), 143.

63. Havelock Ellis, Sexual Inversion (1897), quoted in Chris White, editor, *Nineteenth Century Writings on Homosexuality, A Sourcebook* (London, 1999), 102.

64. Xavier Mayne, *The Intersexes: A History of Simisexualism as a Problem in Social Life* (1908), quoted in White, *Nineteenth Century Writings*, 105.

65. Mayne, *Intersexes*, quoted in White, 110.

66. Mayne, *Intersexes*, quoted in White, 111–112.

67. Edward Carpenter, *Intermediate Types Among Primitive Folk: A Study in Social Evolution* (London, 1914).

68. Diaries of George Ives, quoted in Weeks, *Coming Out*, 119.

69. Walter Pater, *The Renaissance: Studies in Art and Poetry* (1873, repr. New York, 1959), 158.

70. Because of Queensbury's poor orthography, not to mention spelling, there is some doubt as to what he actually wrote. Richard Ellman reads it as 'To Oscar Wilde, ponce and Somdomite'. Ellman, *Oscar Wilde*, 412.

71. Quoted in Ellman, *Oscar Wilde*, 435.

72. Reggie Turner, quoted in Ellman, *Oscar Wilde*, 436.

73. This is what the *National Observer* newspaper called him. Quoted in Ellman, *Oscar Wilde*, 446.

74. Quoted in Weeks, *Coming Out*, 21.

75. E. M. Forster, *Maurice* (London, 1971), 145.

76. Petition of Oscar Wilde to the Home Office, 2 July 1896, TNA HO 45/2514.

77. *The Link*, September 1920, 14. On these ads, see H. G. Cocks, " 'Sporty' Girls and 'Artistic' Boys: Friendship, Illicit Sex and the British 'Companionship' Advertisement 1913–1928." *Journal of the History of Sexuality*, 11, 3 (July 2002), 457–482.

78. William Smyth to Walter Birks, 21 October 1920, *The Link Case*, TNA MEPO 3/283.

Chapter 5: Queer Conflicts: Love, Sex and War, 1914–1967

1. Philip Hoare, Wilde's Last Stand: Decadence, Conspiracy and the First World War (London: Duckworth, 1997), 21.

2. Lord Alfred Douglas, *The Rossiad* (London, 1916), 10.

3. "Abnormal Vice Rampant." *The World*, 15 August 1916.

4. Cited in Hoare, *Wilde's*, 6.

5. Philip Page, "Our New Decadents." *Sunday Express*, 30 November 1924.

6. See, for example, "Jock Greets a Pal in Traditional French Fashion," unref. newspaper in George Ives, *Casebook*, vol. 11, 10. Beinecke Library, Yale University. See also James Gardiner, *Who's a Pretty Boy Then: One Hundred and Fifty Years of Gay Life in Pictures* (London: Serpent's Tale, 1997), 40–41.

7. Cited in Santuna Das, " 'Kiss me, Hardy': Intimacy, Gender, and Gesture in World War I Trench Literature," in *Mordernism/Modernity*, 9, 1 (2002): 51–74, 53.

8. Eric Hiscock, *The Bells of Hell Go Ting-A-Ling-A-Ling* (London, 1976).

9. See Das, "Kiss me, hardy," 54. See also Sarah Cole, "Modernism, Intimacy and the Great War." *English Literary History*, 68 (2001): 469–500, 473.

10. "Private Carpenter," unref. newspaper in Ives, *Casebook*, vol. xi, 1.

11. "Courtship Duet," *Daily Mirror*, 31 August 1918.

12. For Courthard see, *Reynolds*, 1 August 1915. The Wilson case is discussed in David A. Boxwell, "The Follies of War: Cross Dressing and Popular Theatre on the British Front Lines, 1914–1918," in *Modernism/Modernity*, 9, 1 (2002): 1–20, 1.

13. " 'Nancy' Males Ape Females." *Empire News*, 18 May 1919, 9.

14. On women and wartime morality see, for example, A.Woolacott, " 'Khaki and Fever' and its Control: Gender, Class, Age and Sexual Morality on the British Homefront in the First World War." *Journal of Contemporary History*, 29 (1994): 325–347; Hoare, *Wilde's*.

15. Cited in Alkarim Jivani, *It's Not Unusual: A History of Lesbian and Gay Britain in the Twentieth Century* (London: Michael O'Mara, 1997), 56.

16. Kevin Porter and Jeffrey Weeks, *Between the Acts: Lives of Homosexual Men, 1885–1967* (London: Routledge, 1991), 112.

17. Jivani, *Unusual*, 66.

18. Porter, *Between*, 142.

19. Jivani, *Unusual*, 49.

20. Lesley Hall, *Sex, Gender and Social Change Since 1880* (Basingstoke, 2000), 144.

21. Jivani, *Unusual*, 70.

22. John Costello, *Love, Sex and War, 1939–1945* (London, 1986), 162, 172.

23. Porter, *Between*, 142.

24. Quentin Crisp, *The Naked Civil Servant* (1968; London: Fontana/Collins, 1978), 155.

25. Jivani, *Unusual*, 56–57.

26. Porter, *Between*, 78.

27. Porter, *Between*, 134.

28. Porter, *Between*, 64.

29. Porter, *Between*, 141–142.

30. Crisp, *Naked*, 157–158.

31. Philip Page, "Our New Decadents." *Sunday Express*, 30 November 1924; see also Crisp, *Naked*, ch. 3.

32. Porter, *Between*, 26.

33. Porter, *Between*, 36.

34. Bernard Williams, cited in Stephen Humphries, *A Secret World of Sex: Forbidden Fruit, the British Experience, 1900–1950* (London, 1988), 193–194.

35. Kevin Porter, *Between*, 111.

36. "Public house watched," *News of the World*, 30 November 36; "What the Varsity Men Said." *News of the World*, 21 March 37.

37. Porter, *Between*, 76.

38. Gerald Dougherty, cited in Jivani, *Unusual*, 50.

39. Interview with 'Michael' 1 November 2005.

40. Emlyn Williams, cited in Matt Houlbrook *Queer London: Perils and Pleasures of the Sexual Metropolis, 1918–1957* (Chicago: Chicago University Press, 2005), 83.

41. Houlbrook, *Queer*, 85.

42. Crisp, *Naked*, 28.

43. "Lady Austin's Camp Boys." *News of the World*, 26 February, 33; On the Holland Park Avenue case see Matt Houlbrook, "Lady Austin's Camp Boys: Constituting the Queer Subject in 1930s London." *Gender and History*, 14, 1 (2002): 31–61.

44. "Sins of Iniquity," *News of the World*, 29 January, 33.

45. Jivani, *Unusual*, 52.

46. Crisp, *Naked*, 172.

47. "Photographs Taken by Police: Men's Fancy Dress Costumes in Flat Incident." *Reynolds*, 27 March 1927.

48. "Lady Austin," *News of the World.*
49. "Numbered in the Dock; 27 Men Sentenced," *Morning Dispatch*, 28 February, 33.
50. Jivani, *Unusual*, 65. On this point see also Houlbrook, *Queer*, 150.
51. Patrick Higgins, *Heterosexual Dictatorship: Male homosexuality in Post-war Britain* (London: Fourth Estate, 1996), 76.
52. Hall Carpenter Archives, *Walking After Midnight: Gay Men's Life Stories* (London: Routledge, 1989), 67.
53. See Houlbrook, *Queer*, ch. 4.
54. Interview with 'Michael', 1 November 2005.
55. Jivani, *Unusual*, 137.
56. Interview with 'Michael', 2 November 2005.
57. Peter Burton, *Parallel Lives* (London: GMP, 1985), 45.
58. Paul Baker and Jo Stanley, *Hello Sailor!: The Hidden History of Gay Life at Sea* (London: Longman, 2003), 151.
59. Jivani, *Unusual*, 131.
60. "Alleged scenes in a café." *News of the World*, 3 February, 35.
61. Porter, *Between*, 63.
62. Porter, *Between*, 98.
63. "Police Suspicion of Boarding House." *News of the World*, 25 September 1949.
64. Peter Dennis, editor, *Daring Hearts: Lesbian and Gay Lives in 50s and 60s Brighton* (Brighton: QueenSpark, 1992), 104, 13.
65. Dennis, *Daring*, 69.
66. Dennis, *Daring*, 57.
67. Dennis, *Daring*, 56.
68. Dennis, *Daring*, 115.
69. Bob Cant and Susan Hemmings, editors, *Radical Records* (London: Routledge, 1988), 36.
70. Stephen Whittle, "Consuming Difference," in *The Margins of the City: Gay Men's Urban Lives*, edited by Stephen Whittle (Aldershot: Arena, 1994), 32–33.
71. Porter, *Between*, 79–80.
72. See H. G. Cocks, " 'Sporty' Girls and 'Artistic' Boys: Friendship, Illicit Sex and the British 'Companionship' Advertisement, 1913–1928," *Journal of the History of Sexuality*, 11, 3 (July 2002).
73. *News of the World*, 3 December, 40.
74. Cocks, "Sporty."
75. " 'Nancy' Males."
76. H. Montgommery Hyde, *The Other Love: An Historical and Contemporary Survey of Homosexuality in Britain* (London: Heineman, 1970), 203.
77. Porter, *Between*, 138.
78. Dennis, *Daring Hearts*, 53.
79. Terry Castle, *Noel Coward and Radclyffe Hall: Kindred Spirits* (New York: Columbia University Press, 1996), 32–33.
80. Dudley Cave, cited in Sean Cole, Don *We Now Our Gay Apparel: Gay Men's Dress in the Twentieth Century* (Oxford: Berg, 2000), 63.
81. Jivani, *Unusual*, 138.
82. Hyde, *Other*, 201.
83. Hyde, *Other*, 200.
84. Dennis, *Daring*, 29.
85. Interview with Gwladys Cook (n Edwards), 2 November 2005.
86. Houlbrook, *Queer*, 160.
87. Baker, *Hello Sailor!*, 152. See also Houlbrook, 159–160.
88. Dennis, *Daring*, 16.
89. Baker, *Hello*, 150.

90. George Ives, *Diary*, vol. 67, 1 February 1917, 47. Harry Ransom Humanities Research Center, University of Texas at Austin.

91. See, for example, Peter Wildeblood, *Against the Law* (London: Weidenfeld and Nicolson, 1955).

92. For more on this argument, see Houlbrook, *Queer*, part 3; Jivani, *Unusual*, 66–67.

93. Cited in Houlbrook, *Queer*, 168.

94. Matt Houlbrook, "Soldier Heroes and Rent Boys: Homosex, Masculinities, and Britishness in the Brigade of the Guards: *c*.1900–60." *Journal of British Studies*, 42 (3), 2003, 351–388.

95. "What is Wrong with Discipline in the Guards." *Reynolds*, 3 July 1938. Porter, *Between*, 45.

96. "Men who Prey on Guardsmen," *News of the World*, 4 November, 56.

97. See Matt Cook, *London and the Culture of Homosexuality, 1885–1914* (Cambridge: CUP, 2003), ch. 5.

98. Tom Driberg, *Ruling Passions* (London: Jonathan Cape, 1977), 77.

99. "Drama of Two Chums: Separation Leads to Double Tragedy," unreferenced newspaper, 5 March, 23, in Ives, *Casebook*, vol. 15, 31.

100. "Nancy Males."

101. "Two men die." *Daily Mirror*, 15 February, 37.

102. *News Chronicle*, 9.6.38; "For Sixty Years the Perfect Friends." *Sunday Mirror*, 8 March, 39.

103. Hall Carpenter, *Walking*, 19–20.

104. Porter, *Between*, 8.

105. Dennis, *Daring*, 40.

106. Dennis, *Daring*, 40.

107. Ives, *Diary*, vol. 70, 21 May, 17, 118.

108. Houlbook, *Queer*, 134.

109. Edward Hodgson, "Theatre," *Sunday Dispatch*, *c*.October 1929, in Ives, *Casebook*, vol. 26, 44.

110. Temple Thurston, *Defence*, 5 February, 33, in Ives, *Casebook*, vol. 32, 46.

111. Richard Dyer, *The Culture of Queers* (London: Routledge, 2002), 19.

112. "Travestied in Stained Glass." *Morning Post*, 27 February, 33.

113. "She Men: Peter Ross Calls a Crusade." *Referee*, 19 June, 38.

114. "If Guilty They Would be Gassed While in Court." *Reynolds*, 18 December, 38.

115. "Goings On." *Weekend Review*, 4 February, 33.

116. "The Cult of Candour," *Evening News*, 28 December, 21. "Psychoanalysis for Criminals." *Evening Standard*, 27 October, 24.

117. "New Fiction: The Masculine Woman," *Sunday Times*, 5 August, 28.

118. "Porter's Punishment." *News of the World*, 30 October 1932; Ives, *Casebook*, vol. 32, 52.

119. "Sentenced to Surgery," *Reynolds*, 7 March, 37.

120. "Chance for Ex-Priest: Years of Struggle that Amounted to Torture." *News of the World*, 6 June, 37.

121. See Chris Waters, "Havelock Ellis, Sigmund Freud and the State: Discourses of Homosexual Identity in Interwar Britain," in *Sexology in Culture: Labelling Bodies and Desires* (Cambridge: Polity, 1998).

122. Jivani, *Unusual*, 123–125.

123. Humphries, *Secret*, 212–214.

124. Hall Carpenter, *Walking*, 33.

125. Liz Stanley, *Sex Surveyed 1949–1994: from Mass Observations 'Little Kinsey' to the national surveys and Hite Report* (London: Taylor and Francis, 1995), 199–203.

126. *The Practitioner*, 1 April, 54.

127. Jivani, *Unusual*, 89.

128. Cited in Hyde, *Other*, 226–227.

129. "The Squalid Truth," *The Sunday Pictorial*, 25 September, 55.

130. Douglas Warth, "Evil Men," *Sunday Pictorial*, 25 May, 52.

131. "Scandal Exposed by the Writing on the Wall." *News of the World*, 23 November, 52.

132. "The Man Who Spun a Web of Vice." *News of the World*, 18 November, 56.

133. "Ten Men of Shame." *News of the World*, 20 May, 56.

134. "Sailor Cleared of Manslaughter." *News of the World*, 26 October, 47.

135. "Victim in Tale of a Trap is Acquitted." *News of the World*, 23 November, 47.

136. "He killed man who dressed as a woman." *News of the World*, 26 November, 50; "Self Defence Plea After a Death: Manslaughter Verdict." *News of the World*, 13 May, 51.

137. Houlbrook, *Queer*, 181.

138. Statistics for sodomy also include bestiality cases. Jeffrey Weeks, *Coming Out: Homosexual Politics in Britain, from the Nineteenth Century to the Present* (London: Quartet, 1977), 158.

139. For more on this argument, see Houlbrook, *Queer* and Higgins, *Heterosexual*, 266.

140. Porter, *Between*, 127.

141. Porter, *Between*, 132.

142. Hall-Carpenter, *Walking*, 52.

143. Dennis, *Daring*, 38.

144. Dennis, *Daring*, 38.

145. Hugh David, *On Queer Street: A Social History of British Homosexuality, 1895–1995* (London: HarperCollins, 1997), 164–165.

146. "The Problem of Homosexuality: Report by Clergy and Doctors." *The Times*, 26 February.

147. "Sentenced Ex-Officer Dies in Cell." *News of the World*, 30 May, 54.

148. Hall, *Sex*, 166.

149. Hall-Carpenter, *Walking*, 70.

150. Jivani, *Unusual*, 121.

151. *Sunday Times*, 28 March, 54.

152. Jivani, *Unusual*, 114; see also Higgins, *Heterosexual*, pt 1.

153. "What the Papers Say about the Report." *Evening News*, 5 September, 57.

154. Letter from Thomas Carhol to the Public Morality Council, 16 February, 59. London Metropolitan Archives, A/PMC/80.

155. Weeks, *Coming*, 171.

156. Weeks, *Coming*, 182.

157. Jivani, *Unusual*, 138, 140.

158. Cited in Hyde, *Other*, 234.

159. Weeks, *Coming*, 170.

160. Alan Sinfield, *Out on Stage: Lesbian and Gay Theatre in the Twentieth Century* (New Haven: Yale, 1999), 271.

161. Jivani, *Unusual*, 148.

162. Weeks, *Coming*, 176.

163. Dennis, *Daring*, 28.

164. Jivani, *Unusual*, 149.

165. See Houlbrook, *Queer*, ch. 10.

166. Jivani, *Unusual*, 149.

167. Houlbrook, *Queer*, pt. 4.

Chapter 6: From Gay Reform to Gaydar, 1967–2006

1. Lisa Power, *No Bath But Plenty of Bubbles* (London: Cassell, 1995), 147.

2. Power, *No Bath*, 141.

3. Power, *No Bath*, 155.

4. Power, *No Bath*, 149.

5. Power, *No Bath*, 141.

6. Hall Carpenter Archives, *Walking After Midnight: Gay Men's Life Stories* (London: Routledge, 1989), 140.

7. Power, *No Bath*, 224–225.

8. Power, *No Bath*, 219.

9. Power, *No Bath*, 193.

10. Power, *No Bath*, 198.

11. *What is the GAA?* (Brighton, 1978).

12. Hall Carpenter, *Walking*, 72.

13. Kevin Porter and Jeffrey Weeks, *Between the Acts: Lives of Homosexual Men, 1885–1967* (London: Routledge, 1991), 19.

14. Bob Cant and Susan Hemmings, editors, *Radical Records* (London: Routledge, 1988), 156.

15. Power, *No Bath*, 89.

16. Porter, *Between*, 70.

17. Jeffrey Weeks, *Coming Out: Homosexual Politics in Britain, from the Nineteenth Century to the Present* (London: Quartet, 1977), 214.

18. Cant, *Radical*, 92.

19. Hall Carpenter, *Walker*, 108.

20. Porter, *Between*, 71.

21. Tom Driberg, *Ruling Passions* (London: Jonathan Cape, 1977), 16.

22. Porter, *Between*, 112.

23. Power, *No Bath*, 266.

24. Cant, *Radical*, 52.

25. Hall Carpenter, *Walking*, 138.

26. Porter, *Between*, 33.

27. Peter Dennis, editor, *Daring Hearts: Lesbian and Gay Lives in 50s and 60s Brighton* (Brighton: QueenSpark, 1992), 37.

28. Hall Carpenter, *Walking*, 121.

29. Rukus! Federation Ltd, *The Queen's Jewels: a Memory in Progress* (London, 2005).

30. Rukus!

31. Hall Carpenter, *Walking*, 182.

32. Alkarim Jivani, *It's Not Unusual: A History of Lesbian and Gay Britain in the Twentieth Century* (London: Michael O'Mara, 1997), 175.

33. Richard Dyer, *The Culture of Queers* (London: Routledge, 2002), 67.

34. See Wilhelm von Gloeden, *Taormina* (London: GMP, 1985).

35. See Rupert Smith, *Physique: the Life of John S Barrington* (London: Serpent's Tale, 1997).

36. Jivani, *Unusual*, 174.

37. Dennis, *Daring*, 94.

38. Weeks, *Coming*, 222.

39. L. Trenchard and H. Warren, *Something to Tell You: The Experiences and Needs of Young Lesbians and Gay Men in London* (London, 1984), 112.

40. Burton, *Parallel*, 52.

41. Dennis, *Daring*, 107.

42. Dennis, *Daring*, 107.

43. Paul Baker and Jo Stanley, *Hello Sailor! The Hidden History of Gay Life at Sea* (London: Longman, 2003), 101–102.

44. Jivani, *Unusual*, 176.

45. Thanks to Matt Jones for discussion on this point.

46. Terry Sanderson, *Gay Times*, May 1998, 33–35.

47. CHE, *Attacks on Gay People: A Report of the Commission on Discrimination* (London, 1980), 17–18.

48. *CHE Conference Gazette* (1979). London Metropolitan Archive Box BO4/158.

49. Trenchard, *Something*, 59.

50. Trenchard, *Something*, 59.

51. Socialist Workers Party, *Out, Proud and Fighting* (1988).

52. Simon Watney, *Policing Desire: Pornography, AIDS and the Media* (London: Comedia, 1987), 87.

53. Cited in Boze Hadleigh, *Sing Out!: Gays and Lesbians in the Music World* (London: Robson, 1999), 194.

54. Interview with John, 20 May 2006.

55. See Alan Sinfield, "The Sussex Programme and its Context," in *Open Lives, Safe Schools: Addressing Lesbian and Gay Issues in Education* (Bloomington: Indiana University Press, 1996).

56. Cited in Simon Garfield, *The End of Innocence: Britain in the Time of AIDS* (London: Faber, 1994), 33.

57. *Gay Scotland*, July/August 1983, 10.

58. Garfield, *Innocence*, 245.

59. Stephen Mayes and Lyndall Stein, *Positive Lives: Responses to HIV – A Photodocumentary* (London: Cassell, 1993).

60. Garfield, *Innocence*, 46.

61. Nick Bridgmont, *AIDS to Identity* (MA thesis, University of Westminster, 1996).

62. Watney, *Imagine*, 6.

63. The World Health Organisation reported in 1990 that rates per million of population in Europe ranged from 41/million in Greece to 235/million in France. The UK rate stood at 72/million, the Netherlands at 104/million, Italy at 142/million, Denmark at 148/million and Spain at 192/million. Garfield, *Innocence*, 192.

64. Mayes, *Positive*, 106.

65. Interview with Lisa Power, 3 May 2006.

66. Garfield, *Innocence*, 197.

67. Garfield, *Innocence*, 226.

68. Health Protection Agency website http://www.hpa.org.uk/infections/topics_az/hiv_sti/hiv/ Jun.5 06. With thanks to Victoria Field of the Terrence Higgins Trust for her help in interpreting these statistics.

69. Mayes, *Positive*, 68.

70. Derek Jarman, *Smiling in Slow Motion*, edited by Keith Collins (London: Century, 2000), 373.

71. Garfield, *Innocence*, 50.

72. Body Positive Strathcyde Information Unit, *HIV and AIDS: A Brief History* (2004).

73. Mayes, *Positive*, 120–121.

74. Conservatives for the Family Campaign, *HIV Infected Citizens: Charter of Responsibility* (27 September 1991).

75. *Daily Mail*, 3 October 1985.

76. Mayes, *Positive*, 86.

77. Jivani, *Unusual*, 188.

78. Mayes, *Positive*, 77.

79. Jarman, *Smiling*, 326.

80. Mayes, *Positive*, 96.

81. Mayes, *Positive*, 69.

82. Watney, *Policing*, 7.

83. Mayes, *Positive*, 76.

84. Hall Carpenter, *Walking*, 109.

85. Adam Mars Jones, *The Guardian*, 15 March 1995.

86. Derek Jarman, *At Your Own Risk: A Saint's Testimony* (London: Hutchinson, 1992), 134.

87. Cant, *Radical*, 246.

88. Baker, *Hello*, 103.

89. Hall Carpenter, *Walking*, 123, 172.

90. Interview with David, 5 November 2005.

91. Peter Weatherburn, *Andrew Hunt and Ford Hickson, Project Sigma: The Sexual Lifestyles of Gay and Bisexual Men in England and Wales* (Cardiff, 1992). See also A. M. Coxon, *Between the Sheets: Sexual Diaries and Gay Men's Sex in the Era of AIDS* (London: Cassell, 1996).

92. A. M. Coxon, *The Gay Lifestyle and the Impact of AIDS* (Cardiff, 1985).

93. Weatherburn, *Project*, 34.

94. Coxon, *Between*, 146.

95. Graham Hart and Pail Flowers, *A Survey of Gay Men's Sexual Behaviour in Glasgow* (Glasgow, 1996).

96. *Daily Express*, 17 March 1987.

97. Colin Spencer, *Homosexuality: A History* (London: Fourth Estate, 1995), 381.

98. Interview with David, 5 November 2005.

99. Burton, *Parallel*, 194.

100. *Time Out*, 5–12 September 1990; *Independent* 29 July 1990.

101. Geraint John, "Cock and Bull Story." *City Limits*, 25 October–1 November 1990.

102. Peter Tatchell, "Has Britain Become the Least Tolerant Country in Europe." *Tribune*, 29 June 1990.

103. Jivani, *Unusual*, 196.

104. Interview with Lisa Power, 3 May 2006.

105. *Gay Times*, May 1992.

106. Interview with Lisa Power, 3 May 2006.

107. Jivani, *Unusual*, 199.

108. *Gay Times*, August 1992.

109. *Pink Paper*, 3 July 1988, 8–9; *Sunday Times*, 6 July 1997, 24.

110. Hall Carpenter, *Walking*, 136.

111. "Sorting Out the Real Men From the Waifs and Strays." *The Guardian*, 28 April 1994.

112. Dennis, *Daring*, 62.

113. "Mister Trouble Maker." *Boyz*, 3 December 1994, 8.

114. *Lesbian and Gay Parenting Conference*, November 1998, London Metropolitan Archive moo34959.

115. See Stephen Whittle, "Consuming Differences: The Collaboration of the Gay Body with the Cultural State," in *The Margins of the City: Gay Men's Urban Lives*, edited by Stephen Whittle (Aldershot: Arena, 1994).

116. Peter Tatchell, "Let Us Cease These Gay Campaigns." *Pink Paper*, June 1999.

117. Jeffrey Weeks, Brian Heaphy and Catherine Donovan, *Same Sex Intimacies: Families of Choice and Other Life Experiments* (London: Routledge, 2001), 19.

118. Dyer, *Culture*, 16.

119. John Davidson, *Gay Britain: The Complete Guide to Gay Society in Britain* (Downham Market: D&I, 1989).

120. Tim Edwards, *Cultures of Masculinity* (London: Routledge, 2006), 160–161.

Author Biographies

H. G. Cocks is a lecturer in history at Birkbeck College, University of London, and author of *Nameless Offences: Homosexual Desire in the Nineteenth Century* (2003).

Matt Cook is a lecturer in history at Birkbeck College, University of London, and author of *London and the Culture of Homosexuality, 1885–1914* (2003).

Robert Mills is a lecturer in English at King's College London and author of *Suspended Animation: Pain, Pleasure and Punishment in Medieval Culture* (2005).

Randolph Trumbach is a professor of history at Baruch College and the Graduate Center, City University of New York, and author of *The Rise of the Egalitarian Family* (1978) and *Sex and the Gender Revolution, vol. 1: Heterosexuality and the Third Gender in Enlightenment London* (1998).

Index

Illustrations

1. Tomb effigy of Richard Lionheart, King of England. Fontevrault, France. Thirteenth century. The passionate expressions of love between Richard and Philip Augustus of France have provoked much speculation among modern historians about the king's sexual identity.

2. The Wilton Diptych. Richard II being presented to the Virgin and Child (depicted in the adjoining panel, not shown) by St Edmund, St Edward the Confessor and St John the Baptist. c.1395–9. Associating Richard with three virginal saints may have been an attempt to pass off his childless first marriage as a deliberately chaste union, countering claims that attributed it to unmanliness.

3. Lot and the inhabitants of Sodom. Drawing in manuscript of the Old English Hexateuch. First half of eleventh century. In the biblical account of the destruction of Sodom the transgressions of the city's inhabitants are notoriously imprecise, but here homoeroticism appears to be at issue.

4. Torture and execution of Hugh Despenser at Hereford. Illuminated miniature by Loyset Liedet in manuscript of Jean Froissart, Chroniques. Fifteenth century. Despenser, a close adviser of Edward II, was described by the French chronicler Froissart as a 'heretic and sodomite' in an account of his execution for treason.

5. Benjamites flee into wilderness; Bulgars and Albigensians engaged in illicit kissing and embracing. *Bible moralisée manuscript.* 1230s. This manuscript compares the biblical Benjamites, described in Judges 19–20, with medieval heretics and sodomites.

6. Impalement of crowned male. Gothic ivory comb. Fourteenth century (?). This scene, which may depict the murder of Edward II with a red-hot poker, is not necessarily designed to present the victim as a sodomite.

7. Tomb slab of Sir William Neville and Sir John Clanvowe. 1391. These two knights, who died in Constantinople a few days apart, were buried in a common grave and may have been sworn brothers.

8. Abraham's wife given over to pharaoh; heretics and princes of the world kissing and embracing. *Bible moralisée manuscript*. 1230s. Sodomy was sometimes depicted in terms of practices such as kissing and embracing, gestures that were also part of the language of passionate male friendship.

9. Daniel Mytens: King James I. 1621. As a middle-aged, bearded man, King James's would have taken the dominant sexual role with younger beardless men.

10. William Larkin (attrib): The First Duke of Buckingham. *c.*1616. Beardless and in his early twenties, Buckingham would have taken the passive sexual role with James. He was famous for his long fine legs.

11. Lord Castlehaven. Frontispiece to
*The Arraigment and Conviction of Mervin
Lord Audley*, Earl of Castlehaven. 1643.
Castlehaven is a notorious example of
a nobleman who had sexual relations
with members of his household, both
male and female.

12. R. B. Parkes, Edward Kynaston,
mezzotint. 1889 (thought for a long time
to be based on a painting by Lely). Boy
actors like Kynaston (Pepys: 'the loveliest
lady that I ever saw') exerted a powerful
fascination over both men and women.

13. John Hayls: Samuel Pepys. 1666.
Pepys is an example of a man attracted to
both women and adolescent males, though
he did not necessarily act on his desire for
the latter.

14. Jacob Huysmans (attrib.): John
Wilmot, The Earl of Rochester. *c.*1675.
A Restoration rake attracted to both
adolescent boys and women, Rochester
was part of a circle of like-minded men,
such as the second Duke of Buckingham
and Sir Charles Sedley.

The Women-Hater's Lamentation:

OR

A New Copy of Verfes on the Fatal End of Mr. *Grant*, a Woollen-Draper, and two others that Cut their Throats, or Hang'd themfelves in the *Counter*; with the Difcovery of near Hundred more that are Accufed for unnatural difpifing the *Fair Sex*, and Intriguing with one another.

To the Tune of, *Ye pretty Sailors all.*

I.

YE injur'd *Females* fee
  Juftice without the Laws,
Seeing the Injury,
  Has thus reveng'd your Caufe.

II.

For thofe that are fo blind,
  Your Beauties to defpife,
And flight your Charms, will find
  Such Fate will always rife.

III.

Of all the Crimes that Men
  Through wicked Minds do act,
There is not one of them
  Equals this Brutal Fact.

IV.

Nature they lay afide,
  To gratifie their Luft;
Women they hate befide,
  Therefore their Fate was juft.

V.

Ye *Women-haters* fay,
  What do's your Breafts infpire,
That in a Brutal way,
  You your own Sex admire?

VI.

Woman you difapprove,
  (The chief of Earthly Joys)
Yoh that are deaf to Love,
  And all the Sex defpife.

VII.

But fee the fatal end
  That do's fuch Crimes purfue;
Unnat'ral Deaths attend,
  Unnat'ral Lufts in you.

VIII.

A Crime by Men abhor'd,
  Nor Heaven can abide
Of which, when *Sodom* fhar'd,
  She juftly was deftroy'd.

IX.

But now, the fum to tell,
  (Tho' they plead Innocence)
Thefe by their own Hands fell,
  Accus'd for this Offence.

X.

A Hundred more we hear,
  Did to this Club belong,
But now they fcatter'd are,
  For this has broke the Gang.

XI.

Shop-keepers fome there were,
  And Men of good repute,
Each vow'd a Batchelor,
  Unnat'ral Luft purfu'd.

XII.

Ye *Women-Haters* then,
  Take Warning by their Shame,
Your Brutal Lufts reftrain,
  And own a Nobler Flame.

XIII.

Woman the chiefeft Blifs
  That Heaven e'er beftow'd:
Oh be afham'd of this,
  You're by bafe Luft fubdu'd.

XIV.

This piece of Juftice then
  Has well reveng'd their Caufe,
And fhews unnat'ral Luft
  Is curfs'd without the Laws.

Licenfed according to Order.

LONDON: Printed for J. Robinfon, in Fetter-Lane, 1707.

15. The Woman-Hater's Lamentation. Broadside. 1707. Depicting one of the earliest mass trials of adult effeminate men who had had sex with each other, this broadside shows the suicide of two of those charged flanking a central image of their crime. These men, it was assumed, hated women.

16. The Complete Beau. Frontispiece to *An Essay in Defence of the Female Sex*, 1696. When he stood in the pillory charged with attempted sodomy on a boy, the 'beau' Captain Rigby dressed fashionably – but not as a woman.

17. Jonathan Wild in the Condemned Hold. From a *True and Genuine Account*, attributed to Defoe, 1725. Wild is the supposed author of one of the descriptions of sodomites in the early eighteenth century.

18. Kingsbury (attrib): A Milliner's Shop. 1787. King George III, his wife and their daughters are served here by young, effeminate, well-dressed milliners.

This is not the **T H I N G:**

O R,

M O L L Y E X A L T E D.

Tune, *Ye Commons and Peers.*

YE Reverſers of Nature, each *dear* little Creature,
  Of ſoft and effeminate ſight,
See above what your fate is, and 'ere it too late is,
  Oh, learn to be—all in the *Right.*
    Tol de rol.

II.
On the FAIR of our Iſle ſee the Graces all ſmile,
  All our Cares in this Life to requite ;
But ſuch Wretches as You', Nature's Laws wou'd undo,
  For you're *backward*—and not in the *Right.*
    Tol de rol.

III.
Can't Beauty's ſoft Eye, which with Phœbus may vie,
  Can't her roſy Lips yield ye Delight?
No:—they all afford ſweets, which each Man of Senſe meets,
  But not *You*,—for you're not in the *Right.*
    Tol de rol.

IV.
Where's the tender Connection, the Love and Protection,
  Which proceed from the conjugal Rite?
Did you once but know *this,* ſure you'd ne'er do amiſs,
  But wou'd always be—all in the *Right.*
    Tol de rol.

V.
The *Sov'reign* of ALL, who created this *Ball,*
  Ordain'd that each Sex ſhould unite ;
Ordain'd the ſoft *Kiſs,* and more permanent Bliſs,
  That ALL might be—all in the *Right.*
    Tol de rol.

VI.
But a Race ſo deteſted, of Honour diveſted,
  The Daughters of *Britain* invite,
Whom they leave in the Lurch, to well flog 'em with Birch ;
  Shou'd they flay 'em they're—all in the *Right.*
    Tol de rol.

VII.
Preſs ye *Sailors,* perſiſt, come ye *Soldiers,* inliſt,
  By *Land* or by *Sea* make 'em fight,
And then let *France* and *Spain,* call their Men home again,
  And ſend out their WIVES—to be *Right.*
    Tol de rol.

VIII.
Now tho'many good Men, have ſo frolickſome been,
  Our Pity and Mirth to excite,
Yet may theſe worthy Souls have the uppermoſt *Holes*
  In the PILLORY ;—all is but *Right.*
    Tol de rol. &c.
      Ab 1763.

To be had at the *Bee-Hive, Strand* ; and at all the Print and Pamphlet Shops in *Great Britain* and *Ireland.*

19. This is not the Thing, or Molly Exhalted. Broadside. 1763. The reaction of women to sodomites as they stood in the pillory in London was notably hostile.

20. Trial at the Old Bailey Court from *Life & Actions of Moll Flanders* (London, 1723, a chapbook pirate version of Daniel Defoe's novel). Accounts of men tried in this courtroom are the principal source of information on eighteenth-century sodomy.

The ARSE BISHOP JOSLIN G a SOLDIER. or Do as I say, not as I do.

21. The Arse-Bishop Josling a Soldier: Percy Jocelyn, Bishop of Clogher, Compromised. From Anon: *The Arse Bishop Josling a Soldier, or-Do as I say Not as I do.* 1822. Despite injunctions against publicity, homosexual offences involving the upper classes were widely reported and quickly became notorious.

22. Confirmation or the Bishop and the Soldier. From *A Correct Account of the Horrible Occurrence*. 1822. An unintended result of the publicity surrounding sensational cases was to advertise places where men might meet each other for sex.

23. Anne Hurle for Forgery and Methuselah Spalding [for an unnatural offence] on their way to Execution at Newgate, 1804. From W. Jackson: *New and Complete Newgate Calendar*. 1818. The general expansion of criminal justice contributed to the increase of prosecutions for 'unnatural crimes'.

24. Disgraceful Proceedings in Manchester: Men Dressed as Women. From *Illustrated Police News*. 9 October 1880. Fancy dress balls provided a useful excuse for cross-dressing, but unless secrecy was maintained they could be subject to police raids.

25. Men in Women's Clothes: the Dressing Room. From *Illustrated Police News*. 21 May 1870. In their lodgings at St Pancras, the respectable Ernest Boulton and Frederick Park would transform themselves into 'Stella' and 'Fanny' before a night on the town.

26. Young Men Charged With Appearing in Women's Clothes. From *Illustrated Police News*. 14 May 1870. Far from seeking secrecy, 'Stella' and 'Fanny' enjoyed celebrity status, frequenting the West End, and even appearing on stage.

27. Men in Women's Clothes. From *Illustrated Police News*. 28 May 1870. Accused of conspiring to commit sodomy, the defendants pleaded that their dressing as women was no more than a fascination with private theatricals – and won.

28. The War Memorial to the 24th Infantry Division in Battersea Park, London, by Eric Kennington, unveiled by Lord Plumer (left) and the Bishop of Southwark (right), 11 October 1924. Here, the soldiers are stoical, courageous, and also closely bonded; the sculptor depicts them holding hands in the face of adversity.

29. The Dumbells Concert Party, formed from the 3rd Canadian Division in France: Big Beauty Chorus – Marie and the Boys. 1914–1918. Drag was seen as a harmless form of troop entertainment, but led to arrests on the streets of London, Edinburgh and Gateshead during the war.

30. Tea at Lyons Corner House. 1926. Waitresses ensured that a section of the Corner House in London's Piccadilly Circus was reserved for queer clientele in the 1910s and 20s.

31. Chorus boys back stage at London's Adelphi Theatre, 1930. 'John' remembers bantering in polari with other members of the chorus in the 1930s, and the theatre continued to be associated with camp flamboyance and sexual 'deviance'.

" Oh, sir, spare a copper."

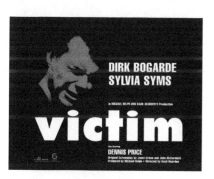

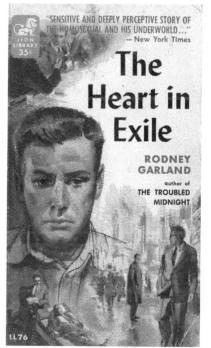

32. 'O Sir, spare a copper'. From *Men Only: A Man's Magazine*. November 1936. The 'queen' was part of a visible and vibrant queer street 'scene' in London in the 1920s and 1930s.

33. *Victim*, starring Dirk Bogarde. 1961. The reform agenda was pressed in the 1950s and 1960s in films and novels depicting the misery and isolation of 'homosexual' men forced to live beyond the law.

34. Cover of *The Heart in Exile* by Rodney Garland. Lion Library. 1956. This cover to Garland's 1952 novel shows the 'homosexual' cruising, drinking and seeking psychoanalytic help for his plight.

Physique pictorial

36. The first Gay Pride march, London, 1972. 1,000 people marched from Trafalgar Square to Hyde Park – a show of unity which belied the rifts that had by this time emerged in the Gay Liberation Front.

VOL. 7 NO. 4   35¢

35. Cover of *Physique Pictorial*, vol.7, no.4. Winter 1957. American imports like *Physique Pictorial* carried photos of confident, muscled men, who – cartoons like this one suggested – might also be queer.

37. Bang Disco. 1970s. Launched in 1976 at the Astoria in London's Charing Cross Road, Bang! was Britain's first American-style gay club.

38. Gay Liberation Front badges from the 1970s. Badges provided a simple way for gay men and lesbians to be out and proud.

39. South London Gay Centre, 78 Railton Rd, Brixton, London. *c*.1975. Some lesbians and gay men experimented with communal living, and ran a gay centre from squats in Railton Road in the 1970s.

40. Culture Club backstage: Boy George with band members Mikey Craig, Roy Hay and Jon Moss. 1980s. The music scene of the 1970s and 1980s provided a succession of role models for gay men experimenting with sex and style – from David Bowie and Elton John to Holly Johnson and Boy George.

41. Lesbians and gays support the miners. 1985. Many gay men and lesbians saw sexuality politics in a wider context and were involved in trade union, feminist and anti-racist campaigns.

42. AIDS memorial panel *c.*1993. By 1993 Ken had embroidered the names of 130 friends and acquaintances in Brighton who had died of AIDS-related illnesses.

43. Mardis Gras parade, Trafalgar Square, London. 2004. Legal changes in the early 2000s meant there was much to celebrate, though many felt that gay life had been comodified and depoliticised.

44. *Pink Paper*, December 2005. Within four months of the legislation coming into force on 5 December 2005, over 2,200 lesbian and 4,300 gay male couples had registered their civil partnerships in Britain.

Lightning Source UK Ltd.
Milton Keynes UK
UKHW020308130219
337169UK00009B/625/P